The Lighting Pattern Book For Homes

Second Edition

Russell P. Leslie

Kathryn M. Conway

LIGHTING RESEARCH CENTER
Rensselaer Polytechnic Institute
Troy, New York

McGraw-Hill
New York   San Francisco   Washington, D.C.   Auckland   Bogotá
Caracas   Lisbon   London   Madrid   Mexico City   Milan
Montreal   New Delhi   San Juan   Singapore
Sydney   Tokyo   Toronto

Library of Congress Cataloging-in-Publication Data

Leslie, Russell P.
    The lighting pattern book for homes / Russell P. Leslie, Kathryn M. Conway — 2nd ed.
      p.   cm.
    Includes bibliographical references (p.   ).
    ISBN 0-07-038079-1
    1. Dwellings—Lighting.   2. Electric power—Conservation.
3. Electric lighting.   4. Interior decoration.   I. Conway, Kathryn M.   II. Title
TK4255.L47   1996
621.32'28—dc20
                                                     96-41380
                                                        CIP

Rensselaer Polytechnic Institute, Troy, New York

© 1993, 1996 by Rensselaer Polytechnic Institute. All rights reserved. Printed in the United States of America. Except as permitted under the United States Copyright Act of 1976, no part of this publication may be reproduced or distributed in any form or by any means, or stored in a data base or retrieval system, without the prior written permission of the publisher.

First edition 1993

Second edition 1996

This edition published by
McGraw-Hill, a division of
the McGraw-Hill Companies, Inc.

Rensselaer

LRC
Lighting Research Center

01 00 99 98 97 96   3 2

ISBN 0-07-038079-1

McGraw-Hill books are available at special quantity discounts to use as premiums and sales promotions, or for use in corporate training programs. For more information, please write to the Director of Special Sales, McGraw-Hill, 11 West 19th Street, New York, NY 10011 or contact your local bookstore.

Dedication

In the preface of *Cummings' Architectural Details* by Marcus Fayette Cummings, we find sentiments from our environs that curiously antedate our intent in writing this book.

All of the designs given are new and original, and have never before been produced in any architectural book.

It is not supposed by the author that its contents will add much to the resources of architects, who are located in the larger cities, but those who have a country practice, such as he enjoys, may find in the illustrations valuable hints. No attempt has been made to illustrate any well-defined style of architecture…

The author has not undertaken to initiate a new style; such a thing may be produced some time in the future, but it is probable that instead of one American style being produced we shall have a multitude of styles, each one stamped by the genius and individuality of its author, and each possessing more or less merit.

What has been aimed at is this: to present a mass of architectural details, easy of construction, pleasing in form, and generally of an inexpensive character, and all so designed that a great variety of selections may be made from them, which, when combined in a building, will produce a harmonious whole; and it is believed by the author that this work will be found to be of value, that its design is practicable; for there are hundreds of towns and villages, in all the States of the Union, in which the wants of the people continually demand the erection of buildings… which in the hands of the builder and workman may be made elegant, and pleasing in all their features, provided they have at hand a guide such as this book is intended to be.

M. F. Cummings, Architect
Troy, New York, 1873

The Lighting Pattern Book for Homes is designed in the spirit of traditional architectural pattern books. It gives model designs and components of designs that can be adapted to your particular building and style. As such, it is dedicated to all those who strive to create practical homes that harmonize with rather than deplete our environment.

Sponsors

Bonneville Power Administration

California Institute for Energy Efficiency

Empire State Electric Energy Research Corporation

Lighting Research Center, Rensselaer Polytechnic Institute

New York State Energy Research and Development Authority

Niagara Mohawk Power Corporation

North Carolina Alternative Energy Corporation

Contents

Foreword

Practicing professionals, producers of products, and researchers in lighting have been searching for methods and materials to save energy. Indeed the message about energy conservation and concern for the environment has now, in some fashion, reached almost everyone on Earth. In the world of buildings, the direction of this conservation effort has been focused on the design of energy-efficient commercial, industrial, and institutional projects.

The first standard for energy conservation in new building design in the United States was produced in 1975. This standard was translated into code language by the states and was used as the basis for the energy conservation portion of their building codes. Over the last 20 years or so, almost every structure erected in North America has been using less energy as a result of the requirements of these codes. Furthermore, energy conservation standards and codes are continually being refined to take advantage of the lessons gained from the new buildings constructed under their mandate.

One of those lessons brought into focus how large the portion of energy consumed by lighting was in some facilities. Lighting standards, practice, and equipment were then altered to answer the challenges raised by the concerns for energy conservation and the environment. The turnabout made in the area of commercial lighting has taken, in some instances, a true revolution to accomplish.

The continuing evolution of lighting and energy conservation is now about to enter into everyone's home. This entry will be in practice and not just in spirit. This book is intended to help make that arrival a welcome one: to provide good lighting while saving energy.

This book is not for lighting professionals. It is an idea book for all of the various people who work in the realm of the residence. It contains the best information that has been learned and compiled on conserving energy through better lighting since the effort began. It is an instrument to make good lighting and energy conservation synonymous.

This is my "Hello" to all the allied professionals who will be carrying forward lighting-related energy conservation to people's homes everywhere. From the utility representative to the home center salesperson, from the electrical contractor to the interior designer, from lighting showrooms to architect/engineer offices, *The Lighting Pattern Book for Homes* can be a resource to all of you, a tool for providing good lighting to benefit whomever you are serving.

Welcome to the era of residential energy conservation through improved lighting.

Howard Brandston
FIES, FCIBSE, FIALD

Preface

We all use lighting in our homes. Lighting is a significant consumer of electricity and accounts for 6 to 20 percent of residential utility bills. The power plants that generate this electricity place a societal burden on our air quality and nonrenewable energy reserves. "Conserve energy and save the environment," we frequently are told. Monthly greetings from our electric utility company and the environmental catalogs that we receive are stuffed with promotions for "green" lighting technologies, such as compact fluorescent lamps.

Yet compact fluorescent lamps are only one of many options for lighting homes efficiently. Other lamps can be more appropriate for certain tasks; some convert electricity more efficiently to light. Turning lamps off when they are not needed is perhaps our greatest energy-saving opportunity. How many of us have bellowed to our children, "Turn off the lights!"? Many modern lighting control technologies make turning off the lamps easier. Lighting efficiency also involves lighting only the things that we wish to see. The luminaires and lamps we choose can either swallow much of the light before it ever leaves the luminaire, or they can aim the light precisely where it is needed. This book offers technologies and designs that can transform our habitats into more efficient homes.

People hold strongly to the belief that fluorescent lighting is not good lighting for the home. "It gives me headaches; it flickers; it makes people look green; it buzzes; it looks institutional." These are common responses that energy-efficiency advocates hear when they suggest fluorescent lighting for homes. Choosing appropriate technologies can help us overcome these negative beliefs about fluorescent lighting, but people have not yet fully accepted such technologies. We hope that this book will give you the tools you need to step beyond misconceptions about fluorescent lighting.

Also, we must remember why we put lighting in our homes. We need to see, create a comfortable atmosphere, and be safe and secure. The mission of Rensselaer's Lighting Research Center is to change architecture through lighting that is more energy efficient and responsive to people's needs. We know that energy-efficient lighting designs must suit all your needs— aesthetic, economic, and practical.

What can we do to encourage efficient home lighting? As an architect, one of us was exasperated when trying to specify proper efficient lighting technologies in a timely fashion during the rapid decision-making process of home construction. Frustration prompted this book, which is designed to guide lighting decisions quickly and wisely. We have supplemented our experiences in architecture and visual communication with the technical expertise of many world-class experts in lighting design, lighting applications, and human factors.

Our sponsors recognized the potential value of a comprehensive book on residential lighting. With their input, we expanded our audience of lighting decision-makers far beyond the architect. We wrote this book for facility managers considering lighting improvements; utility lighting conservation program managers choosing technologies to promote through incentive programs; state energy officers considering code and voluntary programs to encourage lighting energy efficiency; lighting equipment manufacturers searching for new products and ways to market many existing products; electricians, builders, remodelers, and designers of manufactured homes looking for good lighting for their customers; and of course, residents.

Use this book to select and design efficient lighting. Share it with everyone you encounter in the process of designing and building homes. Join us in saving energy and enjoying well-designed lighting.

Russell P. Leslie
Kathryn M. Conway

Acknowledgments

The research, development and production of this book was sponsored by Bonneville Power Administration, California Institute for Energy Efficiency, Empire State Electric Energy Research Corporation, New York State Energy Research and Development Authority, Niagara Mohawk Power Corporation, North Carolina Alternative Energy Corporation, and Rensselaer Polytechnic Institute's Lighting Research Center. The authors especially thank the individuals from each of these organizations who made the sponsorship possible, graciously hosted roundtables, and reviewed manuscripts: Sheila Bennett, Mechanical Engineer, Residential Technology, and Doug Couch, Public Utilities Specialist, Bonneville Power Administration; James Cole, Director, California Institute for Energy Efficiency; Frank Porretto, Program Manager, Empire State Electric Energy Research Corporation; James Barron, Senior Project Manager, New York State Energy Research and Development Authority; Terry McHugh, Project Officer, Research and Development, Niagara Mohawk Power Corporation; Diana Woolley, Senior Project Manager, and Lynn Schrum, Senior Engineering Project Manager, North Carolina Alternative Energy Corporation; and Mark Rea, Director, Lighting Research Center.

The book is truly the product of a team effort and the authors wish to acknowledge the major contributions made by Brenda Ryan, Executive Director of the Public Utility Commission of Texas, who spent the summer of 1992 at the Lighting Research Center as a Visiting Professor and Lighting Application Specialist, and Steve Meyers, graduate research assistant. Ryan developed the first drafts of many of the lamp and luminaire descriptions, the techniques, and the designs. Meyers assisted with the designs. Jason Beckstead, Post-Doctoral Research Associate, Christina Dimitry, Research Assistant, and Rea conducted the research upon which the authors based the hours of residential lighting use estimates. Sally Sledge, Application Engineer, Fail-Safe Lighting, began the research for the typical designs when she was a Lighting Research Center Research Assistant; this work was accomplished through the Niagara Mohawk Energy Efficient Seed Research Program.

Pamela Schemenaur, Lighting Research Center Manager of Outreach Education, outlined many of the luminaire descriptions, rewrote sections of the lamp descriptions, and provided extensive review and advice on lighting applications. Dorene Maniccia, Lighting Research Center Lighting Application Specialist, provided technical review and developed the first draft of the controls chapter.

The typical designs and alternatives proposed by the authors, Ryan, and Meyers were critiqued and expanded during early-morning "charettes" held during the summer of 1992. Lighting Research Center participants included Peter Boyce, Christopher Cuttle, and Robert Davis, respective Heads of the Research and Development in Human Factors, Graduate Education, and Research and Development in Efficient Lighting programs. Other early risers and critics included Howard Brandston, Adjunct Professor and Partner, H.M. Brandston and Partners; Catherine Luo, Technical Writer; Maniccia; and Schemenaur.

The progress from concept to manuscript was facilitated by approximately one hundred professionals who participated in roundtables held in the fall of 1992 at the North Carolina Alternative Energy Corporation Lighting Resource Center in Research Triangle Park; the Niagara Mohawk Lighting Research Laboratory in Watervliet, New York; the Lighting Design Lab in Seattle, Washington; and the Pacific Energy Center in San Francisco, California. Special thanks are due to the manufactured housing industry of North Carolina.

Many thanks are due to the reviewers who read through the hundreds of pages of the draft manuscript: Marcia Ward, Consultant; William Blitzer, Consultant, and Henry Muller, Chief Designer, The Genlyte Group; W. S. (Gus) Baker, Lighting Specialist, and Dave Brook, Extension Energy Agent, Oregon State University Extension Service; Jamie Barrett, Energy Analyst, Davis, Naomi Miller, Manager of Design Applications, and Rea, all of the Lighting Research Center; and Schrum, North Carolina Alternative Energy Center.

Production of this book was facilitated by many Lighting Research Center staff and students, including: Lenda Leonard, Senior Secretary, Karoline Harrington, Secretary, and Laura Canon, Research Assistant. The economic analyses in the Design chapter were performed by Krystof Pavek, Research Assistant. Amy Fowler, Lighting Research Center Technical Editor, provided editorial review. Joseph Ceterski, Researcher, compiled the bibliography.

We also gratefully acknowledge the design and production efforts and encouragement of Nager Reynolds Design, Westport, Connecticut and Catherine Luo, Lighting Research Center Technical Writer. The lamp, luminaire, and control illustrations were done by Bruce Kaiser of Kaiser Illustration, Watervliet, New York; the cover and the technique and design illustrations were done by Mark Patrizio of Kemp Building Graphics, Waterford, New York. Robert Richardson, Portsmouth, Rhode Island, compiled the index. We located the excerpt for the dedication in *Victorian Architectural Details*, published in 1978 by the American Life Foundation and Study Institute.

How To Use This Book

Use *The Lighting Pattern Book for Homes* as a guide to selecting efficient lighting for the home. You can enter the book in several ways.

Using a Lighting Technique

If you have a lighting technique or practice in mind, such as wall washing or accent lighting, use the Table of Contents to find the appropriate page in the Techniques chapter. Each Technique gives design guidance and refers you to luminaires that will give the desired effect. The Techniques entitled "Task and Special Purpose" refer you to the introductions to rooms, in the Designs chapter.

Lighting or Relighting a Room

If you are choosing lighting for a specific room or space in a home or are looking for some energy-efficient alternatives to typical home lighting, use the table of contents to find your room in the Designs chapter. For each room, we offer options for replacing the lamps, luminaires, or controls, and designs for remodeling or new construction. Use these designs as prototypes for your own designs, adapting the style to your taste. Refer to the Lamps, Luminaires, and Controls chapters to learn more about the recommended technologies. Each set of rooms includes an economic analysis of the designs.

Calculating Savings

"The numbers" can help us choose a lighting design. If you want to calculate the annual energy savings, the annual operating cost savings, or a simple payback for installing efficient lighting equipment, use the worksheet and tables in the Economics chapter. We provide many analyses of energy-efficient designs in the Designs chapter; see the bar charts that accompany each set of designs.

Using a Lighting Technology

If you need information about a particular lighting technology, use the Table of Contents to find that technology in the Lamps, Luminaires, or Controls chapters. Read the opening pages of each chapter first and also read the introduction to each type of technology. Combine lamps, luminaires, and controls to create lighting designs. References to alternative technologies, techniques, and rooms in the Designs chapter that show the technology are provided at the end of each type. Tables 3, 4, and 5 in the Economics chapter give data about many lamps used in homes.

Locating More Information

See the Glossary and Appendix for an explanation of the many terms used in this book. Refer to the Associations and Further Reading lists at the end of the book to learn more about lighting.

People, Energy, and Light

Understanding a few basics about people, energy, and light will help you light homes usefully, efficiently, and attractively. Read this chapter before you use the rest of the book, and refer back to it; refer to the Glossary for definitions of the italicized terms in this chapter.

People

Light enables us to see. When light enters our eyes, it excites microscopic structures at the back of our eyes. These structures, known as rods and cones, send messages to our brains. The messages form our perceptions of the objects and phenomena around us. These perceptions include *color, brightness,* and *contrast.* Light can enter our eyes in a direct path from a light source, or it can enter our eyes after it bounces off surfaces. When light shines on an opaque object, some of it is absorbed by the object, and some of it is reflected; we see the part that is reflected. Likewise, our perception of the color of objects is determined by the light reflected from them.

Contrast helps us distinguish shapes, edges, and details on the surface of objects. Contrast is the ratio of the brightness of one area to the brightness of adjacent areas. This page has high contrast between the black letters and the white area around them. In most circumstances, the more contrast that a shape, edge, or detail has, the better we can see it.

Of course, the ability to see depends not only on the light that is available in homes, but also on the visual abilities of the residents. Each person's eyes may differ: normally we all see best as young adults and experience a decline in our ability to see as we age. The older we are, the more light we need to see things as well as we did when we were young. Many people have visual disabilities; they need to be considered when designing and selecting lighting.

As we go through the cycle of each day, and as we move from one space to another, we experience both bright and dark spaces. Our eyes have a marvelous capacity to adjust to different levels of light; this is called adaptation. Everyone at times has been jolted awake from the darkness of sleep by a bright light: for a short period, we cannot see well and must squint. Quickly, though, our eyes adapt. Stepping into a dark staircase from a sunny hallway, we may need to pause a moment before our eyes are able to discern the steps. We can, eventually, see in very dim conditions, but not in complete darkness. A dim night light can help us navigate through the clutter in a child's room, or guide us to the bathroom; it provides enough light for orientation, but not enough for us to see details or to read.

Color, brightness and contrast perception, visual ability, age, and adaptation are all *human factors* that we need to consider when lighting homes. We also need to be sensitive to residents' beliefs, preferences, and behaviors regarding lighting. People's beliefs may guide their preferences and behaviors, even if the beliefs are not based in fact. Negative beliefs about lighting can thwart efforts to encourage efficient lighting in homes. This book attempts to show how we can use light efficiently while allowing people to see and to be comfortable. The following chapters note the disadvantages as well as the advantages of various lighting technologies and designs to help people avoid the problems that can give rise to negative experiences and beliefs. Also, a wide variety of designs is offered in hopes that many aesthetic preferences can be met.

No one knows the diversity of lighting beliefs and preferences better than those who help people choose lighting for their homes. Selecting technologies and using them effectively is a true challenge. Consider all the professionals that can be involved in lighting homes: architects, builders, contractors, distributors, electricians, facility managers, interior designers, lighting designers, salespersons, and utility representatives. Also consider all the places and occasions that people can buy lighting technologies—from the common "light bulb" picked up at the grocery store to the once-in-a-lifetime purchase of a crystal chandelier, lighting a home is not a straightforward activity.

Other complicating factors in lighting a home are electricity, safety, and the need for a qualified professional to install most luminaires and controls. People must seriously weigh the costs and hassles of changing a lighting design in their home. Thus it is important to make careful choices that provide flexible and long-lasting lighting installations, whether replacing luminaires, remodeling, or building a new home. When remodeling and building anew, state and local building codes must be followed, especially for multi-family housing. Some codes contain articles that specify types of lighting technologies, or levels of light for certain areas. For instance, kitchens in California homes must contain at least one luminaire that operates a fluorescent lamp.

The activities and behaviors of residents have an impact on lighting homes, too. People need to conduct many more types of activities at home than they do in other places, particularly workplaces. The homes that are covered in this book are modest, and each room may have to serve several functions. For example, the kitchen is used for preparing food, eating, and socializing, but it may also be used for reading, writing, and hobbies. The lighting techniques that are used must satisfy these and other needs.

Intuitively, we expect that the more a room is used, the more the lighting in that room will be used. Thus the number of hours per day that the lights are on in the kitchen will probably exceed the number of hours that the lights are used in the bedrooms. The Economics chapter gives more information on this topic. Of course, we all know that the lights stay on unless they are turned off, and we know that people may forget to turn off lights when they are not needed. Energy-conserving habits should include using daylight when it is available, dimming lights if lower light outputs are acceptable, and turning off lights whenever they are not needed. In some areas of the home, automatic controls can supplement or substitute for manual controls. Making lighting controls easily accessible enables residents to make the best use of a lighting design.

Energy

Understanding a bit about energy will help you fully take advantage of today's lighting technologies. This book deals with light that is created and controlled by means of the electricity that is supplied by a utility company to the home. Knowing that most electricity is generated and transmitted at a cost to ourselves and our environment can inspire residents to want to save electricity. Additionally, many organizations, including the United States Environmental Protection Agency, environmental groups, affordable housing advocates, and utility companies, conduct programs that are intended to reduce residential demand for electricity.

Most people understand that appliances consume electricity, but they may not realize that the *lamps* (bulbs) and *luminaires* (fixtures) scattered throughout their homes are appliances, too. In fact, it would be best to think of lamps and luminaires all together as one appliance, because lighting accounts for 6 to 20 percent of the electricity consumed in homes. When people choose a refrigerator or dishwasher, they are likely to seek information on the label that will tell them how much it will cost to operate the appliance each year. They may also be willing to pay more for a more efficient appliance, because they will recover the added expense in a few months or years. It is far more difficult to calculate efficiency and savings for lighting, because there are many types of lighting technologies used throughout the home. Nevertheless, such calculations can be done, and the Economics chapter provides a helpful worksheet. To satisfy consumers' demands for information and to comply with new United States federal legislation, manufacturers of lamps soon will be listing more details about energy and light quality on packaging. Some independent groups are also encouraging manufacturers to provide more information, and are offering "seals of approval" to help consumers choose environmentally acceptable products.

Before using the worksheet, though, note that the *power* that is used to create light in the home is measured in a unit called the *watt*. One thousand watts equals one *kilowatt*. Lamps operate with a specific range of watts; the maximum watts in the range is used to label the *wattage* of the lamp. For example, common incandescent A-lamps (light bulbs) are available in a variety of wattages, including 40-watt, 60-watt, 75-watt, and 100-watt. *Ballasts* and some *controls* also consume power.

The amount of electric energy supplied to a lighting technology to operate it over time is measured in *watt-hours*. It is the result of multiplying *input power*, measured in watts, by time, measured in hours. Utility companies bill residential customers for the number of *kilowatt-hours* (kWh) they use. For example, ten 100-watt lamps operated for 1 hour would use 1 kilowatt-hour of energy (10 lamps × 100 watts × 1 hour = 1 kWh). Thus energy used for lighting can be saved either by reducing the amount of power required for lighting or by reducing the amount of time that the lighting is used. The cost per kilowatt-hour varies considerably in North America: some customers pay as little as $0.03 per kilowatt-hour while others pay as much as $0.18 per kilowatt-hour.

The amount of light that is produced by a lamp, or its *light output*, is measured in *lumens*. The *efficacy* of a lamp is the ratio of lumens produced to watts consumed. This *lumen-per-watt* (LPW) ratio is similar to the miles-per-gallon ratio used for automobiles, in that a higher ratio indicates a more efficacious lamp. The lumen-per-watt ratio is an important factor for selecting lamps. The Lamps and Economics chapters contain tables that list light output and wattage for lamps commonly used in homes. As a result of the Energy Policy Act of 1992, several types of lamps, including some cool white fluorescent lamps and reflector lamps, will soon be phased out of the market in the United States due to their low efficacies. Other, higher-efficacy lamps exist that can be used to replace these low-efficacy lamps.

Efficacy is used to rate lamps; *efficiency* is the measure used for luminaires. Efficiency expresses the light output from a luminaire as a percentage of the light output from the lamps. For example, if a luminaire contains one fluorescent lamp that emits 1000 lumens, and the luminaire in turn emits 900 lumens, then the luminaire has an efficiency of 90 percent. Choose luminaires with high efficiencies to make the best use of energy.

Some lighting technologies, particularly lamps that require electronic ballasts, do more than consume power: they can also affect the *power quality* in a home. Power quality refers to the characteristics of the current and voltage supplied to electrical equipment. Poor power quality can cause inefficient operation of the utility company's equipment and may also interfere with other electrical equipment in the home. Potential problems with certain technologies are noted in the text that describes the technology, and in the captions in the Designs chapter. Also, a more detailed explanation of lighting and power quality is given in the Appendix.

Light

Light is a form of energy that stimulates our eyes. Light has several characteristics that can be measured. These characteristics are not well understood by many people, and the vocabulary used to describe them is rather technical. Nevertheless, familiarity with these characteristics is essential to creating successful and efficient lighting designs.

As noted previously, the amount of light emitted by a lamp is measured in lumens. In homes, this light output is important because it illuminates our surroundings. When the light emitted by a lamp falls on a surface, it is best referred to as *illuminance*, although it is sometimes called light level. Illuminance is measured in units called *footcandles* (lumens per square foot) or *lux* (lumens per square meter). Generally, casual activities require approximately 20 footcandles; more visually demanding activities such as preparing food or reading require approximately 50 footcandles; and difficult-to-see tasks like sewing require approximately 150 footcandles. These recommended illuminances vary based on the age of the person performing the work, the size and contrast of the task materials, and the speed and accuracy with which the work must be performed. The designs should provide enough light for the tasks that typically are conducted in each room. If more precision is required when designing a lighting system, consult the Illuminating Engineering Society of North America's *Lighting Handbook*.

Another characteristic of light that is helpful to understand is *distribution*. Distribution includes both the direction in which the light moves, and the amount, or intensity of light that moves in a particular direction. For example, think of the beam of light emitted by an automobile headlight. The luminaire directs most of the light forward, in a narrow beam. This *light distribution pattern* differs from that created by the small luminaire inside the automobile, above the passengers. Inside, the luminaire has a very diffuse and broad light distribution pattern. Choose technologies that distribute light to the area where it is most needed. If light is distributed to an area where it is not needed, it is wasted, and the design is not efficient. The Lamps and Luminaires chapters give specific information on light distribution for each of the technologies.

The most frequently mentioned characteristic of light in homes is color. When people talk about light that is "like daylight," they usually have the yellowish, or "sunny" color of light from incandescent lamps in mind. Yet consider the wide range of colors of daylight: a cloudy day has a grey-blue color; sunsets are orange, red, and purple. As the hours pass in the day, the color of light changes, too. Even so, incandescent lamps emit the most familiar color of light in homes. One of the purposes of this book is to persuade people that incandescent lamps are not the only option for lighting homes; in fact, fluorescent lamps can produce a wide range of colors of light that are suitable for people, their furnishings, and the architecture of the home.

Color is characterized in two ways: by its color temperature and by its ability to render colors. *Correlated color temperature* (CCT) describes the color appearance of the light in terms of its perceived warmth or coolness. If "pure white" is considered to be neutral, then a "yellow white" is warm and a "blue white" is cool. Correlated color temperature is measured on the Kelvin scale. A low correlated color temperature, less than 3100 K, identifies a warm white light, such as that emitted by an incandescent lamp. A high correlated color temperature, more than 4000 K, identifies a cool white light, such as that produced by an overcast sky.

The *color rendering index* (CRI) measures the effect of light on the perceived color of objects. To determine the color rendering index, the color appearances of eight standard color chips are measured with special equipment under a reference light source with the same correlated color temperature as the lamp being evaluated. Then the eight color chips are measured under the lamp being evaluated. If these colors are exactly like those measured under the reference source, the rated color rendering index for the lamp is 100. If the measured color of the eight standard chips shifts from the reference condition, the color rendering index is less than 100.

A low color rendering index indicates that some colors may appear unnatural when illuminated by the lamp. Incandescent lamps render color like the reference source does so they typically have color rendering indices of 95 to 100. Cool white fluorescent lamps have a color rendering index of 62; premium fluorescent lamps are available with color rendering indexes of 80 and above. Both the correlated color temperature and the color rendering index of each lamp are given in the Lamps and Economics chapters.

In the Designs chapter, the alternatives to typical lighting designs incorporate the basic principles described in this chapter. Each design considers people and their activities in a particular room of the home, offers ways to use lighting energy responsibly, and maximizes the quality of light that is available from a variety of technologies.

Techniques

Techniques are ways to "arrange" or distribute the light in a space to achieve a desired effect. For example, a room may contain luminaires that distribute light uniformly to all surfaces, or luminaires that distribute light mainly to the walls and ceiling, or luminaires that distribute light only to a few objects. Illuminance describes the amount of light that reaches a surface.

The techniques in this chapter are general and can be used for many areas of the home. Daylight is covered only briefly here because this book focuses on electric sources of light; daylight is an important light source for homes and is treated at length in many other books. Daylight and the techniques of Ambient lighting, Indirect lighting, and Wall Washing all can create a general, diffuse light distribution in a space. Other techniques that are used for more specific light distribution are Accent and Task lighting, and lighting for Special Purposes. Each technique is described and illustrated in this chapter, and appropriate luminaires are suggested. The Designs chapter shows examples of these techniques applied in various rooms of the home.

Daylight

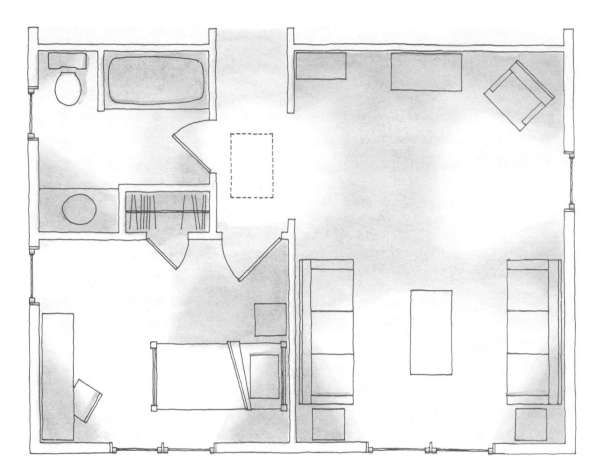

Like electric lighting, daylighting has sources, luminaires, and controls. Daylight sources are the direct sun, the sky which can diffuse the sun's light, and surfaces surrounding a building that can reflect sun or sky light into the building. Daylight luminaires are the windows and skylights that admit daylight into the building. Examples of daylight controls are tinted glass and films, blinds, curtains, overhangs, and shades that reduce the brightness and change the distribution of daylight, and sensors and switches that control electric lighting in the daylit space.

Homes often have generous amounts of daylight, and residential building codes require that most rooms have windows. Typical residential rooms are small enough so that daylight can reach deep into the room, particularly if windows are located high on the wall. Daylighting only becomes an energy-efficient strategy if electric lamps are dimmed or turned off when daylight provides adequate illumination. Depending on climate or building orientation, the use of windows and skylights can have a positive or negative effect on a home's heating or cooling requirements. For instance, windows that are located below table height do not add much lighting benefit but may add considerably to the home's heating and cooling loads.

Daylight may introduce some lighting problems. Windows or skylights can cause direct and reflected glare on television and computer screens, cause some fabrics and artwork to fade, and can cause thermal discomfort. These problems are magnified when direct sunlight enters the room. Often people will counteract these problems by closing shades, blinds, or curtains, thus reducing or eliminating daylight and increasing the need for electric lighting.

Most daylit rooms average 10 to 12 hours per day of potentially avoided electric lighting; the proper use of electric lighting controls maximizes the energy savings available when daylight is used in a lighting design. For a simple yearly estimate of daylighting energy savings potential in kilowatt-hours, multiply the number of hours that lamps in a room would be on during the day times 365 days times the watts consumed by the lamps and divide by 1000.

Windows and skylights provide a view and are free of lighting energy costs; however, in terms of initial cost, windows and skylights are more expensive than an equal area of solid wall. Windows also can provide emergency egress and/or natural ventilation. Daylighting has excellent color qualities and can provide ample illuminance, although the intensity and color of daylight varies with season, time of day, and weather. Windows and skylights can provide solar heating benefit, but also can cause excessive solar heat gain and/or heat loss.

Use daylight in as many spaces as possible to reduce daytime electric lighting energy use. Small windows or skylights usually provide adequate light for moving around the home. In new construction or a major remodeling, consider installing a window or skylight in hallways, baths, and foyers. In larger rooms, windows on more than one wall will give balanced light distribution throughout the room, help reduce direct glare, and provide cross ventilation.

In order to avoid direct and reflected glare, position desks and seating for conversation and reading so that people are not facing the windows. Alternatively, adjust blinds to redirect sun to the ceiling. Transparent curtains and shades can soften direct sunlight. In rooms with windows on only one wall, people seated with their backs against the window may appear as silhouettes to others in the room, who may experience discomfort by trying to see a backlit face against the bright window.

Locate tasks that require more light nearer to windows. For instance, place a hobby or homework table next to a window. In bathrooms, a small window behind or beside the toilet often provides adequate illumination. Thus the maintenance problems of a window in the tub enclosure are avoided and the wall space above the sink is available for a mirror. Furthermore, the window is well-positioned for the task of reading! A window with a high sill permits privacy as well as daylight.

In rooms with television or computer screens, place the screen so that it does not reflect the image of the window in the screen. Hold a mirror in the proposed location of the screen. If you can see the image of a window, lamp, or luminaire in the mirror when it is viewed from the intended sitting position, the screen will also reflect that image. Direct sunlight can cause discomfort when the resident is watching television, working at the computer, or reading. Nonetheless, for many other less visually demanding tasks, sunlight enlivens the room.

Automatic daylight dimmers that are controlled by photosensors are impractical for most residences because of their high price. Photosensors are practical for operating luminaires that are used all night for security. Provide separate switches for luminaires in various parts of the room to allow residents to use only the luminaires that they need during the day.

Ambient

Ambient lighting provides the general illumination for a space and enables people to move around the home. Ambient lighting suffices for non-visually demanding activities such as conversation or television viewing. Ambient lighting can be provided by many types of luminaires. Most rooms in homes are small enough so that one or two luminaires will provide adequate ambient light.

Avoid high illuminances for ambient lighting, unless visually demanding tasks (such as reading or crafts) are done throughout the room. Lower illuminances can save energy because lower-wattage lamps can be used. For maximum efficiency, combine low ambient illuminances with local accent or task lighting for work areas.

Luminaires: Ceiling-Mounted Diffusers, Suspended, Recessed Downlights, Architectural, Wall-Mounted Sconces or Diffusers, Table and Floor Lamps

Indirect

The technique of indirect lighting uses one or more luminaires to direct light onto the ceiling and upper walls of a room; the ceiling and upper walls act as reflectors and distribute the light evenly throughout the room. This technique is also referred to as uplighting. For highest efficiency, the walls and ceiling should be painted white, or a very light color. Indirect lighting minimizes shadows and reflected glare. It is especially appropriate for tasks involving glossy paper, or reflective surfaces such as computers or televisions. For other critical visual tasks, a supplementary task light may be required.

Use fluorescent lamps for greatest energy savings. Clean luminaires regularly because dust and insects collect on or in the luminaires and reduce light output. Avoid lighting ceilings and walls that have surface imperfections.

Luminaires: Suspended Uplights, Coves, Valances, Track or Adjustable Heads (Wall-Mounted), Floor Lamps

Wall Washing

Wall washing illuminates a vertical surface to an acceptably uniform brightness. Wall washing draws attention to the wall, and can be used to accentuate an entrance, fireplace, or artwork. The light reflected from matte surface walls can make a room appear bright and will provide a soft, diffuse light in the room. Paint walls white or a light color for greatest efficiency. Wall washing can make spaces such as hallways or narrow rooms appear more spacious.

Wall washing is achieved by placing luminaires in or on the ceiling or on the floor at regular intervals. The spacing between the luminaires and between the luminaires and the wall determines the brightness of the surface. The spacing can be calculated so that the wall is evenly illuminated, or illuminated in a regular pattern that creates a scalloped effect. Follow the manufacturers' recommendations for spacing the luminaires.

If wall washing is used for ambient light in a room, provide additional lighting for special purposes where needed, or locate tasks that need high illumination, such as reading or sewing, near the walls. Mount the luminaires close enough to the wall so that people seated nearby will not receive direct glare. Do not wall wash windows or mirrors because the image of the lamps and luminaires may be reflected.

Several other cautions pertain to wall washing. Dark surfaces reflect far less light than do white surfaces, so more light should be directed onto them if they are to be perceived as being wall washed. Luminaires mounted close to the wall create a grazing effect on textured surfaces. This can be an advantage if the texture is attractive, but should be avoided where the wall has surface irregularities resulting from poor-quality drywall taping or sanding.

Luminaires: Ceiling-Mounted Track or Adjustable Heads, Recessed Wall Wash, Soffits, Valances

Accent

Accent lighting, also called highlighting, emphasizes objects by focusing light directly on them. Accent lighting is used inside and outside the home to feature locations such as an entrance or to create dramatic effects. Also, points of visual interest can be created by highlighting artwork, fireplaces, plants, textured walls, or architectural details. However, be selective when using accent lighting because overuse can create a space that appears to be unorganized or cluttered.

Accent lighting is achieved by properly locating directional luminaires. For highest efficiency, luminaires should be located as close as possible to the object they illuminate. To select an appropriate luminaire and lamp, consult Table 3 in the Economics chapter, or manufacturers' data for beam spreads and intensity values. Low-voltage parabolic aluminized reflector (PAR) and multi-faceted reflector (MR) lamps are available with very narrow beams that are appropriate for small objects. These lamps are energy efficient because little light is wasted as stray light.

Avoid glare by using proper mounting locations and aiming angles. Manufacturers' catalogs often provide product-specific guidelines. Choose luminaires that have baffles or shields because glare is a special concern when using accent lighting.

Switch accent luminaires separately from other luminaires in the room so that the resident can use the accent luminaires only when they are needed. This also permits the resident to limit the time that sensitive objects such as photographs and artwork are exposed to light.

Create effective highlights and save energy by reducing the ambient light in the space surrounding the accented object. Additionally, choose background colors that contrast strongly with the highlighted object to reduce the light output required to achieve a dramatic effect. For example, place a white object on a dark background.

Luminaires: Ceiling-Mounted Track or Adjustable Heads, Suspended Downlights, Recessed Accent

Task

Task lighting provides increased light for specific tasks in a room that may already have some ambient lighting. Task lighting is especially appropriate for seeing small objects or objects of low contrast. For example, a person who is sewing would need extra light to easily see black stitches on black fabric. Task lighting can also provide increased illuminances for tasks that are critical, such as reading directions on a bottle of medicine. Some residential appliances, including sewing machines, range hoods, refrigerators, and upright vacuum cleaners, have built-in task lighting.

Always consider the tasks that will be performed in a room before designing the lighting. Plan for multiple uses of rooms, and for various arrangements of furniture. Remember that as people age, they need more light for critical tasks.

In the Designs chapter, the introductions to some rooms suggest task lighting techniques, as follows. To light counters, refer to Kitchen designs; to light desks, refer to Home Office designs; to light tables, refer to Dinette and Dining Room designs.

Luminaires: Ceiling-Mounted Diffusers, Ceiling-Mounted Track or Adjustable Heads, Suspended, Recessed Downlights, Recessed Wall Wash, Architectural, Under-Cabinet, Table and Desk Lamps

Special Purposes

Lighting for special purposes includes techniques that are useful in specific places or for specific purposes.

In the Designs chapter, the introductions to some rooms suggest techniques for lighting for special purposes, as follows. To light artwork, plants, or televisions, refer to Living Room designs; to light mirrors, refer to Bathroom designs; for lighting for reading in bed or for closets, refer to Bedroom designs; for security lighting, refer to Outdoor Spaces designs.

For more information refer to the indicated luminaires

Artwork: Ceiling-Mounted Track or Adjustable Heads, Recessed Wall Wash, Recessed Accent, Soffits, Valances, Artwork

Plants: Suspended Downlights, Shelf or Display Cabinet, Under-Cabinet

Televisions: Ceiling-Mounted Diffusers, Suspended, Recessed Downlights, Architectural, Wall-Mounted Sconces or Diffusers, Table and Floor Lamps

Mirrors: Ceiling- and Wall-Mounted Diffusers, Recessed Downlights, Soffits, Valances, Vanity Lights, Medicine Cabinet

Reading in Bed: Ceiling-Mounted Track or Adjustable Heads, Recessed Downlights, Soffits, Valances, Table and Desk Lamps, Night Light

Closets: Ceiling-Mounted Diffusers, Recessed Downlights, Night Light

Security: Ceiling-Mounted, Recessed, Soffits, Wall-Mounted, Exterior

Designs

A design involves the selection of one or more appropriate techniques for lighting a room, and then the selection of appropriate luminaires, lamps, and controls. The design arranges these technologies in the room to support the residents' activities and to enhance the appearance of the room. To create a comprehensive design, you must also consider the room size and shape; styles of architecture and furnishings; the price, availability, and energy requirements of the technologies; and the effort needed to install the equipment. Considering all these factors may seem intimidating at first, so this chapter is arranged to help you quickly identify some designs that you can adapt for your needs.

Typical and energy-efficient alternative designs

This chapter illustrates 36 rooms and outdoor spaces with typical lighting designs and 111 alternatives for replacing the lamps, controls, and luminaires or for remodeling or newly constructing these rooms. Note that many of these rooms are modest in size. They are practical and economical models for average homes. Use the typical designs to identify combinations of lamps, luminaires, and controls that are or would be likely to be used in your rooms. Then look at the alternative designs for energy-efficient ideas.

All of the designs were created without windows so that they could be modified for many building types and furniture arrangements. Nonetheless, be sure to use daylight wherever it is appropriate. See Daylight in the Techniques chapter for more information.

The typical rooms and their lighting designs serve as starting-points for evaluating the energy-efficient alternatives. Building audits, expert opinion, and examinations of plans for manufactured, low-income, and middle-income homes were used to establish the typical designs.

The suggested alternatives to the typical designs were reviewed by lighting experts to ensure that the quality is equal to or better than the typical design. See the descriptions with each design for any adjustments that affect quality. Note that even though the typical design for a particular room may be found in many homes, it may not be the best choice for your purposes: always consider the needs of the residents and the potential for energy savings to be gained from the alternative designs.

Style

Luminaires for homes usually are chosen for their decorative appearance, or style. To avoid issues of style, the luminaires illustrated in this chapter are as simple and unadorned as possible; the general types of luminaires and the lamp or lamps that they contain are the important features to consider for design and energy-efficiency. Different styles of luminaires can be substituted for the illustrated luminaires if the lamps and light distribution are similar. For instance, sconces can be found in a wide variety of styles. Choose styles that will suit the residents' preferences.

Annual operating costs

All of the alternative designs have lower annual operating costs than the typical designs. Refer to the bar graphs shown with each set of designs to see the annual lamp replacement and energy costs for each design. If a design is suggested as "optional," it is not shown in the graph. The assumptions for average hours of lighting use, average hours of use per lamp operation (hours per start), dimming, and occupancy are listed with each graph. Lamp prices, life, and input power are taken from Tables 3, 4, and 5 in the Economics chapter. The lamp life is adjusted for each design to reflect the impact of switching and dimming. All of the economic analyses use the procedure shown in the Economics Worksheet.

Effort versus savings

Electricity rates in North America vary widely, from as low as $0.03 to as high as $0.18 per kilowatt-hour (kWh). The bar graphs assume an electricity rate of $0.10 per kWh. If your cost of electricity is different, use a simple multiplier to estimate your annual energy cost. For example, if the annual energy cost on the graph is $8.00 per year and the electricity rates are $0.03, $0.06, or $0.14 per kWh, the multipliers will be 0.3, 0.6 or 1.4 respectively. Thus annual electricity cost of the designs for those rates is $2.40 ($8.00 x 0.3), $4.80 ($8.00 x 0.6), or $11.20 ($8.00 x 1.4). Remember, though, that the annual lamp costs will not change.

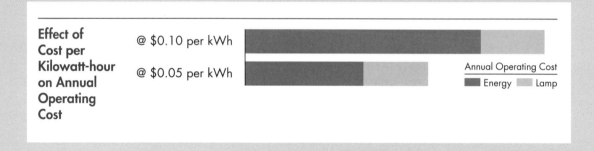

Effect of Cost per Kilowatt-hour on Annual Operating Cost

@ $0.10 per kWh

@ $0.05 per kWh

Annual Operating Cost
■ Energy ■ Lamp

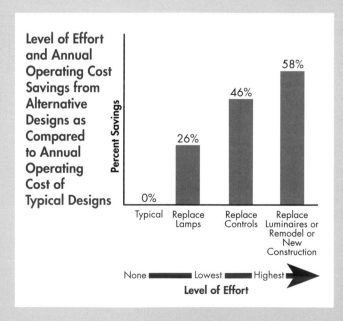

Level of Effort and Annual Operating Cost Savings from Alternative Designs as Compared to Annual Operating Cost of Typical Designs

Percent Savings

0% Typical
26% Replace Lamps
46% Replace Controls
58% Replace Luminaires or Remodel or New Construction

None ■ Lowest ■ Highest ➤
Level of Effort

The average percentage reduction in annual operating cost for the 111 alternative designs compared to the typical designs is 47 percent. Annual operating cost savings increase as the level of effort required to install the alternative design increases. Generally, the least effort is required to replace a lamp. More effort is required to replace a luminaire or control. Remodeling and new construction require the most effort. The "Replace Lamps" alternatives save an average of 26 percent in annual energy cost compared to the typical designs. The "Replace Controls" alternatives save an average of 46 percent. The "Replace Luminaires" and the "Remodel or New Construction" alternatives save an average of 58 percent.

Kitchens

Give special consideration to lighting counters, as this is the primary task area in kitchens. Where possible locate the sink in front of a window for good use of daylighting. Locate luminaires near the areas of greatest use and on both sides of the primary work areas to control glare. Install downlights over the counter 1 to 2 feet from the wall, but avoid locating them over the upper wall cabinets. To minimize shadows, avoid locating the lamp behind the person using the counter. Use under-cabinet luminaires to avoid shadows under overhead cabinets.

Small Kitchen

Typical

A ceiling-mounted diffuser containing three 60-watt incandescent A-lamps and controlled by a wall-mounted switch provides ambient lighting. Note that the location of the luminaire can cause shadows to be cast on the countertop. A range-hood luminaire provides lighting for cooking.

Replace lamps

Replace the A-lamps with three 52-watt halogen A-lamps, or use electronically ballasted 18-watt screwbase compact fluorescent lamps. If the luminaire is fully enclosed, check the fit of the replacement lamps.

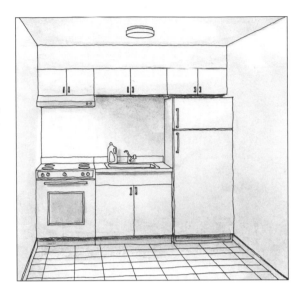

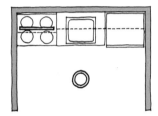

Replace luminaires

To reduce annual operating cost and to enjoy higher light output, install a ceiling-mounted diffuser containing two 32-watt, 4-foot T8 RE730 linear fluorescent lamps and one electronic ballast. Retain the wall-mounted switch.

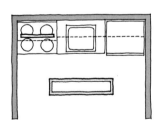

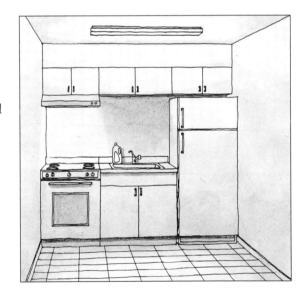

Annual Operating Cost at $0.10 per kWh

	Annual Operating Cost	
Typical		$22.00
Replace Lamps (halogen A-lamps)		$21.00
Replace Lamps (CFL)		$13.00
Replace Luminaires		$7.50

Annual Operating Cost
■ Energy ■ Lamp

CFL = compact fluorescent lamp
For all of the lamps, assume 3 hours of use per day and 2 hours per start.

Medium Kitchen 1

Typical

Four recessed downlights, without reflectors, each containing one 100-watt incandescent A-lamp, provide ambient lighting and lighting for the counter. One wall-mounted switch controls the downlights.

Replace lamps

Replace each A-lamp with a 50-watt halogen PAR30 flood lamp.

Replace controls

For the typical design, replace the wall-mounted switch with a manual-on/manual-off motion detector.

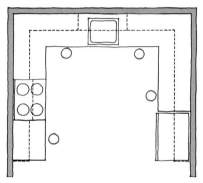

Replace luminaires

If lower light output is acceptable, modify each of the recessed downlights with a conversion kit that houses a reflector, a magnetic ballast, and two 13-watt compact fluorescent twin-tube lamps.

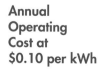
Annual Operating Cost at $0.10 per kWh

	Annual Operating Cost
Typical	$48.00
Replace Lamps	$41.50
Replace Controls	$33.50
Replace Luminaires	$19.00

Annual Operating Cost
■ Energy   ■ Lamp

For all of the lamps, assume 3 hours of use per day and 2 hours per start. The motion detector factor is 70 percent.

Medium Kitchen 2

Typical

A ceiling-mounted diffuser containing four 40-watt, 4-foot T12 cool white linear fluorescent lamps and two magnetic ballasts provides ambient lighting. Task lighting for the sink is provided by one under-cabinet luminaire containing two 20-watt, 2-foot T12 cool white linear fluorescent lamps and one magnetic ballast. The hood of the stove contains a luminaire. The ceiling and under-cabinet luminaire are controlled separately by two wall-mounted switches.

Replace lamps

Replace the lamps with 34-watt, 4-foot T12 RE730 and 20-watt, 2-foot T12 RE730 linear fluorescent lamps to provide better color and slightly lower annual operating cost.

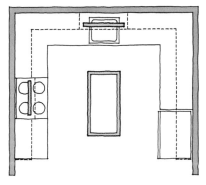

Replace luminaires

Replace the existing luminaire with a similar luminaire that houses four 32-watt, 4-foot T8 RE730 linear fluorescent lamps and one electronic ballast. Optionally, if a lower light output is acceptable, install a luminaire that contains only two or three lamps. Replace the under-cabinet luminaire with a similar luminaire that houses two 17-watt, 2-foot T8 RE730 linear fluorescent lamps and one electronic ballast. If the same number of lamps is used, it may not be necessary to install a new luminaire. It will, however, be necessary to install a new ballast to operate the T8 lamps. This must be done by an electrician, or someone qualified to perform electrical wiring.

Remodel or new construction

To create a different light distribution pattern, two coves, each containing one 32-watt, 4-foot T8 RE730 linear fluorescent lamp and one electronic ballast, provide uplighting and ambient lighting for the kitchen. Three under-cabinet luminaires and one valance over the sink each containing one 17-watt, 2-foot T8 RE730 linear fluorescent lamp and one magnetic ballast provide lighting for the counter. The valance is controlled by a wall-mounted switch; the under-cabinet luminaires have luminaire-mounted switches. The cove luminaires are controlled separately by two wall-mounted switches.

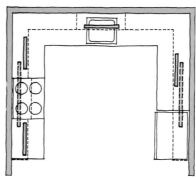

Annual Operating Cost at $0.10 per kWh

Typical	$28.50
Replace Lamps	$27.50
Replace Luminaires	$20.50
Remodel or New Construction	$20.00

Annual Operating Cost
■ Energy ■ Lamp

For all of the lamps, assume 3 hours of use per day and 2 hours per start.
The luminaire in the range hood is not included in the analysis.

Medium Kitchen 3

Typical

Eight 40-watt, 4-foot T12 cool white linear fluorescent lamps with four magnetic ballasts provide the ambient lighting from this luminous ceiling. One wall-mounted switch controls all of the lamps. Some installations may have eight magnetic ballasts, one for each lamp.

Replace lamps

To improve color and slightly lower the light output, replace the lamps with 34-watt, 4-foot T12 RE730 lamps. If the space is overlit and each lamp has its own ballast, consider removing four of the lamps, and replacing the other four with 40-watt, 4-foot T10 lamps.

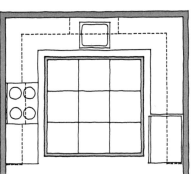

Replace luminaires

To improve the efficiency of the luminous ceiling, paint the ceiling cavity white to increase reflectance, and clean or replace old diffusers. Replace the lamps with eight 32-watt, 4-foot T8 RE730 lamps. Replace the magnetic ballasts with electronic ballasts. Optionally, wire the lamps to two wall-mounted switches so that either four or eight of the lamps can be switched to give two levels of light output. Optionally, use four dimmable electronic ballasts and one wall-mounted dimmer.

Replace luminaires

If the space is grossly overlit, replace the lamps with four 32-watt, 4-foot T8 RE730 lamps with electronic

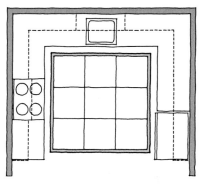

ballasts, controlled by one wall-mounted switch. This design gives significantly less light output than the original design, but it is probably sufficient and perhaps more visually comfortable for ambient lighting. Under-cabinet luminaires may be needed to light the counters.

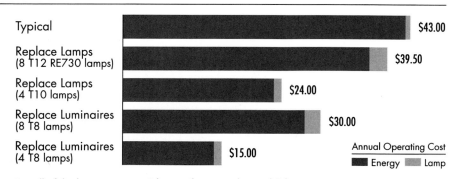

Annual Operating Cost at $0.10 per kWh

	Annual Operating Cost
Typical	$43.00
Replace Lamps (8 T12 RE730 lamps)	$39.50
Replace Lamps (4 T10 lamps)	$24.00
Replace Luminaires (8 T8 lamps)	$30.00
Replace Luminaires (4 T8 lamps)	$15.00

Annual Operating Cost
■ Energy　■ Lamp

For all of the lamps, assume 3 hours of use per day and 2 hours per start.

Large Kitchen

Typical

Seven ceiling-mounted track heads and one suspended downlight, each containing one 75-watt incandescent A-lamp, provide ambient lighting and lighting for the counters. Two wall-mounted switches control the two types of luminaires.

Replace lamps

If lower light output is acceptable, replace the A-lamps in the track heads with 60-watt halogen A-lamps. Optionally, for track heads that are designed for R-lamps, replace the lamps with 50-watt halogen PAR-lamps. Replace the A-lamp in the suspended downlight with one electronically ballasted 18-watt globe screwbase compact fluorescent lamp if a slightly lower light output is acceptable and any existing diffuser can be removed.

Replace controls

For the typical design, replace the switch for the track heads with a dimmer or, optionally, with a motion detector.

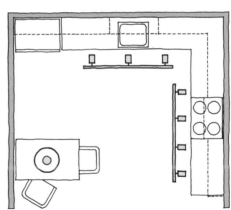

Replace luminaires

Without altering the layout of the tracks, replace the existing seven track heads with four track heads, each containing one 39-watt, 16.5-inch fluorescent twin-tube lamp and one electronic ballast. Replace the A-lamp in the suspended downlight with one electronically ballasted 18-watt globe screwbase compact fluorescent lamp if a lower light output is acceptable and any existing diffuser can be removed. Control both types of luminaires with wall-mounted switches.

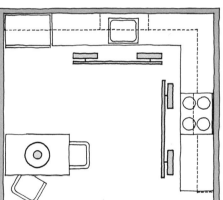

CONTINUED

Designs

Remodel or new construction

This design offers a different light distribution pattern, especially on the counters where light is provided by four under-cabinet luminaires, each containing one 13-watt, 21-inch warm white T5 linear fluorescent lamp and one magnetic ballast. One ceiling-mounted diffuser and one suspended downlight each containing three 13-watt compact fluorescent twin-tube lamps and one magnetic ballast provide ambient lighting.

The ceiling-mounted luminaires are controlled by a wall-mounted switch and the T5 lamps are controlled by one manual switch or optionally by switches mounted on each luminaire.

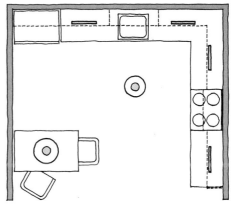

Annual Operating Cost at $0.10 per kWh

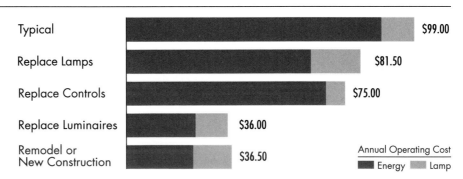

	Annual Operating Cost
Typical	$99.00
Replace Lamps	$81.50
Replace Controls	$75.00
Replace Luminaires	$36.00
Remodel or New Construction	$36.50

Annual Operating Cost
■ Energy   ▨ Lamp

For all of the lamps, assume 4 hours of use per day and 2 hours per start. Lamps with dimmers are dimmed 50 percent of the time they are operated, to 50 percent light output as perceived by the human eye; the other 50 percent of the time, they are operated at full light output.

Dining Rooms

These designs illustrate areas of the home containing a table used primarily for eating, although other tasks such as food preparation and doing homework may also be done at these tables. A dining room is often a separate room; a dinette may be part of a kitchen area or a separate alcove. Use these designs for any area of the home used for dining.

Where possible, locate the table near a window to take advantage of daylighting. The most important function in dining rooms is seeing what is on the table and the people around it, so supplement ambient light with a luminaire over or near the table. Consider using the wall washing technique if the table is against a wall and the wall is a light color. In small rooms, a single luminaire over the table often can provide task lighting for the table as well as ambient lighting. Use dimming where the table is used for different tasks such as dining and homework.

Small Dinette

Typical

One 100-watt incandescent A-lamp in a ceiling-mounted diffuser provides ambient lighting. The control is a wall-mounted switch.

Replace lamps

If a lower light output is acceptable, replace the A-lamp with a 75-watt halogen A-lamp.

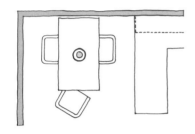

Replace luminaires

Install a simple ceiling-mounted diffuser containing a magnetically ballasted 32-watt, 12-inch circline RE730 fluorescent lamp controlled by a wall-mounted switch. Optionally, consider a more sophisticated luminaire that is suspended close to the ceiling and offers better control of glare.

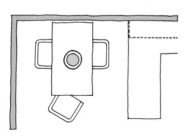

Remodel or new construction

A soffit provides ambient lighting with light output equal to or higher than the typical design. The soffit contains one 32-watt, 4-foot T8 RE830 linear fluorescent lamp with one magnetic ballast, controlled by a wall-mounted switch.

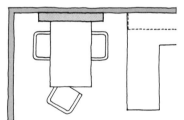

Note that this design drastically changes the distribution of light in the room; the light is reflected off the wall and ceiling rather than being directed down onto the center of the table. The walls must be painted a light color to ensure high reflectance.

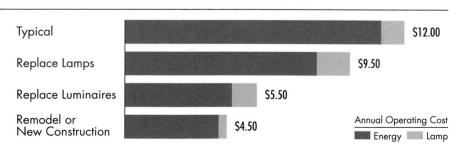

Annual Operating Cost at $0.10 per kWh

	Annual Operating Cost
Typical	$12.00
Replace Lamps	$9.50
Replace Luminaires	$5.50
Remodel or New Construction	$4.50

Annual Operating Cost
■ Energy ■ Lamp

For all of the lamps, assume 3 hours of use per day and 2 hours per start.

Medium Dinette

Typical

A 75-watt incandescent A-lamp in the suspended downlight provides both ambient lighting and lighting for the table. A wall-mounted switch controls the luminaire.

Replace lamps

If a slightly lower light output is acceptable, replace the A-lamp with either a 60-watt halogen A-lamp or with an electronically ballasted 18-watt globe screwbase compact fluorescent lamp. For the latter option, remove any diffusing lens or globe from the luminaire.

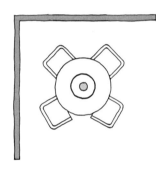

Replace luminaires

Replace the existing luminaire with a ceiling-mounted diffuser containing two 13-watt compact fluorescent twin-tube lamps and one magnetic ballast. Retain the wall-mounted switch.

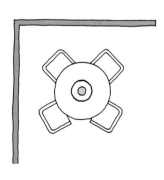

Remodel or new construction

Install a valance for both wall washing and ambient lighting. This design offers greater light output because the valance contains two 32-watt, 4-foot T8 RE730 linear fluorescent lamps with one electronic ballast. The luminaire is controlled by a wall-mounted switch.

Annual Operating Cost at $0.10 per kWh

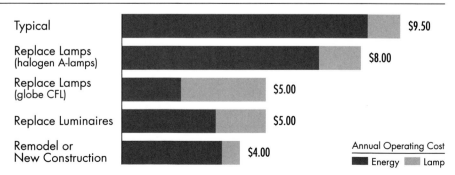

	Annual Operating Cost
Typical	$9.50
Replace Lamps (halogen A-lamps)	$8.00
Replace Lamps (globe CFL)	$5.00
Replace Luminaires	$5.00
Remodel or New Construction	$4.00

Annual Operating Cost
■ Energy ■ Lamp

CFL = compact fluorescent lamp
For all of the lamps, assume 3 hours of use per day and 2 hours per start.

Dining Room

Typical

A chandelier containing five 60-watt incandescent A-lamps illuminates the table and provides ambient lighting. It is controlled by a wall-mounted switch, as are two sconces that also provide ambient lighting. Each sconce also contains one 60-watt incandescent A-lamp.

Replace lamps

Replace the A-lamps with 52-watt halogen A-lamps. Consider installing a dimmer to vary the light output.

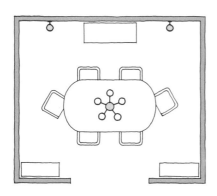

Remodel or new construction

If lower light output is acceptable, install sconces that each contain one 13-watt compact fluorescent twin-tube lamp and one magnetic ballast. Replace the chandelier with two suspended downlights, each containing two 13-watt compact fluorescent twin-tube lamps and one magnetic ballast. Two luminaires are needed to provide even light distribution on the table. One wall-mounted switch controls both suspended luminaires; another switch controls the sconces.

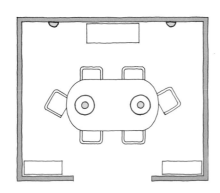

Remodel or new construction

Replace the sconces with two recessed accent luminaires, each containing one 50-watt halogen PAR30 lamp. Replace the chandelier with four recessed downlights with louvers to control glare; each downlight contains two 13-watt compact fluorescent twin-tube lamps and one magnetic ballast. Separate wall-mounted switches control the downlights and the recessed accent luminaires.

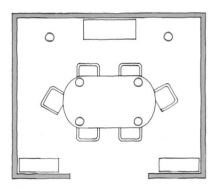

Annual Operating Cost at $0.10 per kWh

Typical	$42.00
Replace Lamps	$39.50
Remodel or New Construction*	$11.50
Remodel or New Construction**	$26.00

Annual Operating Cost
■ Energy ▪ Lamp

* Sconces and two suspended luminaires ** PAR30, compact fluorescent twin-tube
For the lamps in the sconces and recessed accent luminaires, assume 1 hour of use per day and 1 hour per start. For the lamps in the chandelier, the suspended luminaires, and the recessed luminaires over the table, assume 3 hours of use per day and 2 hours per start.

Designs

35

Living Rooms

The living room designs support many activities, including conversation, reading, and viewing television.

Locate luminaires near places where reading or other visually demanding tasks will be done. Use table or floor lamps, which can be relocated as the furniture arrangement changes. For watching television, use low-level ambient lighting.

Locate the television so that the images of light sources, including windows, are not reflected from the television screen into the eyes of the viewer. For greater viewing comfort, avoid windows or bright lamps and luminaires on the wall directly behind the television. Switch lamps separately in a living room with a television, or use dimmers to reduce ambient light when there are no other simultaneous visual tasks such as reading.

Living rooms may also have artwork on the walls. Avoid direct sunlight on paintings, prints, and drawings to reduce fading. To highlight artwork, use accent lighting or wall washing techniques. Position the lamp to avoid reflected glare, especially for shiny surfaces or glass-covered artworks. Locate low-wattage lamps close to the artwork to save energy while maintaining illumination; however, do not locate them so close that they would discolor or burn the artwork. See the Accent technique for more information. To reveal texture and form on sculptures, try lighting one side of the form more than the other to create shadows. Switch the artwork luminaires separately to avoid long exposure to light on sensitive artwork.

Plants have special lighting requirements that can be met economically and efficiently in the home. A simple system of linear fluorescent lamps, positionable luminaires, and a timer can be integrated into shelving, display cabinets, or free-standing benches. Consult a lamp catalog or a garden center for guidance on lamp selection.

Small Living Room 1

Typical

Two table lamps, each containing one 100-watt incandescent A-lamp, provide ambient lighting and lighting for television viewing; one table lamp is controlled by a wall-mounted switch.

Replace lamps

If a lower light output is acceptable, replace the A-lamps with either 75-watt halogen A-lamps or with magnetically ballasted 26-watt screwbase compact fluorescent lamps. Note that electronically ballasted lamps may interfere with the television remote control. Make sure that the weight of the compact fluorescent lamps does not make the table lamps top-heavy or otherwise unbalanced. Also, do not use compact fluorescent lamps in dimmable table lamps.

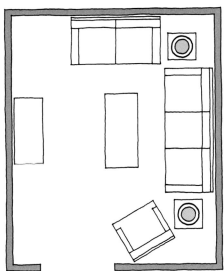

Annual Operating Cost at $0.10 per kWh		
Typical		$24.00
Replace Lamps (halogen A-lamps)		$19.50
Replace Lamps (CFL)		$10.00

Annual Operating Cost
■ Energy ■ Lamp

CFL = compact fluorescent lamp
For all of the lamps, assume 3 hours of use per day and 2 hours per start.

Small Living Room 2

Typical

One ceiling-mounted diffuser containing four 60-watt incandescent A-lamps provides ambient lighting and is controlled by a wall-mounted switch.

Replace lamps

Replace the A-lamps with 52-watt halogen A-lamps.

Replace controls

For the typical design, replace the wall-mounted switch with a dimmer; however, do not use a dimmer with compact fluorescent lamps.

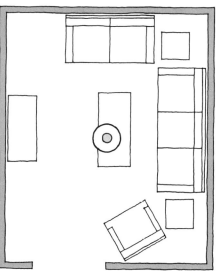

Replace luminaires

One ceiling-mounted diffuser containing two 13-watt compact fluorescent twin-tube lamps and one magnetic ballast provides ambient lighting. A table lamp containing two 13-watt compact fluorescent twin-tube lamps and a magnetic ballast provides lighting for television viewing and reading. A wall-mounted switch controls the diffuser.

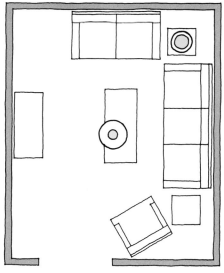

Annual Operating Cost at $0.10 per kWh

	Annual Operating Cost	
Typical		$29.50
Replace Lamps		$28.00
Replace Controls		$21.50
Replace Luminaires		$9.50

Annual Operating Cost
■ Energy ■ Lamp

For all of the lamps, assume 3 hours of use per day and 2 hours per start. Lamps with dimmers are dimmed 50 percent of the time they are operated, to 50 percent light output as perceived by the human eye; the other 50 percent of the time, they are operated at full light output.

Medium Living Room 1

Typical

One ceiling-mounted diffuser containing three 60-watt incandescent A-lamps provides ambient lighting and lighting for television viewing and is controlled by a wall-mounted switch. One table lamp containing one 75-watt incandescent A-lamp also provides ambient lighting; it is controlled by a wall-mounted switch.

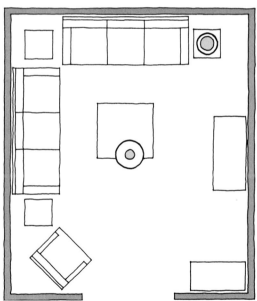

Replace lamps

Replace the A-lamps in the diffuser with 52-watt halogen A-lamps, and the one in the table lamp with a 60-watt halogen A-lamp if a slightly lower light output is acceptable near the table lamp.

Replace controls

For the typical design, replace the control for the diffuser with a motion detector.

Remodel or new construction

For a different light distribution pattern in the living room, install a valance containing three 32-watt, 4-foot T8 RE830 linear fluorescent lamps and one electronic ballast to provide ambient lighting, wall washing, and lighting for television viewing and reading. One table lamp containing two 13-watt compact fluorescent lamps and one magnetic ballast also provides ambient lighting. Both the valance and the table lamp are controlled by wall-mounted switches. Optionally, the valance could be controlled by a wall-mounted dimmer if a dimming ballast is installed.

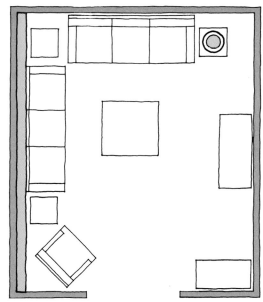

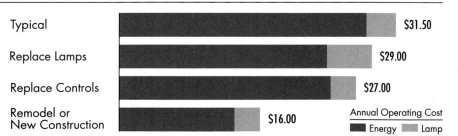

Annual Operating Cost at $0.10 per kWh		
Typical		$31.50
Replace Lamps		$29.00
Replace Controls		$27.00
Remodel or New Construction		$16.00

Annual Operating Cost
■ Energy ■ Lamp

For all of the lamps, assume 3 hours of use per day and 2 hours per start. The motion detector factor is 80 percent.

Medium Living Room 2

Typical

A ceiling fan luminaire with four 60-watt A-lamps provides ambient lighting. Two floor lamps, each containing a three-level 50/100/150-watt lamp, provide lighting for reading. The lamps in the fan luminaire are controlled by a wall-mounted switch.

Replace lamps

To reduce glare, and if lower light output is acceptable, replace the 60-watt lamps with 42-watt halogen A-lamps.

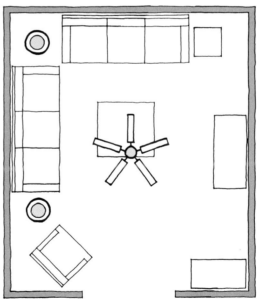

Remodel or new construction

Remove the light kit from the ceiling fan. For ambient lighting, install a valance that contains three 32-watt, 4-foot T8 RE830 linear fluorescent lamps and an electronic ballast. Optionally, install a dimming electronic ballast. Two table lamps each contain two 13-watt compact fluorescent twin-tube lamps and one magnetic ballast. Wall-mounted switches control the valance and the table lamps.

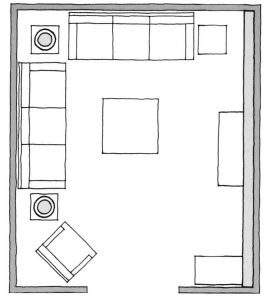

Annual Operating Cost at $0.10 per kWh

Typical		$55.00
Replace Lamps		$48.50
Remodel or New Construction	$21.00	

Annual Operating Cost
■ Energy ■ Lamp

For all of the lamps, assume 3 hours of use per day and 2 hours per start. For the three-level lamp, assume that the average wattage during use is 100 watts.

Large Living Room 1

Typical

Four recessed downlights, each containing one 75-watt R30 lamp, provide ambient lighting. Two table lamps, each containing two 60-watt A-lamps, provide lighting for reading. A recessed accent luminaire containing a 75-watt R30 lamp highlights the fireplace and is controlled by a separate wall-mounted switch.

Replace lamps

Replace the five R30 lamps with five 50-watt PAR30 halogen flood lamps and the four 60-watt lamps with 52-watt halogen A-lamps. Alternatively, replace the four 60-watt lamps with four electronically ballasted 18-watt screwbase compact fluorescent twin-tube lamps, if they fit in the luminaires.

Replace controls

For the typical design, replace the wall-mounted switch for the four recessed downlights with a motion detector. Optionally, install dimmers for the table lamps but do not use dimmers with compact fluorescent lamps.

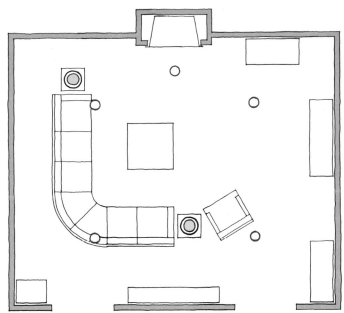

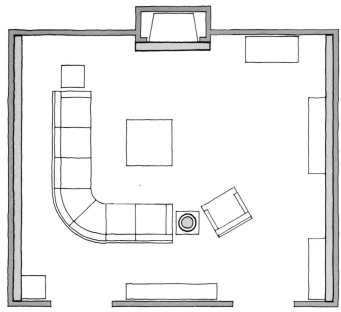

Remodel or new construction

For a different light distribution pattern in the living room, two valances and one soffit, containing a total of seven electronically ballasted 40-watt, 5-foot T8 linear fluorescent RE830 lamps, provide ambient lighting. Depending upon the dimensions of the room, 4-foot lamps could also be used in these architectural luminaires. The table lamp contains two 13-watt compact fluorescent twin-tube lamps and one magnetic ballast. The valances and soffit each are controlled by a wall-mounted switch.

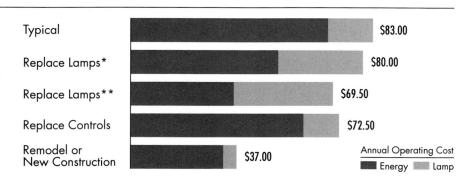

Annual Operating Cost at $0.10 per kWh

Typical	$83.00
Replace Lamps*	$80.00
Replace Lamps**	$69.50
Replace Controls	$72.50
Remodel or New Construction	$37.00

Annual Operating Cost
■ Energy ■ Lamp

* PAR30, halogen A-lamps ** PAR30, compact fluorescent twin-tube
For all of the lamps, assume 3 hours of use per day and 2 hours per start.
The motion detector factor is 80 percent.

Large Living Room 2

Typical

Twelve recessed downlights, each containing one 150-watt R40 lamp, provide ambient lighting. The perimeter and interior lamps are controlled by separate wall-mounted switches.

Replace lamps

Replace the 150-watt lamps with 60-watt IR PAR38 halogen flood lamps or alternatively, if lower light output is acceptable, with 50-watt PAR30 halogen flood lamps.

Replace controls

For the typical design, replace the wall-mounted switches with dimmers.

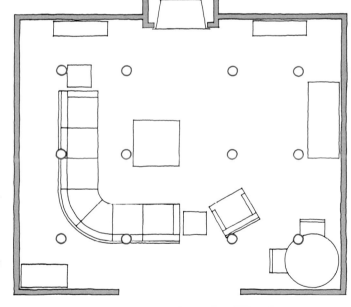

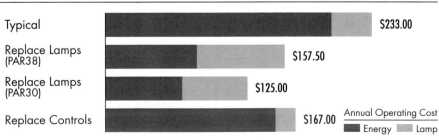

Annual Operating Cost at $0.10 per kWh		
Typical		$233.00
Replace Lamps (PAR38)		$157.50
Replace Lamps (PAR30)		$125.00
Replace Controls		$167.00

Annual Operating Cost
■ Energy ■ Lamp

For all of the lamps, assume 3 hours of use per day and 2 hours per start. Lamps with dimmers are dimmed 50 percent of the time they are operated, to 50 percent light output as perceived by the human eye; the other 50 percent of the time, they are operated at full light output.

Large Living Room 3

Typical

A ceiling fan luminaire with one 150-watt A-lamp provides ambient lighting; it is controlled by a wall-mounted switch. A table lamp containing one 60-watt A-lamp and a suspended downlight containing one 100-watt A-lamp also provide ambient lighting and lighting for reading. The suspended luminaire is controlled by a wall-mounted switch. The ceiling-mounted track with four adjustable heads, each containing one 75-watt R30 lamp, washes the wall and artwork with light. The track luminaire is controlled by a wall-mounted switch.

Replace lamps

If lower light output is acceptable, replace the 150-watt lamp in the fan luminaire with a 100-watt halogen A-lamp. Replace the lamp in the table lamp with an electronically ballasted 18-watt screwbase compact fluorescent lamp, using a harp extender if needed. Remove the diffuser and replace the lamp in the suspended luminaire with an electronically ballasted 18-watt globe screwbase compact fluorescent lamp.

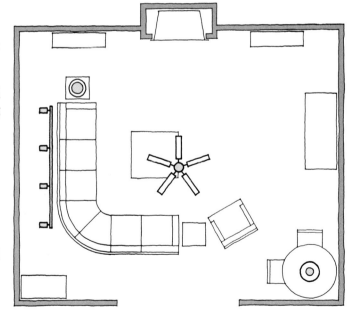

Replace the 75-watt lamps in the track heads with 50-watt PAR30 halogen lamps.

Replace controls

For the typical design, replace the wall-mounted switches with dimmers. Install a socket and cord dimmer on the table lamp. Do not use dimmers with compact fluorescent lamps.

CONTINUED

Remodel or new construction

A ceiling fan luminaire with one 75-watt halogen A-lamp provides ambient lighting; it is controlled by a wall-mounted dimmer. For a different light distribution pattern in the living room, two valances, containing a total of eight 32-watt, 4-foot T8 RE830 linear fluorescent lamps, provide ambient lighting; they are electronically ballasted and controlled by two wall-mounted switches. Depending upon the dimensions of the room, 5-foot lamps could be used in the valances. A luminaire containing two 13-watt, 21-inch T5 linear fluorescent warm white lamps provides lighting for objects in the cabinets; it is controlled by a luminaire-mounted switch.

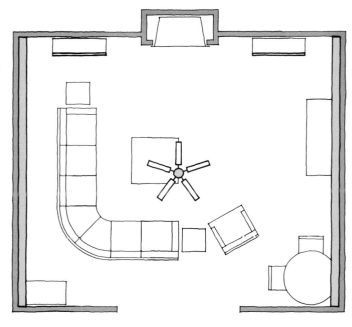

Annual Operating Cost at $0.10 per kWh

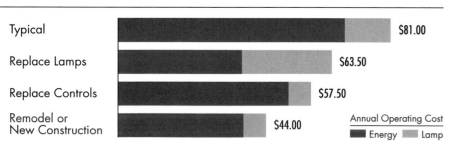

	Annual Operating Cost
Typical	$81.00
Replace Lamps	$63.50
Replace Controls	$57.50
Remodel or New Construction	$44.00

Annual Operating Cost
■ Energy ■ Lamp

For all of the lamps, assume 3 hours of use per day and 2 hours per start. Lamps with dimmers are dimmed 50 percent of the time they are operated, to 50 percent light output as perceived by the human eye; the other 50 percent of the time, they are operated at full light output.

Designs

Bathrooms

An important visual task in a bathroom is viewing oneself in the mirror. Direct the light to the person, not to the mirror. Use light from both sides of the mirror to reduce shadows on the face. If a single luminaire is used above the mirror, use one that is at least 2 feet long to avoid casting shadows under the chin; avoid reflector lamps because they may cast harsh shadows. Use a light-colored countertop to reflect light under the chin. Also avoid locating the lamp behind the persons viewing the mirror, to prevent their faces from being in a shadow. Use rare-earth fluorescent lamps for bathroom mirrors to provide good color.

Half Bath

Typical

One exhaust fan and luminaire combination containing one 100-watt incandescent A-lamp provides ambient lighting and is controlled by a wall-mounted switch.

Replace lamps

If lower light output is acceptable, replace the 100-watt A-lamp with one 75-watt halogen A-lamp.

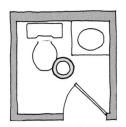

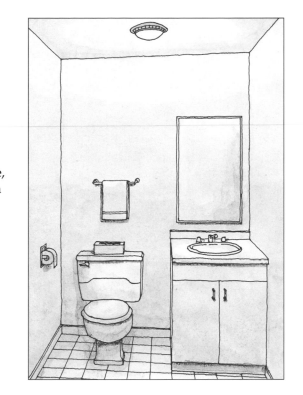

Remodel or new construction

For more light output, install one wall-mounted vanity light containing two 20-watt, 2-foot T12 RE730 linear fluorescent lamps with one magnetic ballast, controlled by a wall-mounted switch.

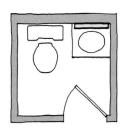

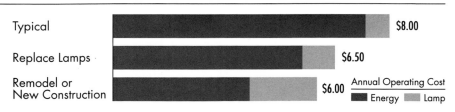

Annual Operating Cost at $0.10 per kWh

	Annual Operating Cost
Typical	$8.00
Replace Lamps	$6.50
Remodel or New Construction	$6.00

Annual Operating Cost
■ Energy   ■ Lamp

For all of the lamps, assume 2 hours of use per day and 30 minutes per start.

Small Bath

Typical

One vanity light containing three 60-watt G25 incandescent lamps controlled by a wall-mounted switch provides ambient lighting and lighting for the mirror.

Replace lamps

Replace each G25 lamp with one electronically ballasted 15-watt globe screwbase compact fluorescent lamp. Note that the high cost of the globe compact fluorescent lamps can be offset by the annual energy savings.

Optionally, if lamps are operated all night for orientation in the typical design, add a ¼-watt or 7½-watt night light and use it instead of the other lamps.

Replace controls

For the typical design, replace the wall-mounted switch with a motion detector.

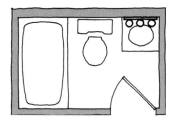

Replace luminaires

One wall-mounted vanity light containing two 18-watt, 10.5-inch fluorescent twin-tube lamps and one electronic ballast controlled by a wall-mounted switch provides ambient lighting and lighting for the mirror.

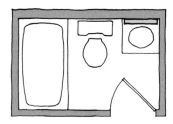

Remodel or new construction

Install a soffit containing one 32-watt, 4-foot T8 RE730 linear fluorescent lamp and one electronic ballast controlled by a wall-mounted switch.

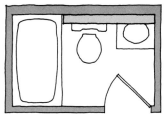

Annual Operating Cost at $0.10 per kWh

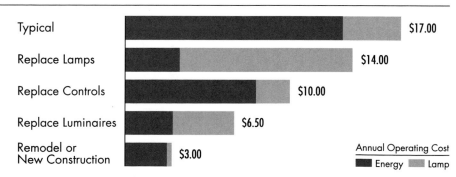

	Annual Operating Cost
Typical	$17.00
Replace Lamps	$14.00
Replace Controls	$10.00
Replace Luminaires	$6.50
Remodel or New Construction	$3.00

Annual Operating Cost
■ Energy   ■ Lamp

For all of the lamps, assume 2 hours of use per day and 30 minutes per start. The motion detector factor is 60 percent.

Medium Bath 1

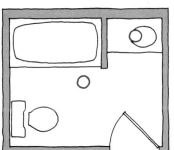

Typical

Two recessed downlights, each containing one 75-watt R30 flood lamp and each controlled by a wall-mounted switch, provide ambient lighting and lighting for the mirror.

Replace controls

For the typical design, rewire the downlights so that they both are controlled by a wall-mounted motion detector.

Replace luminaires

Modify each of the downlights using a conversion kit that houses a reflector, a magnetic ballast and two 13-watt compact fluorescent twin-tube lamps.

Remodel or new construction

A soffit containing one 25-watt, 3-foot T8 RE730 linear fluorescent lamp and one electronic ballast provides ambient lighting and lighting for the mirror. One ceiling-mounted diffuser containing two 13-watt compact fluorescent twin-tube lamps and one magnetic ballast provides ambient lighting. The luminaires are separately controlled by wall-mounted switches.

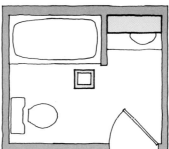

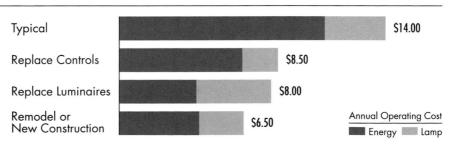

Annual Operating Cost at $0.10 per kWh			
Typical			$14.00
Replace Controls			$8.50
Replace Luminaires			$8.00
Remodel or New Construction			$6.50

Annual Operating Cost
■ Energy ■ Lamp

For all of the lamps, assume 2 hours of use per day and 30 minutes per start. The motion detector factor is 60 percent.

Typical

One luminaire mounted on the medicine cabinet contains four 60-watt A-lamps and provides mirror lighting; a ceiling-mounted diffuser with one 60-watt A-lamp provides ambient lighting.

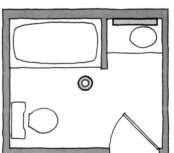

Replace lamps

If lower light output is acceptable, replace the four 60-watt lamps with either two 75-watt halogen A-lamps, or two electronically ballasted 27-watt screwbase compact fluorescent lamps. Note that the luminaire will not be evenly lit; this may be unacceptable to some residents. Check the size of the compact fluorescent lamps to make sure they fit in the luminaire. Use a 52-watt halogen A-lamp to replace the 60-watt lamp in the diffuser.

Remodel or new construction

Install three sconces, each containing two 13-watt compact fluorescent twin-tube lamps and one magnetic ballast. Optionally, install sconces that contain electronic ballasts. The sconces are controlled by one wall-mounted switch.

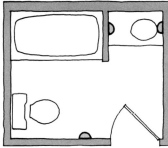

Annual Operating Cost at $0.10 per kWh		
Typical		$24.50
Replace Lamps (halogen A-lamps)		$17.50
Replace Lamps (CF, halogen A-lamps)		$15.00
Remodel or New Construction		$12.50

Annual Operating Cost
■ Energy ■ Lamp

CF = compact fluorescent
For all of the lamps, assume 2 hours of use per day and 30 minutes per start.

Large Bath

Typical

Two wall-mounted vanity lights, each containing four 40-watt G25 incandescent lamps, provide ambient lighting and lighting for the mirror. One recessed downlight (enclosed with a lens) containing one 60-watt incandescent A-lamp provides lighting in the shower. Another recessed downlight contains one 250-watt R40 heat lamp.

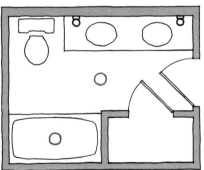

Replace controls

Replace the wall-mounted switches for the vanity lights and the heat lamp with interval timers.

Replace luminaires

Two wall-mounted vanity lights, each containing two 18-watt, 10.5-inch long twin-tube fluorescent lamps and one magnetic ballast, provide ambient lighting and lighting for the mirror. One recessed downlight containing two 13-watt compact fluorescent twin-tube lamps and one magnetic ballast provides lighting in the shower. This design retains the recessed downlight that contains one 250-watt R40 heat lamp. Each type of luminaire is controlled by a separate wall-mounted switch.

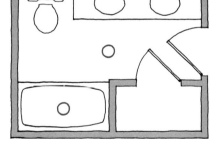

CONTINUED

Remodel or new construction

Install a soffit containing two 40-watt, 5-foot T8 RE730 linear fluorescent lamps and one electronic ballast to provide ambient lighting. For lighting in the shower, install one recessed downlight (enclosed with a lens) containing two 13-watt compact fluorescent twin-tube lamps and one magnetic ballast. This design also retains the recessed downlight with a 250-watt R40 heat lamp, but the downlight is controlled by an interval timer. The other luminaires are controlled separately by wall-mounted switches.

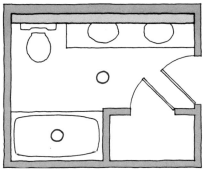

Annual Operating Cost at $0.10 per kWh

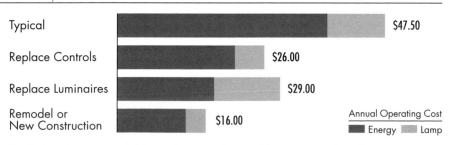

	Annual Operating Cost
Typical	$47.50
Replace Controls	$26.00
Replace Luminaires	$29.00
Remodel or New Construction	$16.00

Annual Operating Cost
■ Energy ■ Lamp

For the heat lamp, assume 1 hour of use per day, but 30 minutes per day when it is controlled by a timer. For the other lamps, assume 2 hours of use per day and 30 minutes per start, but 1 hour of use per day if they are controlled by a timer.

Designs

Bedrooms

Provide a separately switched task light for reading in bed. Consider using wall-mounted luminaires with adjustable arms so that they can be positioned to direct light onto the reading material and to avoid glare. Locate the switch so that it is accessible from the bed. To avoid potential burns, be sure that the luminaires are secure, especially those containing incandescent lamps. Locate the luminaire above the head of the bed to minimize shadows. For orientation at night, use a low-wattage night light plugged into an electrical outlet instead of operating a hall or closet light.

Some bedrooms have luminaires in the closet. Consider using the room's ambient lighting for shallow closets because supplementary lighting for closets is not always necessary. Clothes-closet storage areas, as defined by the National Electric Code, may not contain unenclosed incandescent or fluorescent lamps. An enclosed surface-mounted luminaire with incandescent lamps may be used in closets if the luminaire is at least 12 inches away from the storage area (6 inches for a luminaire with fluorescent lamps). Enclosed recessed luminaires (with incandescent or fluorescent lamps) must be at least 6 inches away from the storage area. If a closet luminaire is likely to be left on, consider using a timer or luminaires with fluorescent lamps. Locate surface-mounted luminaires so that they do not interfere with placing objects on the shelf. Do not locate the luminaire directly over the storage shelf; instead, place it on the opposite wall, near the ceiling.

Small Bedroom

Typical

One table lamp containing one 75-watt incandescent A-lamp provides ambient lighting and lighting for the table, as does one desk lamp containing one 60-watt incandescent A-lamp. The table lamp is plugged into an electrical outlet that is controlled by a wall-mounted switch.

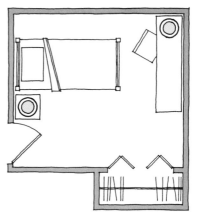

Replace lamps

If less light output is acceptable, replace the A-lamp in the table lamp with a 60-watt halogen A-lamp. Replace the A-lamp in the desk lamp with a 52-watt halogen A-lamp.

Replace lamps

If the luminaires are large enough, replace the A-lamps in the table and desk lamps with electronically ballasted screwbase compact fluorescent lamps of 26-watts and 20-watts, respectively.

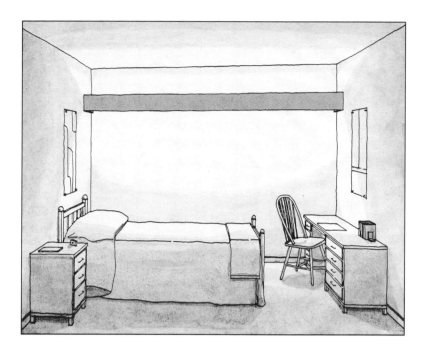

Remodel or new construction

A valance with a louver containing two 34-watt, 4-foot T12 RE730 linear fluorescent lamps and one electronic ballast provides ambient lighting. This design creates a different light distribution pattern, but still provides suitable lighting for the bed and desk.

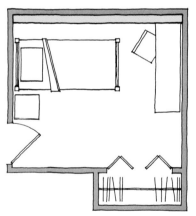

Annual Operating Cost at $0.10 per kWh

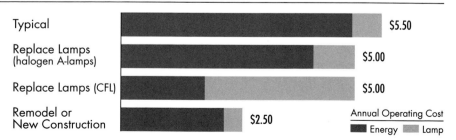

	Annual Operating Cost
Typical	$5.50
Replace Lamps (halogen A-lamps)	$5.00
Replace Lamps (CFL)	$5.00
Remodel or New Construction	$2.50

Annual Operating Cost — ■ Energy ▪ Lamp

CFL = compact fluorescent lamps
For all of the lamps, assume 1 hour of use per day and 30 minutes per start.

Children's Bedroom

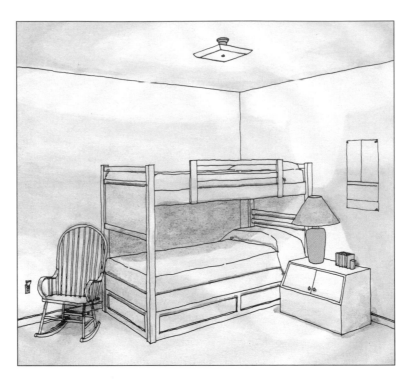

Typical

One ceiling-mounted diffuser containing two 60-watt incandescent A-lamps provides ambient lighting and is controlled by a wall-mounted switch. One desk lamp containing one 60-watt incandescent A-lamp provides lighting for the desk and bed. Lighting in the closet is provided by one ceiling-mounted luminaire containing one 60-watt incandescent A-lamp.

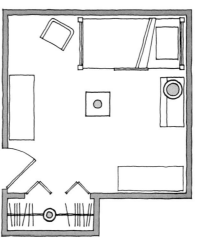

Replace lamps

Replace all of the 60-watt lamps with 52-watt halogen A-lamps. If any of the lamps are operated for orientation or for a sense of security, add a night light that contains a photosensor.

Replace controls

For the typical design, control the ceiling-mounted luminaire with a motion detector, and the luminaire in the closet with an interval timer.

Replace luminaires

Replace the ceiling-mounted luminaire with one that contains a 32-watt, 12-inch RE730 circline lamp. Replace the remaining 60-watt lamps with 52-watt halogen A-lamps.

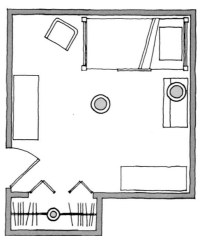

CONTINUED

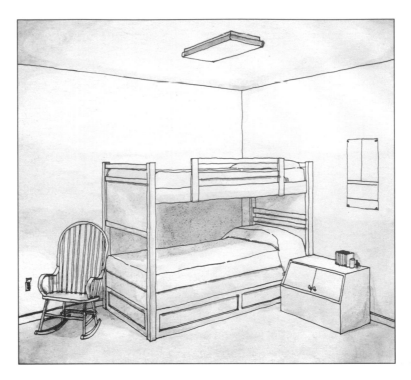

Replace luminaires

Install a ceiling-mounted diffuser that contains two 20-watt, 2-foot T12 RE730 linear fluorescent lamps and one magnetic ballast. One ceiling-mounted diffuser containing one 20-watt, 2-foot T12 RE730 linear fluorescent lamp and one magnetic ballast controlled by a wall-mounted switch provides lighting in the closet.

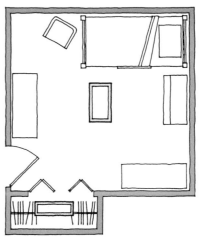

Annual Operating Cost at $0.10 per kWh

	Annual Operating Cost
Typical	$24.50
Replace Lamps	$23.00
Replace Controls	$13.50
Replace Luminaires	$12.50
Replace Luminaires	$11.50

Annual Operating Cost
■ Energy ■ Lamp

Assume 4 hours of use per day for the lamps in the ceiling-mounted luminaire, 1 hour of use per day for the lamps on the desk and in the closet. Assume 2 hours per start for lamps in the ceiling-mounted luminaire and 1 hour per start for the desk lamp. The motion detector or timer reduction factor is 50 percent.

Designs

Large Bedroom

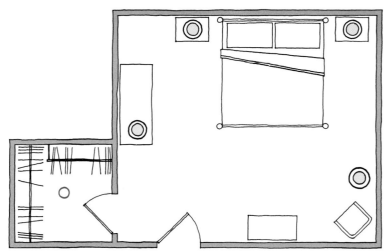

Typical

Three table lamps and one floor lamp, each containing one 75-watt incandescent lamp, provide ambient lighting and lighting for the mirror and the bed. A wall-mounted switch controls the floor lamp. One recessed downlight containing one 60-watt incandescent A-lamp provides lighting for the closet and is controlled by a wall-mounted switch.

Replace lamps

Replace the 75-watt A-lamps with 60-watt halogen A-lamps if lower light output is acceptable. Replace the lamp in the closet with a 52-watt halogen A-lamp.

CONTINUED

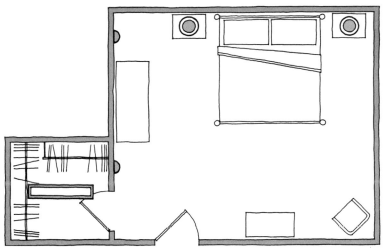

Remodel or new construction

Two sconces, each containing one 13-watt compact fluorescent twin-tube lamp and one magnetic ballast, provide ambient lighting. Two table lamps, each containing an electronically ballasted 18-watt screwbase compact fluorescent quad-tube lamp, provide lighting for the bed. The sconces are controlled by a wall-mounted switch. One ceiling-mounted diffuser containing one 34-watt, 4-foot T12 RE730 linear fluorescent lamp and one magnetic ballast provides lighting in the closet; this luminaire is controlled by a wall-mounted switch.

Remodel or new construction

One sconce containing one 13-watt compact fluorescent twin-tube lamp and one magnetic ballast, and one soffit containing three 32-watt, 4-foot T8 RE730 linear fluorescent lamps and one electronic ballast provide ambient lighting and lighting for the bed. The sconce and the soffit are controlled by separate wall-mounted switches. One ceiling-mounted diffuser containing one 32 watt, 4-foot T8 RE730 linear fluorescent lamp and one magnetic ballast provides lighting in the closet; this luminaire is controlled by a wall-mounted switch.

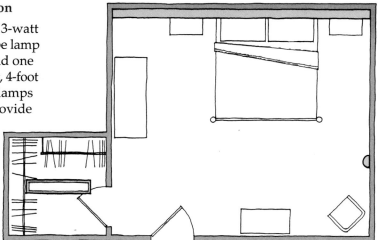

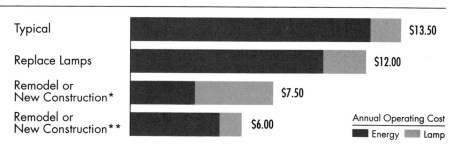

Annual Operating Cost at $0.10 per kWh

Typical		$13.50
Replace Lamps		$12.00
Remodel or New Construction*		$7.50
Remodel or New Construction**		$6.00

Annual Operating Cost
■ Energy ■ Lamp

* Compact fluorescent twin-tube, compact fluorescent quad-tube, T12
** Compact fluorescent twin-tube, T8, T8
For the lamps in the bedroom, assume 1 hour of use per day and 30 minutes per start.
For the lamp in the closet, assume 30 minutes of use per day.

Home Office

Some homes contain an office. These home office designs also can be used for parts of family rooms or bedrooms that have a desk.

Supplement ambient lighting with a task light for the desk. To reduce reflected glare, avoid placing lamps or windows directly in front of the person at the desk. Locate the lamp to the left of a right-handed person and to the right of a left-handed person. Lighting from the side reduces glare and minimizes shadows on the task.

For home offices with a computer, use low-level ambient lighting. Use a supplementary task light when working simultaneously with printed material, shielding the lamp from the computer screen. Locate the terminal so that the images of lamps and windows are not reflected from the screen into the eyes of the viewer. For greater comfort, avoid windows and bright lamps and luminaires on the wall directly behind the computer screen.

Home Office

Typical

One ceiling-mounted diffuser containing four 60-watt A-lamps provides ambient lighting and is controlled by a wall-mounted switch. A desk lamp contains a 75-watt A-lamp.

Replace lamps

Replace the lamps in the diffuser with 52-watt halogen A-lamps. Replace the 75-watt lamp with an electronically ballasted 20-watt screwbase compact fluorescent quad-tube lamp. Check the fit of the compact fluorescent lamp in the desk lamp.

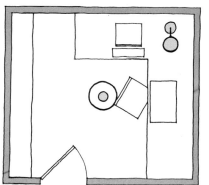

CONTINUED

Designs

Replace luminaires

Replace the diffuser with a 2-foot by 2-foot ceiling-mounted luminaire that contains two 34-watt T12 RE730 U-shaped fluorescent lamps and one electronic ballast. Replace the desk lamp with one that contains an 18-watt compact fluorescent quad-tube lamp and one magnetic ballast.

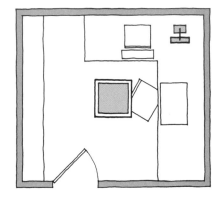

Remodel or new construction

Install a valance over the desk. The valance contains two 32-watt, 4-foot T8 RE730 linear fluorescent lamps and one electronic ballast and is controlled by a wall-mounted switch. Optionally, use a dimming ballast and dimmer switch. For the option of higher light output over the desk area, use four lamps wired in pairs to separate switches. Install a soffit over the shelves. The soffit contains two 32-watt, 4-foot T8 RE730 linear fluorescent lamps and one electronic ballast and is controlled by a wall-mounted switch. Use a desk lamp that contains an 18-watt compact fluorescent quad-tube lamp and one magnetic ballast.

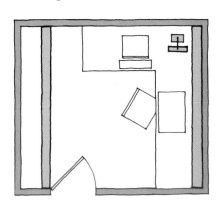

Remodel or new construction

Install two recessed wall wash luminaires near the shelves and two recessed downlights over the desk. Each luminaire contains two 13-watt compact fluorescent twin-tube lamps and one magnetic ballast. Each type of luminaire is controlled by a separate wall-mounted switch. Use a desk lamp that contains one 13-watt compact fluorescent twin-tube lamp and one magnetic ballast.

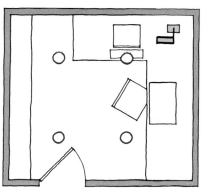

Annual Operating Cost at $0.10 per kWh

Typical	$26.00
Replace Lamps	$21.50
Replace Luminaires	$10.00
Remodel or New Construction (T8)	$12.50
Remodel or New Construction (CFT)	$14.50

Annual Operating Cost
■ Energy ■ Lamp

CFT = compact fluorescent twin-tube
For all of the lamps, assume 2 hours of use per day and 2 hours per start.

Stairs and Hallways

Foyers are the entry vestibule to a home. Ambient lighting usually is sufficient for foyers and hallways. Accent lighting can provide visual interest. See Ambient and Accent techniques for more information.

Foyer with Open Stair

Typical

A chandelier containing five 60-watt candle lamps provides ambient lighting and is controlled by three-way wall-mounted switches.

Replace lamps

If lower light output is acceptable, replace the 60-watt lamps with 40-watt candle lamps.

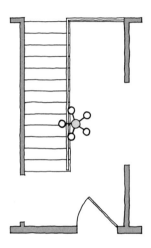

Remodel or new construction

A valance containing two 32-watt, 4-foot T8 RE730 linear fluorescent lamps provides ambient lighting and wall washing. This design provides a higher light output than the other designs and distributes light more evenly on the stairs.

CONTINUED

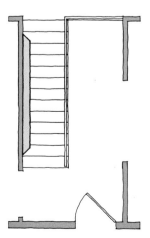

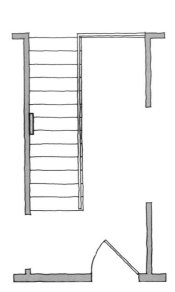

Remodel or new construction

Replace the chandelier with a wall-mounted diffuser containing one 32-watt, 12-inch RE730 circline lamp.

Annual Operating Cost at $0.10 per kWh

	Annual Operating Cost	
Typical		$29.00
Replace Lamps		$20.50
Remodel or New Construction*		$10.00
Remodel or New Construction**		$8.00

Annual Operating Cost
■ Energy ▨ Lamp

*T8 **Circline
For all of the lamps, assume 4 hours of use per day and 1 hour per start.

Designs

Closed Stair

Typical

Two recessed downlights, each containing one 100-watt A-lamp, provide ambient lighting; they are controlled by three-way wall-mounted switches.

Replace lamps

Replace the 100-watt lamps with 50-watt PAR30 halogen flood lamps.

Replace controls

If the stairs are not used frequently and residents leave the lamps operating for many hours, as they might for a basement or attic stair, consider replacing the wall-mounted switches with electronic interval timers. Inform residents that the control should be activated each time a person uses the stairs, to avoid the luminaire switching off while the person is on the stairs.

Replace luminaires

Modify each of the downlights with a conversion kit that houses a reflector, a magnetic ballast, and two 13-watt compact fluorescent twin-tube lamps.

For higher light output than the compact fluorescent lamps provide, replace the downlight luminaires with ceiling-mounted diffusers, each containing one 32-watt, 12-inch RE730 circline lamp.

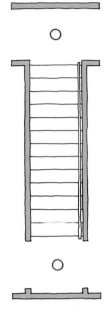

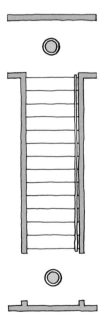

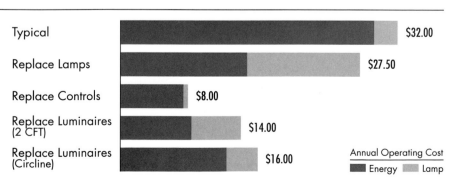

Annual Operating Cost at $0.10 per kWh

	Annual Operating Cost
Typical	$32.00
Replace Lamps	$27.50
Replace Controls	$8.00
Replace Luminaires (2 CFT)	$14.00
Replace Luminaires (Circline)	$16.00

Annual Operating Cost: ■ Energy ■ Lamp

CFT = compact fluorescent twin-tube
For all of the lamps, assume 4 hours of use per day and 1 hour per start.
If an interval timer is used, assume 1 hour of use per day.

Hallway

Typical

Three recessed downlights, each containing one 50-watt R20 lamp, provide ambient lighting. They are controlled by three-way wall-mounted switches.

Replace lamps

If the luminaire housings are large enough, replace each 50-watt lamp with an electronically ballasted 15-watt screwbase compact fluorescent lamp with an integral reflector. Add a night light if the lamps in the hallway are operated for orientation.

Replace luminaires

Modify each of the recessed downlights with a conversion kit that houses a reflector, a magnetic ballast, and one 13-watt compact fluorescent quad-tube lamp.

Remodel or new construction

For a different light distribution pattern, two sconces, each containing one 13-watt compact fluorescent twin-tube lamp and a magnetic ballast, provide ambient lighting. They are controlled by a three-way wall-mounted switch.

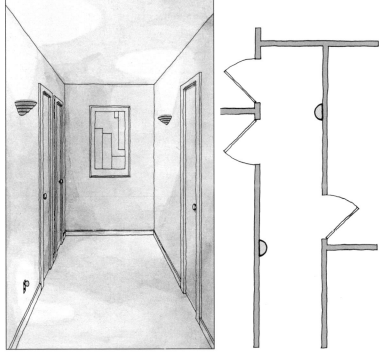

Annual Operating Cost at $0.10 per kWh

	Annual Operating Cost
Typical	$33.00
Replace Lamps	$21.00
Replace Luminaires	$13.50
Remodel or New Construction	$7.50

Annual Operating Cost
Energy   Lamp

For all of the lamps, assume 4 hours of use per day and 1 hour per start.

Multi-Family Common Spaces

Some common spaces in multi-family housing lack windows or skylights and therefore require long hours of use of electric lighting. Well-designed lighting can help residents or visitors understand the space and locate the entry and exits quickly. Entries and exits can be highlighted; see the Accent Technique for more information. Refer to the local building codes for information on requirements for and placement of exit signs and other emergency lighting.

Multi-Family Lobby

Typical

One ceiling-mounted luminaire containing three 40-watt G16.5 lamps provides ambient lighting and is controlled by a switch in a remote location.

Replace lamps

Replace the 40-watt lamps with electronically ballasted 11-watt globe screwbase compact fluorescent lamps, if the luminaire will accommodate their size.

Replace controls

For the typical design, install a dimming motion detector. Do not, however, use this control with compact fluorescent lamps.

Replace luminaires

Replace the luminaire with one that contains two 13-watt compact fluorescent twin-tube lamps and one magnetic ballast. Optionally, choose a luminaire that contains a 32-watt circline lamp.

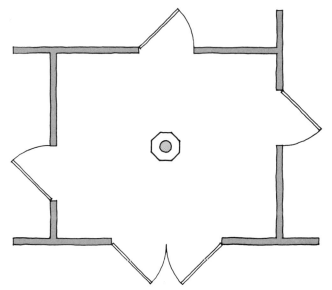

Remodel or new construction

For a different light distribution pattern in the lobby, install three sconces, each containing one 13-watt compact fluorescent lamp and one magnetic ballast. The sconces are controlled by a switch at a remote location.

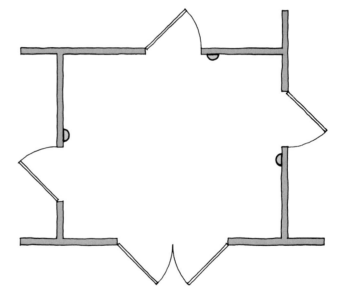

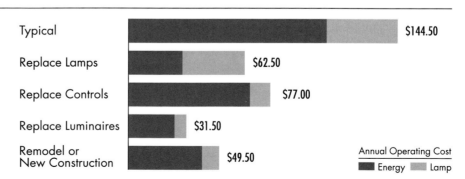

Annual Operating Cost at $0.10 per kWh		
Typical		$144.50
Replace Lamps		$62.50
Replace Controls		$77.00
Replace Luminaires		$31.50
Remodel or New Construction		$49.50

Annual Operating Cost
■ Energy ■ Lamp

For all of the lamps, assume 24 hours of use per day. Lamps with dimming motion detectors are dimmed 75 percent of the time they are operated, to 50 percent light output as perceived by the human eye; the other 25 percent of the time, they are operated at full light output.

Multi-Family Corridor

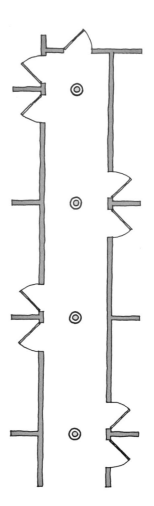

Typical

Four ceiling-mounted luminaires, each containing one 60-watt incandescent A-lamp, provide ambient lighting.

Replace lamps

Remove the globe diffusers and replace each A-lamp with one magnetically ballasted 18-watt globe screwbase compact fluorescent lamp.

Replace controls

For the typical design, install a motion detector that is designed for hallways.

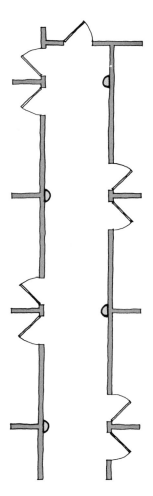

Remodel or new construction

Four wall-mounted diffusers, each containing one 18-watt compact fluorescent quad-tube lamp and one magnetic ballast, provide ambient lighting.

Annual Operating Cost at $0.10 per kWh

	Annual Operating Cost
Typical	$236.50
Replace Lamps	$106.50
Replace Controls	$59.00
Remodel or New Construction	$102.50

Annual Operating Cost
■ Energy　■ Lamp

For all of the lamps, assume 24 hours of use per day. For lamps controlled by a motion detector, assume 30 minutes per start and a motion detector factor of 25 percent.

Multi-Family Fire Stair 1

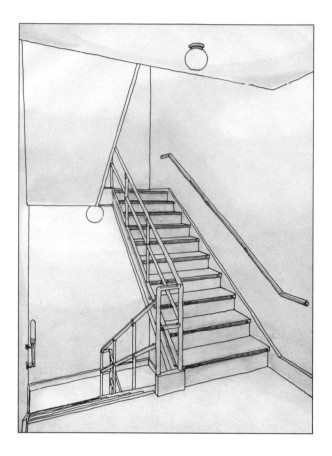

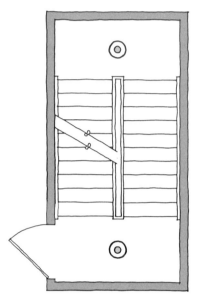

Typical

One ceiling-mounted diffuser or porcelain socket containing one 150-watt A-lamp provides ambient lighting for each landing of the staircase.

Replace lamps

If lower light output is acceptable, replace each 150-watt lamp with one 100-watt halogen A-lamp. Alternatively, replace each 150-watt lamp with one 35-watt high-pressure sodium lamp with a screw-in adapter for the ballast. Note that the light that is emitted will be yellow-white.

Replace controls

For the typical design, install a wall-mounted interval timer system that can be activated at each floor.

Replace luminaires

To maintain light output, install ceiling-mounted diffusers, each containing one 22-watt and one 32-watt circline lamp.

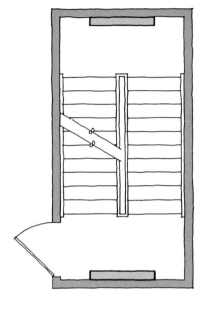

Remodel or new construction

A valance on each landing
contains one 32-watt, 4-foot T8
RE730 linear fluorescent lamp and
one electronic ballast.
Alternatively, also install a wall-
mounted interval timer system
that can be activated at each floor.

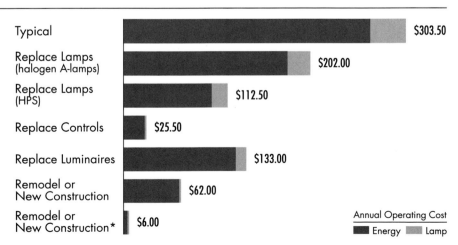

**Annual
Operating
Cost at
$0.10 per kWh**

Typical	$303.50
Replace Lamps (halogen A-lamps)	$202.00
Replace Lamps (HPS)	$112.50
Replace Controls	$25.50
Replace Luminaires	$133.00
Remodel or New Construction	$62.00
Remodel or New Construction*	$6.00

Annual Operating Cost
■ Energy   ■ Lamp

HPS = high pressure sodium   * With timer
For all of the lamps, assume 24 hours of use per day. For lamps that are controlled by a
timer, assume 2 hours of use per day and 15 minutes per start.

Multi-Family Fire Stair 2

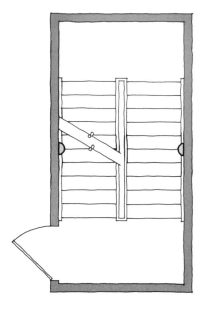

Typical

A wall-mounted diffuser on each flight of stairs contains one 100-watt A-lamp and provides ambient lighting.

Replace lamps

If lower light output is acceptable, replace the 100-watt lamp with a 75-watt halogen A-lamp.

Replace controls

For the typical design, install a wall-mounted interval timer system that can be activated at each floor.

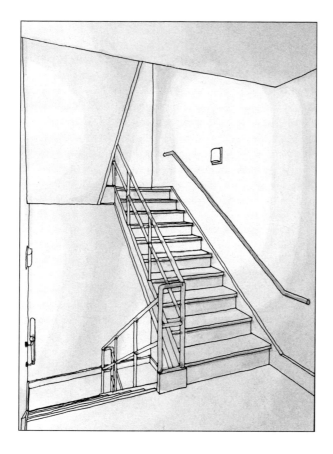

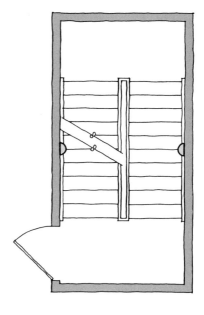

Replace luminaires

A wall-mounted diffuser on each flight of stairs contains one 35-watt high-pressure sodium lamp and provides ambient lighting. Note that the light that is emitted will be yellow-white. Also, many high-intensity discharge lamps require several minutes to relight. This could cause a problem for people using the stairwell after a power interruption, so consult manufacturers' data to select an appropriate lamp for this design. Optionally, use a luminaire that contains a fluorescent lamp.

Annual Operating Cost at $0.10 per kWh

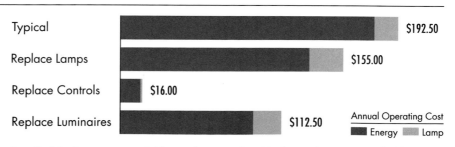

	Annual Operating Cost
Typical	$192.50
Replace Lamps	$155.00
Replace Controls	$16.00
Replace Luminaires	$112.50

Annual Operating Cost
■ Energy ■ Lamp

For all of the lamps, assume 24 hours of use per day. For lamps that are controlled by a timer, assume 2 hours of use per day and 15 minutes per start.

Outdoor Spaces

Exterior lighting is used for safety, security, and decoration. Lighting outdoor spaces can also make them usable spaces for relaxation, recreation, and work at night. Light objects and the landscape to provide an attractive outdoor view from inside the home at night. Light pathways to prevent accidents. Light the back and sides of a home to give residents a sense of security, but avoid creating large, harsh shadows where intruders might hide. For instance, supplement entry lighting with exterior flood lamps to eliminate dark corners. If the entry is visible to neighbors, intruders may be discouraged. Use ceiling-mounted or recessed luminaires for porches and entries with an overhang; also consider using wall-mounted sconces on either side of the door.

Entry 1

Typical

Two sconces, each containing one 60-watt incandescent A-lamp, provide ambient lighting. They are controlled by a wall-mounted switch inside the building.

Replace lamps

Replace each A-lamp with a 52-watt halogen A-lamp.

Replace lamps

If the lamp is protected by an enclosed luminaire, and the temperature does not fall below 0° Fahrenheit (-18° Celsius), install an electronically ballasted 20-watt screwbase compact fluorescent lamp if the luminaire is large enough to hold the lamp. If the temperature does not fall below 32° Fahrenheit (0° Celsius), a magnetically ballasted screwbase lamp could be used.

CONTINUED

Annual Operating Cost at $0.10 per kWh

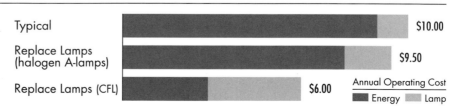

	Annual Operating Cost
Typical	$10.00
Replace Lamps (halogen A-lamps)	$9.50
Replace Lamps (CFL)	$6.00

Annual Operating Cost
■ Energy ▢ Lamp

CFL = compact fluorescent lamp
For all of the lamps, assume 2 hours of use per day and 2 hours per start.

Entry 2

Typical

Two sconces, each containing one 60-watt incandescent A-lamp, provide ambient lighting. They are controlled by a wall-mounted switch inside the building.

Replace lamps

If the lamp is protected by an enclosed luminaire and the temperature does not fall below 0° Fahrenheit (-18° Celsius), install an electronically ballasted 20-watt screwbase compact fluorescent lamp if the luminaire is large enough to hold the lamp. If the temperature does not fall below 32° Fahrenheit (0° Celsius), a magnetically ballasted screwbase lamp could be used.

Replace luminaires

Install one luminaire that contains two 60-watt incandescent A-lamps and a motion detector or, optionally, a photocell. The motion detector switches the lamps on when motion is detected, regardless of light levels. The photocell switches the lamps on when outdoor light levels fall below normal daylight levels. Thus, luminaires with a motion detector must be switched off during the daytime, either manually or by an automatic timer or a photocell. Also, take care to adjust the sensitivity of the motion detector to avoid false starts. Note that frequent switching on and off of luminaires by a motion detector in a busy area may be annoying or alarming to some residents.

Annual Operating Cost at $0.10 per kWh		
Typical		$59.00
Replace Lamps		$29.00
Replace Luminaires		$29.50

Annual Operating Cost
■ Energy ■ Lamp

For all of the lamps, assume 12 hours of use per day and 12 hours per start. The motion detector factor is 50 percent.

Floodlight 1

Typical

One wall-mounted luminaire containing two 150-watt PAR38 lamps provides ambient lighting for an area adjacent to the home.

Replace lamps

If slightly lower light output is acceptable, replace each 150-watt lamp with a 60-watt IR PAR38 lamp or optionally with a 90-watt halogen PAR38 lamp.

Annual Operating Cost at $0.10 per kWh

Typical — $25.50

Replace Lamps — $17.50

Annual Operating Cost
■ Energy ■ Lamp

For all of the lamps, assume 2 hours of use per day and 2 hours per start.

Floodlight 2

Typical

One wall-mounted luminaire containing two 150-watt PAR38 lamps provides ambient lighting for an area adjacent to the home.

Replace lamp

If slightly lower light output is acceptable, replace each 150-watt lamp with a 60-watt IR PAR38 lamp or optionally with a 90-watt halogen PAR38 lamp.

Replace luminaire

If the lamps usually burn all night, or night and day, and if slightly lower light output is acceptable, install one luminaire that contains two 60-watt IR PAR38 lamps and a photocell and a motion detector. The lamps are switched on when both motion is detected and the photocell indicates that outdoor light levels have fallen below normal daylight levels. Also, take care to adjust the sensitivity of the motion detector to avoid false starts.

Annual Operating Cost at $0.10 per kWh

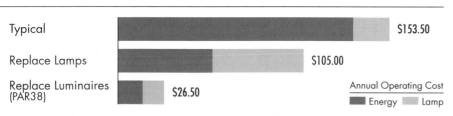

	Annual Operating Cost
Typical	$153.50
Replace Lamps	$105.00
Replace Luminaires (PAR38)	$26.50

Annual Operating Cost
■ Energy ■ Lamp

For all of the lamps, assume 12 hours of use per day and 12 hours per start. The motion detector factor is 25 percent.

Pole-Mounted Light

Typical

One pole-mounted luminaire containing one 75-watt A-lamp provides ambient lighting for a small area close to the home or along a walkway.

Replace lamps

If the lamp is protected by an enclosed luminaire and the temperature does not fall below 0° Fahrenheit (-18° Celsius), install an electronically ballasted 18-watt screwbase compact fluorescent lamp if the luminaire is large enough to hold the lamp. If the temperature does not fall below 32° Fahrenheit (0° Celsius), a magnetically ballasted screwbase lamp could be used.

Annual Operating Cost at $0.10 per kWh

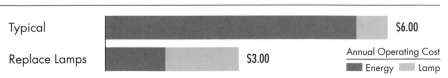

	Annual Operating Cost
Typical	$6.00
Replace Lamps	$3.00

Energy Lamp

For all of the lamps, assume 2 hours of use per day and 2 hours per start.

Economics

This chapter provides data on lighting technologies, including typical prices, suggested values for hours of lamp operation in various rooms, and a worksheet that you can use to analyze the costs of using the lighting in your designs.

To complete an economic analysis, you must compare one design to another. Design 1 can be the existing lighting system, the common practice used by a builder, or any other point of reference that you find useful. Design 2 is the new lighting design that is being compared to Design 1. If your goal is energy efficiency or lower operating costs, examine several alternative designs and compare them to each other and to Design 1.

First identify two designs for comparison; then choose the analyses of interest to you:

To estimate the annual energy saved by installing an alternative design, complete the worksheet, items A through I. The annual energy saved is I, the difference between the annual energy use of Design 1 and the annual energy use of Design 2.

To estimate the annual operating cost, including energy and lamp replacement costs, saved by installing an alternative design, complete the worksheet, items A through Q. The annual operating cost saved is Q, the difference between the annual operating cost of Design 1 and the annual operating cost of Design 2.

To calculate the simple payback of the alternative solution, complete the worksheet, items A through Z. The simple payback is Z, the number of years that must elapse before the annual operating cost savings have paid back the initial incremental cost of the lighting design.

Detailed directions for each line of the worksheet start on the page immediately following the worksheet. You may want to familiarize yourself with these instructions before using the worksheet.

Economics Worksheet

Item	Directions (read instructions for more detail)	Design 1	Design 2	Units
A	Enter lamp/ballast watts			watts
B	Enter number of lamps			
C	Enter power reduction factor (Table 1)			
D	Multiply A by B by C and then divide by 1000			kilowatts (kW)
E	Enter hours of one lamp's daily operation (Table 2)			hours per day
F	Enter motion detector factor (Table 2)			
G	Multiply E by F by 365			hours per year
H	Multiply D by G for annual energy use			kWh per year
I	Subtract H_2 from H_1 for ANNUAL ENERGY SAVINGS			kWh per year

Stop here if you are calculating annual energy savings

Item	Directions (read instructions for more detail)	Design 1	Design 2	Units
J	Enter cost of electricity			dollars per kWh
K	Multiply H by J for annual energy cost			dollars per year
	L_a Enter average rated lamp life (Tables 3–5)			hours
	L_b Enter lamp life multiplier (see instructions)			
L	Multiply L_a by L_b for lamp life			hours
M	Multiply B by G and divide result by L for lamps used per year			lamps per year
N	Enter price of one lamp (Tables 3–5)			dollars per lamp
O	Multiply M by N for annual lamp replacement cost			dollars per year
P	Add O to K for annual operating cost			dollars per year
Q	Subtract P_2 from P_1 for ANNUAL OPERATING COST SAVINGS			dollars per year

Stop here if you are calculating annual operating cost savings

Item	Directions (read instructions for more detail)	Design 1	Design 2	Units
R	Enter amount of incentive, if any			dollars
S	Enter price of lamp(s) (Tables 3–5)			dollars
T	Enter price of ballast(s) (Table 6)			dollars
U	Enter price of luminaire(s) (Table 6)			dollars
V	Enter price of control(s) (Table 6)			dollars
W	Enter total cost of labor			dollars
X	Add S, T, U, V, and W, then subtract R			dollars
Y	From X_2, subtract X_1 for total incremental cost of Design 2			dollars
Z	Divide Y by Q for SIMPLE PAYBACK			years

Instructions and Notes for Economics Worksheet

"Design 1" refers to a typical design, an existing design, or any design against which you will compare another alternative design, "Design 2."

A   Enter the input power of one lamp including the ballast. See Tables 3, 4, and 5 for the default values for some lamps. Note that some lamps have different lamp and ballast combinations. Input power will vary with ballast manufacturer, type of ballast, and number of lamps that are operated per ballast. If the lamp is not listed in Tables 3, 4, or 5, look up the lamp wattage in a manufacturer's catalog and estimate the change in input power due to the ballast using these tables as a guide. Note that incandescent lamps do not have ballasts and that for self-ballasted screwbase compact fluorescent lamps, the ballast wattage is included with the lamp wattage. For a three-way incandescent lamp, enter the highest wattage; step C reduces the wattage for multiple-level switching.

B   Tally the total number of this type of lamp in your Design 1 and Design 2.

C   If the lamps usually are operated at full power, enter 1.

If multiple-level switching is used, estimate the average power reduction. For example, if only half of the lamps are operated most of the time, enter 0.5. If a 50-100-150 three-way incandescent lamp is operated at equal amounts on all three settings, enter 0.67 (100 watts average divided by 150).

If dimmers are used, see Table 1 for the appropriate power reduction factor. Often dimmers are used for occasional variation of illuminance, not for regular reduction of power. If so, enter 1. Using lower-wattage lamps is usually a better economic choice than using higher-wattage lamps that are dimmed all the time.

D   This product is the power of the lamp in Design 1 or Design 2.

E   Estimate the average hours of one lamp's operation per day or see Table 2 for default values. Consider the impact of photocells or timer controls in your estimate. For example, if a security light that operates 24 hours per day is controlled by a photocell, enter 12 hours for the average hours of lamp operation. See F for motion detector hours of use reduction.

F   Enter 1 if no motion detector is used. If a motion detector is used, estimate the fraction of the daily hours of lamp operation in E when the room is occupied or the lamps must be operated, or see Table 2 for default values. For example, if the lamps in a bathroom usually are operated 4 hours per day, but the bathroom is unoccupied for one of these hours, and a motion detector is to be installed, enter 0.75.

G   This product is the annual hours of operation of one lamp.

H   This product is the annual energy use in kWh for all the lamps in Design 1 or Design 2.

I   If I is negative, Design 2 uses more energy than Design 1. If a design includes more than one lamp type in a room or project, calculate H_1 individually for each lamp type in Design 1 and add for H_1 total. Calculate H_2 individually for each lamp type in Design 2 and add for H_2 total. Subtract H_1 total from H_2 total for I total.

J Enter the average cost of electricity for the location being considered in the analysis. Electricity costs in North America range from $0.03 to $0.18 per kWh. In this book $0.10 per kWh is used for all examples. Check with your local utility to verify your rate. Some utilities have seasonal rates that can be averaged to calculate an annual rate.

K This product is the annual energy cost for the lamps in Design 1 or Design 2.

L Multiply L_a by L_b to estimate the lamp life for your designs.

La Look up the average rated lamp life in Tables 3, 4, or 5, or look them up in a manufacturer's catalog.

Lb For incandescent lamps, enter 1.0 because incandescent lamps are not greatly affected by hours of operation per start. If a dimmer is used, however, see Table 1 for a lamp life multiplier for incandescent lamps.

For fluorescent lamps, enter the lamp life multiplier from this table.

*For some compact fluorescent lamps with "soft start" electronic ballasts, the values may be higher than those shown in the chart.

Average hours of lamp operation per start	Lamp life multiplier for fluorescent lamps
continuous	1.8
12	1.5
6	1.2
3	1.0
2	0.9*
1	0.7*
0.5	0.5*
0.25	0.4*

M For a single lamp that lasts longer than a year, this number will be less than 1.0, indicating the fraction of the lamp's life that is attributable to one year of use.

N See Tables 3, 4, and 5 for typical lamp prices. Prices vary and promotions or sales may reduce prices, so check with your local lamp supplier for an accurate price estimate. Ballasts and luminaires last a very long time in residential applications, so their costs are considered only under initial cost, with the exception of self-ballasted compact fluorescent lamps. Self-ballasted compact fluorescent lamps cannot be separated from the ballast; the ballast is replaced at the same time as the lamp and is included in the lamp price.

O This product is the annual lamp replacement cost for Design 1 or Design 2.

P This number includes the annual electricity cost of operating the lamps and the cost of lamp replacement. Note: where there is a labor cost for maintenance or lamp replacement, the annual labor cost may be added here. Although most homeowners do not pay labor costs for lamp replacement, managers of some large facilities may reduce lamp replacement labor costs through the use of longer-life lamps, or through reduced hours of operation due to automatic lighting controls.

Q If Q is negative, Design 2 costs more to operate than Design 1. If a design includes more than one lamp type in a room or project, calculate P_1 individually for each lamp type in Design 1 and add for $P_{1\ total}$. Calculate P_2 individually for each lamp type in Design 2 and add for $P_{2\ total}$. Subtract $P_{1\ total}$ from $P_{2\ total}$ for Q_{total}.

R   Enter the total amount of an incentive, if any is available. If there are no incentives, enter zero. Some electric utilities offer discounts, rebates, promotions, and other incentives to reduce the cost of energy-efficient equipment. For example, if two compact fluorescent lamps are being considered and each has a $5 rebate, R is $10.

S   If Design 1 uses the same number and type of lamps as Design 2, enter zero for both Design 1 and Design 2. If the analysis is a retrofit of an existing installation and if Design 2 uses new lamps, enter zero for Design 1 and enter $(B \times N)_2$ for Design 2. Otherwise, enter $(B \times N)_1$ for Design 1 and $(B \times N)_2$ for Design 2.

T   If Design 1 uses the same number and types of ballasts as Design 2, enter zero for both Design 1 and Design 2. If the analysis is a retrofit of an existing installation, enter zero for Design 1 and the price of the new ballast(s) for Design 2 if Design 2 is using new ballasts. Otherwise enter the ballast prices for both Design 1 and Design 2. See Table 6 for typical ballast prices. Prices vary so check with your ballast supplier for an accurate price estimate.

U   If Design 1 uses the same number and types of luminaires as Design 2, enter zero for both Design 1 and Design 2. If the analysis is a retrofit of an existing installation, enter zero for Design 1 and the price of the new luminaire(s) for Design 2 if Design 2 uses new luminaires. Otherwise enter the luminaire prices for both Design 1 and Design 2. See Table 6 for typical luminaire prices. Prices vary so check with your luminaire supplier for an accurate price estimate.

V   If Design 1 uses the same number and types of controls as Design 2, enter zero for both Design 1 and Design 2. If the analysis is a retrofit of an existing installation, enter zero for Design 1 and the price of the new controls for Design 2 if Design 2 uses new controls. Otherwise enter the new control prices for both Design 1 and Design 2. See Table 6 for typical control prices. Prices vary so check with your control supplier.

W   If the cost of labor to install Design 1 is the same as the cost of labor to install Design 2, enter zero for both Design 1 and Design 2. If the analysis is a retrofit of an existing installation, enter zero for Design 1 and the cost of labor to install Design 2 for Design 2. Otherwise enter the labor costs for installation of both Design 1 and Design 2. Consider the labor costs of the electrical work and any carpentry or repair work that is not included in both cases. Verify costs with your electrician and/or carpenter.

X   This number is the initial cost of Design 1 and Design 2 relative to each other, less any incentives from your electric utility company.

Y   This number is the total incremental cost of Design 2, relative to Design 1. If this number is negative, the initial cost of Design 1 is greater than the initial cost of Design 2, so the payback will be immediate.

Z   Simple payback uses a simplified method to determine the life-cycle cost of a lighting upgrade; it considers only the initial cost and the annual operating cost savings. There are more sophisticated analysis methods that can also include the time value of money, allowance for inflation, and consideration of the owner's expected return-on-investment.

Table 1.
Power Reduction Factors and Lamp Life Multipliers for Dimmers

A person's judgment of how much light output is dimmed differs from the measured amount of dimming recorded by a light meter. To use this table, first read down from the numbers in either the first row, "Percent of Full Light (as perceived by eye)" if you are estimating the percentage of dimming by what you perceive, or read down from the numbers in the second row, "Percent of Full Light Output (as measured)" if you use an instrument to measure the light output. Then, use the third row to choose either dimming that is used all of the time, or dimming that is used only half of the time.

% of Full Light (as perceived by eye)		100	90		75		50	
% of Full Light (as measured)		100	80		56		25	
% of Time on Dimmer*		0	100	50	100	50	100	50
Incandescent Lamps	Power Reduction Factor	1	0.9	.95	0.8	0.9	0.5	.75
	Lamp Life Multiplier	1	2	1.3	8	1.8	20	1.9
Fluorescent Lamps**	Power Reduction Factor	1	0.8	0.9	0.5	.75	0.3	.65

*If dimmers are used only for occasional reduction in illuminance, enter 1.0.

**Fluorescent lamp life is not significantly affected by dimming, so use the value determined by instruction L_b.

Table 2.
Hours of Lamp Use and Motion Detector Factors

Room	Hours of Lamp Use	Motion Detector Factor
Kitchen Area	4	0.7
Kitchen Dining Area	3	0.8
Kitchen Food Preparation Area	3	0.7
Living Room	3	0.8
Main Bathroom	2	0.6
Main Bedroom	1	0.7

Table 3a.
Incandescent Lamp Information

Lamp Type	Rated Lamp Watts	Average Rated Lamp Life (hours)	Light Output (lumens)	CCT (K)	CRI	Typical Price per Lamp ($)
Common Incandescent						
A19, Inside Frost	40	1,000–1,500	460–505	2,800	95+	0.75
A19, Inside Frost	60	1,000	870–890	2,800	95+	0.75
A19, Inside Frost	75	750	1,190–1,220	2,800	95+	0.75
A19, Inside Frost	100	750	1,750	2,800	95+	0.75
A21, Inside Frost	150	750	2,850	2,800	95+	1.75
A21 or T21, Inside Frost	50–100–150	1,200–1,500	580–2,220	2,800	95+	2.00
Candle	40	1,500	—	2,800	95+	1.00
Candle	60	1,500	—	2,800	95+	1.00
C7 Night Light, Clear	7	3,000	45	2,800	95+	1.00
G16.5	40	1,500	245–345	2,800	95+	2.25
G25	40	1,500	370–425	2,800	95+	2.50
G25	60	1,500	660–715	2,800	95+	2.50
G40	60	2,500	576–740	2,800	95+	5.00
Reduced-Wattage and Reduced-Wattage, Long-Life						
Reduced-Wattage A-Lamp	52	1,000	800	2,800	95+	1.00
Reduced-Wattage A-Lamp	67	750	1,130	2,800	95+	1.00
Reduced-Wattage A-Lamp	90	750	1,620	2,800	95+	1.00
Reduced-Wattage A-Lamp	135	750	2,580	2,800	95+	1.25
Reduced-Wattage, Long-Life A-Lamp	52	2,500	700–705	2,800	95+	1.50
Reduced-Wattage, Long-Life A-Lamp	67	2,500	930–945	2,800	95+	1.50
Reduced-Wattage, Long-Life A-Lamp	90	2,500	1,360–1,375	2,800	95+	1.50
Reduced-Wattage, Long-Life A-Lamp	135	2,500	2,105–2,145	2,800	95+	2.00
Halogen						
Halogen A-Lamp	42	3,500	665	3,050	95+	4.00
Halogen A-Lamp	52	3,500	885	3,050	95+	4.00
Halogen A-Lamp	60	3,000	960	3,050	95+	4.00
Halogen A-Lamp	72, 75	2,250–3,500*	1,090–1,300	3,050	95+	4.00
Halogen A-Lamp	100	2,250–3,000*	1,600–1,880	3,050	95+	4.00

CCT = Correlated Color Temperature   CRI = Color Rendering Index
*The economic analyses in the Designs chapter uses 3,000 hours.

Table 3b.
Incandescent Lamp Information

Lamp Type	Rated Lamp Watts	Average Rated Lamp Life (hours)	Light Output (lumens)	Center Beam Candlepower (candelas)	Beam Spread (°)	CCT (K)	CRI	Typical Price per Lamp ($)
Reflector								
R20	50	2,000	410–420	510–550	38–43	2,800	95+	5.00
R30 Flood	75	2,000	830–900	430–470	65–130	2,800	95+	4.50
R40 Flood	150	2,000	1,900	1,300–1,400	59–76	2,800	95+	5.50
R40 Heat Lamp	250	5,000	—	—	—	—	—	15.00
ER30	75	2,000	850	1,200	42	2,800	95+	6.50
PAR38 Flood	75	2,000	750–765	1,750–1,800	30–37	2,800	95+	5.00
PAR38 Flood	150	2,000	1740	3,100–4,000	30–36	2,800	95+	5.00
Halogen PAR16 Narrow Flood	55	2,000	—	1,300	30	3,050	95+	14.00
Halogen PAR20 Narrow Flood	50	2,000–2,500*	560	1,250–1,400	30–32	3,050	95+	9.00
Halogen PAR30 Flood	50	2,000–2,500*	670	1,100–1,600	36–42	3,050	95+	9.00
Halogen PAR38 Flood	45	2,000	540	1,600–1,800	32	3,050	95+	10.00
Halogen PAR38 Flood	90	2,000–2,500*	1,270	3,500–4,000	30	3,050	95+	10.00
Halogen IR PAR38 Flood	60	2,000–2,500*	1,150	3,300	32	3,050	95+	12.00
Tubular-Shaped Halogen								
Tubular-Shaped, RSC Base	300	2,000	5,600–6,000	—	—	3,050	95+	10.00
Tubular-Shaped, RSC Base	500	2,000	10,500–11,100	—	—	3,050	95+	10.00
Tubular-Shaped IR, RSC Base	350	2,000	10,000	—	—	3,050	95+	30.00
Low-Voltage Halogen								
PAR36 Narrow Spot	50	4,000	400	11,000	8	3,050	95+	14.00
MR11 (FTF)**	35	3,000	460	2,750–3,000	20	2,950	95+	14.00
MR16 Flood (BAB)**	20	2,000–4,000	280	460–850	36–40	2,925	95+	12.00
MR16 Flood (EXN)**	50	2,000–4,000	960	1,500–2,500	38–40	3,050	95+	12.00
Bi-pin Halogen	35	2,000	650	—	—	3,050	95+	15.00

CCT = Correlated Color Temperature   CRI = Color Rendering Index

* The economic analyses in the Designs chapter use 2,000 hours.

** The three-letter code is an American National Standards Institute (ANSI) designation that identifies a lamp of a certain beam spread and wattage.

Table 4a.
Fluorescent Lamp Information

Lamp Type	Rated Lamp Watts	Input Power per Lamp (Lamp + Ballast)*				Average Rated Lamp Life (hours)	Light Output (lumens)	CCT (K)	CRI	Typical Price per Lamp ($)
		Magnetic		Electronic						
		1 Lamp/ Ballast	2+ Lamps/ Ballast	1 Lamp/ Ballast	2+ Lamps/ Ballast					
Linear Fluorescent										
12" T5 Cool White	8	10				7,500	390–400	4,200	62	5.00
12" T5 Warm White	8	10				7,500	400	3,000	52	7.00
21" T5 Cool White	13	18				7,500	820–860	4,200	62	6.00
21" T5 Warm White	13	18				7,500	870–880	3,000	52	8.00
24" T12 Cool White	20	32	27			9,000	1,200–1,240	4,200	62	4.00
24" T12 RE730	20	32	27			9,000	1,275–1,300	3,000	70+	6.00
24" T12 RE830	20	32	27			9,000	1,300–1,350	3,000	80+	10.00
24" T8 RE730	17	24	22	22	17	20,000	1,325	3,000	70+	6.00
24" T8 RE830	17	24	22	22	17	20,000	1,400	3,000	80+	7.00
36" T12 Cool White	30	46	42	31	30	18,000	2,200–2,250	4,200	62	5.00
36" T12 Cool White, RW	25	41	37	26	25	18,000	1,925–2,000	4,200	62	6.00
36" T12 RE730, RW	25	41	37	26	25	18,000	2,025–2,350	3,000	70+	9.00
36" T8 RE730	25	33	33	30	24	20,000	2,125	3,000	70+	6.00
36" T8 RE830	25	33	33	30	24	20,000	2,250	3,000	80+	7.00
48" T12 Cool White	40	52	48	46	36	20,000	3,050	4,200	62	2.00
48" T12 Cool White, RW	34	46	42	38	30	20,000	2,650	4,200	62	3.00
48" T12 RE730, RW	34	46	42	38	30	20,000	2,800	3,000	70+	6.00
48" T12 RE830, RW	34	46	42	38	30	20,000	2,900	3,000	80+	10.00
48" T10 RE730	40	52	48	40	36	24,000	3,700	3,000	70+	7.00
48" T8 RE730	32	37	36	34	31	20,000	2,850	3,000	70+	5.50
48" T8 RE830	32	37	36	34	31	20,000	3,050	3,000	80+	7.00
60" T8 RE830	40	50	46	44	37	20,000	3,800	3,000	80+	8.50

CCT = Correlated Color Temperature   CRI = Color Rendering Index   RW = Reduced-wattage

* For two or more lamps, the number is the wattage consumed by one lamp plus its portion of the total ballast wattage. The total system wattage is the total number of lamps in the system multiplied by this number.

Table 4b.
Fluorescent Lamp Information

| Lamp Type | Rated Lamp Watts | Input Power per Lamp (Lamp + Ballast)* | | | | Average Rated Lamp Life (hours) | Light Output (lumens) | CCT (K) | CRI | Typical Price per Lamp ($) |
| | | Magnetic | | Electronic | | | | | | |
		1 Lamp/ Ballast	2+ Lamps/ Ballast	1 Lamp/ Ballast	2+ Lamps/ Ballast					
U-Shaped and Long Twin-Tube										
T12/U6 Cool White	40	52	48	46	36	12,000	2,600	4,200	62	10.00
T12/U6 Rare-Earth	34	52	48	46	36	12,000	2,400	3,000	70+	14.00
T8 U-Shaped Rare-Earth	31	36	35	37	30	20,000	2,800	3,100	80+	12.00
10.5" FT18W Rare-Earth	18	22	20	21	18	20,000	1,250	3,000	80+	13.00
16.5" FT36W Rare-Earth	36, 39	48	43	37	34	12,000	2,900	3,000	80+	15.00
22.5" FT40W Rare-Earth	40	44	41	43	38	20,000	3,150	3,000	80+	15.00
Compact Fluorescent and Circline										
CFT5W	5	7	6			10,000	250	2,700	82	6.00
CFT7W	7	9	8			10,000	400	2,700	82	6.00
CFT9W	9	11	10			10,000	600	2,700	82	6.00
CFT13W	13	15	14			10,000	825–900	2,700	82	7.00
CFQ9W	9	11	10			10,000	575	2,700	82	11.00
CFQ13W	13	15				10,000	860–900	2,700	82	11.00
CFQ18W	18	22				10,000	1,200	2,700	82	13.00
CFQ26W	26	30				10,000	1,800	2,700	82	14.00
6.5" Circline Cool White	20	25				12,000	800	4,200	62	8.00
6.5" Circline Warm White	20	25				12,000	825	3,000	52	8.50
8" Circline Cool White	22	27				12,000	1,025	4,200	62	7.00
8" Circline Warm White	22	27				12,000	1,000	3,000	52	9.00
8" Circline RE730	22	27		22		12,000	1,150	3,000	70+	11.00
12" Circline Cool White	32	42				12,000	1,800	4,200	62	8.00
12" Circline Warm White	32	42				12,000	1,500–2,100	3,000	52	10.00
12" Circline RE730	32	42		30		12,000	2,100	3,000	70+	11.00

CCT = Correlated Color Temperature   CRI = Color Rendering Index

* For two or more lamps, the number is the wattage consumed by one lamp plus its portion of the total ballast wattage. The total system wattage is the total number of lamps in the system multiplied by this number.

Economics

Table 4c.
Fluorescent Lamp Information

Lamp Type		Input Power (Lamp + Ballast Watts)*	Average Rated Lamp Life (hours)	Light Output (lumens)	CCT (K)	CRI	Typical Price per Lamp ($)
Self-Ballasted Compact Fluorescent							
Ballast Type							
Electronic		15	10,000	900	2,700	82	17.00
Magnetic		18	10,000	700	2,800	82	20.00
Electronic		18	10,000	1,100	2,700	81	20.00
Electronic		20	10,000	1,200	2,700	82	20.00
Electronic		22	10,000	1,400	2,700	81	21.00
Electronic		23	10,000	1,550	2,700	82	20.00
Electronic		26,27	10,000	1,550	2,800	84	22.00
Screwbase Compact Fluorescent with Integral Accessories							
Ballast Type	**Accessory**						
Electronic	Globe	11	10,000	450	2,700	82	23.00
Electronic	Globe	15	10,000	700	2,700	82	24.00
Electronic	Globe	18	10,000	1,100	2,700	82	24.00
Magnetic	Capsule	15	9,000	700	2,700	82	18.00
Magnetic	Capsule	18	9,000	750	2,700	82	20.00
Electronic	Capsule	18	10,000	1,100	2,700	82	20.00
Electronic	Reflector	15	10,000	900	2,700	82	23.00
Electronic	Reflector	18	10,000	800	2,700	82	23.00

CCT = Correlated Color Temperature   CRI = Color Rendering Index

* The wattage on the package for self-ballasted compact fluorescent lamps includes both the lamp wattage and the ballast wattage.

Table 5.
High-Intensity Discharge Lamp Information

Lamp Type	Rated Lamp Watts	Input Power (Lamp + Ballast Watts)	Average Rated Lamp Life (hours)	Light Output (lumens)	CCT (K)	CRI	Typical Price per Lamp (S)
High-Intensity Discharge							
High-Pressure Sodium	35	53	16,000	2,250	2,100	22	18.00
High-Pressure Sodium	50	64	24,000	4,000	2,100	22	18.00
High-Pressure Sodium	70	95	24,000	6,300	2,100	22	18.50
High-Pressure Sodium	100	130	24,000	9,500	2,100	22	19.00
Metal Halide	70	95	10,000	5,000–5,200	3,700–4,000	65–70	27.00
Metal Halide	100	125	10,000	8,500–10,000	3,700–4,000	65–70	27.00
Mercury	75	93	16,000–24,000	2,800–3,150	5,700	22–50	23.00
Mercury	100	125	24,000	3,850–4,300	5,700	22–50	17.00
Mercury	175	200	24,000	7,850–7,950	5,700	22–50	17.00

CCT = Correlated Color Temperature   CRI = Color Rendering Index

Table 6.
Typical Price Ranges for Ballasts, Controls, and Luminaires

Ballasts

Magnetic	$15–25
Magnetic Dimming	$30–75
Electronic	$25–65
Electronic Dimming	$30–90

Controls

Switches	$1–10
Door Switches	$10–20
Dimmers for Incandescent Lamps	$5–30
Dimmers for Fluorescent Lamps	$30–150
Motion Detectors	$40–100
Interval Timers	$5–25
Plug and Socket Timers	$10–20

Luminaires

Recessed with Incandescent Lamps	$20–75
Recessed with Compact Fluorescent Lamps	$45–100
Track Lights, per head	$10–50
Wall- or Ceiling-Mounted with Fluorescent or Incandescent Lamps	$10–200
Linear Fluorescent Strips	$10–30
Wall-Mounted Exterior with Incandescent Lamps	$15–200
Wall-Mounted Exterior with High-Pressure Sodium Lamps	$70–150
Exterior Floodlight with PAR-Lamps	$10–20
Exterior with High-Intensity Discharge Lamps	$40–90

Lamps

Commonly known as "light bulbs," electric light sources are called "lamps" in this book to conform to the lighting profession's convention. Lamps discussed in this chapter are organized into three groups: Incandescent, Fluorescent, and High-Intensity Discharge. Within these groups, the following information is given for each type of lamp: Qualities – Color and Light Output; Energy and Cost – Wattage, Efficacy, Life, Cost, and Where to Buy; Use – Installation, Luminaires, Controls, and Cautions; For more information – Designs and Other Lamps. These categories of information are explained below. Use them to compare different lamps. The tables give specific data about the various lamps.

The introductory section for each lamp type describes the directionality of the lamp; some lamps focus their light output in a specific direction. Reflector lamps are directional. Others are nondirectional or diffuse and emit light uniformly in all directions. The common A-lamp is a nondirectional lamp.

Qualities

Color: Some lamps appear "warmer" than others, as explained in the People, Energy, and Light chapter. Lamps also vary in how well they render color in homes. Residents are most accustomed to the warmth and excellent color rendering of incandescent lamps. When selecting lamps, be sure to evaluate correlated color temperature (CCT) and color rendering index (CRI).

Light Output: The total amount of light emitted by a lamp is measured in lumens. Lamps differ in light output. They also differ in the rate at which light output decreases as the lamp ages, a phenomenon called lamp lumen depreciation. A light output rating on a lamp's package is the initial light output rating before the decrease begins. Use lumens to compare the light output of lamps that have similar distributions. The tables in this chapter include the light output for different kinds of lamps.

Energy and Cost

Wattage: The rate at which power is used by a lamp is measured in watts. Energy use and cost are directly related to the wattage and hours of use of a lamp. A lower-wattage lamp will use less energy than a higher-wattage lamp that is operated for the same amount of time. Lamp wattages can be found on the lamp itself and on its packaging; actual wattages for lighting systems that use fluorescent and high-intensity discharge lamps will vary from the listed wattage due to the additional watts that are consumed by the ballast. Low-voltage lamps also require slightly more watts than that which is stated on the lamp or package due to transformer losses.

Efficacy: Some lamps produce more lumens for each watt of power than other lamps. High-efficacy lamps consume less energy than low-efficacy lamps of equal light output. Use efficacy ratings, listed in lumens per watt, to identify lamps that more effectively convert the energy you pay for into light.

Life: Some lamps can last more than 20 times longer than other lamps. The lamp life listed on a package is the average rated lamp life. Actual lamp life will vary and can be influenced by the lamp's operating temperature, starting method, operating cycle, and operation on dimmers.

Cost: The purchase price of lamps should be considered, along with the energy cost of operating the lamp and the frequency of lamp replacements.

Where to Buy: Some lamps are commonly available in supermarkets, discount department stores, or hardware stores. Others must be purchased through electrical suppliers or lighting stores. Many energy-efficient lamps are offered through mail-order catalogs and electric utility promotions.

Use

Installation: Lamps are designed for a particular type of socket and may not always be interchangeable with other lamps. Some lamps require ballasts or transformers. Due to the differences in size, performance under different temperatures, light output, and light distribution, some lamps are preferable for certain installations.

Luminaires: Proper performance of a lamp depends upon its use in a compatible luminaire.

Controls: Some lamps are more easily dimmed or switched than others. See the Controls chapter for more information.

Cautions: Lamps in certain applications can present problems such as noise, fire hazards, lamp failure due to temperature or moisture, or interference with electrical devices.

For more information refer to

Designs: Most lamp types are used in several of the designs in this book. Refer to the listed designs to see an application of the particular lamp type.

Other Lamps: Several lamp options may exist for an application. Consider the other suggested lamps for possible improvements in energy efficiency or light quality. Lamps are listed in the order in which they appear in this chapter.

Incandescent

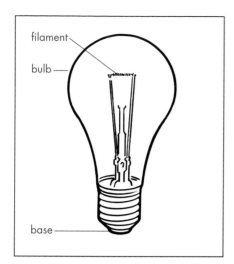

filament

bulb

base

Incandescent lamps convert electric power into light by passing electricity through a filament of coiled tungsten wire, heating it until it glows. The lamps usually are filled with an inert gas mixture consisting primarily of argon. Of the energy that goes into the incandescent filament, only 10 to 15 percent is emitted as light; the rest is emitted as heat.

Incandescent lamps come in a variety of shapes and sizes. The letter designation refers to the shape, and the number indicates the maximum diameter of the lamp in eighths of an inch. For example, A19 lamps are the shape most commonly found in homes, and are 19 eighths of an inch in diameter (2⅜ inches) at the widest point. Different base types are available; the most common type is a medium screwbase. The glass bulb can be clear, diffuse, or even colored, or it can have a reflective coating on the inside. Both directional and nondirectional incandescent lamps are available.

Qualities

Color: Excellent; color temperature decreases when incandescent lamps are dimmed.

Light Output: See the table for each lamp type for light output ratings.

Energy and Cost

Wattage: See the table for each lamp type for wattages.

Efficacy: Low efficacies (from 6 to 20 lumens per watt) compared to fluorescent lamps. Improved-efficacy incandescent lamps are available.

Life: Short (from 750 to 2000 hours) compared to fluorescent lamps. Dimming incandescent lamps extends their life.

Cost: Common A-lamps are inexpensive, but some reflector and specialty lamps are more expensive than fluorescent lamps. See the table for each lamp type for typical incandescent lamp costs.

Where to Buy: A-lamps are readily available in supermarkets, discount stores, and hardware stores, as are most common reflector (R) and parabolic aluminized reflector (PAR) lamps. Lighting stores and electrical suppliers carry special shapes.

Use

Installation: Where lower light output is acceptable, replace an incandescent lamp with a lower-wattage incandescent lamp for energy savings. Use incandescent lamps where excellent color rendering and good optical control of light are essential. Because incandescent lamps have low efficacies, restrict their use to applications where short hours of use are expected, where the lamps are frequently switched, where the lamps will be exposed to extremely cold temperatures, or where there are no other alternatives.

Controls: Easily dimmed.

Cautions: Incandescent lamps become very hot; keep combustible materials away from the lamp.

For more information refer to

Designs: Incandescent lamps commonly are used throughout a home.

Other Lamps: Fluorescent, High-Intensity Discharge

Lamps

Incandescent: Common

Common incandescent lamps come in a variety of shapes and sizes. Decorative candle lamps are often used in chandeliers. Tubular or "showcase" lamps are used in some plug-in desk lamps, furniture-integrated luminaires, and artwork luminaires. Globe lamps (G-lamps) are spherical and typically are used where the lamp can be seen. A three-way lamp has two filaments. When used with a three-level socket, either or both filaments can be lit to provide three levels of light. All common incandescent lamps are nondirectional.

Like many common incandescent lamps, A- and G-lamps are available with either clear or frosted bulbs. As a rule of thumb, use lamps with clear bulbs when you want to see the filament, and frosted lamps when you do not. If the filament is visible, the light will be very intense and the direct glare may be unacceptable to residents. Frosted lamps diffuse the light.

Qualities

Color: Excellent.

Lamp Type	Rated Lamp Watts	Average Rated Lamp Life (hours)	Light Output (lumens)	CCT (K)	CRI	Typical Price per Lamp ($)
Common Incandescent						
A19, Inside Frost	40	1,000–1,500	460–505	2,800	95+	0.75
A19, Inside Frost	60	1,000	870–890	2,800	95+	0.75
A19, Inside Frost	75	750	1,190–1,220	2,800	95+	0.75
A19, Inside Frost	100	750	1,750	2,800	95+	0.75
A21, Inside Frost	150	750	2,850	2,800	95+	1.75
A21 or T21, Inside Frost	50–100–150	1,200–1,500	580–2,220	2,800	95+	2.00
Candle	40	1,500	—	2,800	95+	1.00
Candle	60	1,500	—	2,800	95+	1.00
C7 Night Light, Clear	7	3,000	45	2,800	95+	1.00
G16.5	40	1,500	245–345	2,800	95+	2.25
G25	40	1,500	370–425	2,800	95+	2.50
G25	60	1,500	660–715	2,800	95+	2.50
G40	60	2,500	576–740	2,800	95+	5.00

CCT = Correlated Color Temperature   CRI = Color Rendering Index

Energy and Cost

Efficacy: Low. Improved-efficacy incandescent lamps are available.

Life: Short compared to fluorescent lamps. Longer-life incandescent lamps are available.

Cost: Inexpensive, but decorative or multi-level lamps are more expensive than common A-lamps.

Where to buy: A-lamps are readily available in supermarkets, discount stores, and hardware stores. Lighting stores and electrical suppliers carry special shapes.

Use

Installation: Where lower light output is acceptable, replace a common incandescent lamp with a lower-wattage incandescent lamp for energy savings. Because common incandescent lamps have low efficacies, restrict their use to applications where short hours of use are expected, where the lamps are frequently switched, where decorative lamps are needed, or where there are no other alternatives.

Controls: Easily dimmed.

For more information refer to

Designs: Medium Living Room, Small Bath, Large Bath, Foyer with Open Stair, Multi-Family Lobby

Other Lamps: Reduced-Wattage Incandescent, Halogen A Incandescent, Reflector, Screwbase Compact and Circline Fluorescent

Incandescent: Reduced-Wattage

Reduced-wattage incandescent A-lamps are shaped like other incandescent A-lamps, but the gas fill is different, allowing lower wattages or longer life. Lamps of 25 watts and higher have an argon fill, with a small percentage of nitrogen. The addition of krypton improves efficacy and offers opportunities for longer life. Thus, two types of reduced-wattage A-lamps are available: 1) reduced-wattage, and 2) reduced-wattage with extended life. The table compares the light output, efficacy, and lamp life of three common A-lamps with corresponding reduced-wattage and long-life versions. The data show that standard-life, reduced-wattage lamps have lower light output than common lamps. However, the wattage reduction more than offsets the lower light output, thus giving the reduced-wattage versions a slightly higher efficacy than the common lamps.

Reduced-wattage, long-life incandescent A-lamps are recommended only in applications where replacing lamps is difficult. As the table indicates, life is extended to 2500 hours, but light output is reduced by as much as 30 percent, compared with the corresponding common lamp. As a result, efficacy is also reduced.

Reduced-wattage incandescent lamps have the same nondirectional light distribution as the common A-lamps they may replace.

Comparison of Reduced-Wattage and Common Incandescent A-Lamps

	Rated Lamp Watts	Light Output (lumens)	Efficacy (lumens/watt)	Lamp Life (hours)
Common	100	1,750	17.5	750
	75	1,190–1,220	15.9–16.3	750
	60	870–890	14.5–14.8	1,000
Reduced-Wattage	90	1,620	18.0	750
	67	1,130	16.9	750
	52	800	15.4	1,000
Reduced-Wattage, Long-Life	90	1,360–1,375	15.1–15.3	2,500
	67	930–945	13.9–14.1	2,500
	52	700–705	13.5–13.6	2,500

Qualities

Color: Same as common incandescent lamps.

Light Output: Lower than common incandescent lamps.

Lamp Type	Rated Lamp Watts	Average Rated Lamp Life (hours)	Light Output (lumens)	CCT (K)	CRI	Typical Price per Lamp (S)
Reduced-Wattage and Reduced-Wattage, Long-Life						
Reduced-Wattage A-Lamp	52	1,000	800	2,800	95+	1.00
Reduced-Wattage A-Lamp	67	750	1,130	2,800	95+	1.00
Reduced-Wattage A-Lamp	90	750	1,620	2,800	95+	1.00
Reduced-Wattage A-Lamp	135	750	2,580	2,800	95+	1.25
Reduced-Wattage, Long-Life A-Lamp	52	2,500	700–705	2,800	95+	1.50
Reduced-Wattage, Long-Life A-Lamp	67	2,500	930–945	2,800	95+	1.50
Reduced-Wattage, Long-Life A-Lamp	90	2,500	1,360–1,375	2,800	95+	1.50
Reduced-Wattage, Long-Life A-Lamp	135	2,500	2,105–2,145	2,800	95+	2.00

CCT = Correlated Color Temperature   CRI = Color Rendering Index

Energy and Cost

Wattage: Lower than common incandescent lamps.

Efficacy: Slightly higher than common incandescent lamps, except for long-life lamps, which have lower efficacy than common lamps.

Life: Shorter than fluorescent lamps, but reduced-wattage, long-life incandescent A-lamps last two-and-a-half to three times as long as common incandescent A-lamps.

Cost: Slightly higher than common incandescent lamps.

Where to Buy: Supermarkets, lighting, hardware, and convenience stores.

Use

Installation: Easily replace common lamps. These lamps are best used where a slight reduction in light output will be acceptable. If this is the case, lower-wattage common incandescent lamps should also be considered (that is, 40-watt or 60-watt lamps instead of 60-watt or 75-watt lamps, respectively). Because of their reduced efficacy, long-life lamps should be avoided unless replacing lamps is inconvenient and all other alternatives have been eliminated.

Luminaires: Reduced-wattage A-lamps can screw directly into any luminaire that is designed to operate common incandescent A-lamps.

Controls: Easily dimmed.

For more information refer to

Other Lamps: Halogen A Incandescent, Reflector, Screwbase Compact and Circline Fluorescent

Incandescent: Halogen A

Halogen incandescent lamps have a slightly different shape and a thicker and heavier glass bulb than the common incandescent A-lamps they may replace. Like common incandescent lamps, halogen lamps produce light when electricity is passed through a tungsten filament, heating the filament until it glows. The filament evaporates over a lamp's life, causing the bulb wall to blacken slowly, with loss of light and eventual lamp failure through disintegration of the filament. In halogen lamps, chemicals called halogens are introduced in the gas fill to minimize the problem of filament evaporation. The halogens redirect evaporated tungsten onto the filament, rather than onto the bulb wall. As a result, the light output does not degrade as rapidly as it does with common incandescent lamps, so lamp life is extended.

Although most halogen lamps are dimmable, dimming the lamps reduces their burning temperature. The halogen cycle is most effective when lamps are operating with the hotter interior bulb temperatures that are created with full operation. If these lamps are dimmed regularly during operation and the lamps begin to blacken, operate them briefly at full output. Operating them on dimmer circuits will not offset their longer life nor interfere with the energy and economic advantages of their use in homes.

Halogen incandescent lamps have the same nondirectional light distribution as common A-lamps.

The table compares the light output, efficacy, and lamp life of halogen incandescent lamps with common incandescent lamps.

Comparison of Halogen and Common Incandescent A-Lamps

	Rated Lamp Watts	Light Output (lumens)	Efficacy (lumens/watt)	Lamp Life (hours)
Common	100	1,750	17.5	750
	75	1,190–1,220	15.9–16.3	750
	60	870–890	14.5–14.8	1,000
	40	460–505	11.5–12.6	1,000–1,500
Halogen	100	1,600–1,880	16.0–18.8	2,250–3,000
	72, 75	1,090–1,300	15.1–17.3	2,250–3,500
	60	960	16.0	3,000
	52	885	17.0	3,500
	42	665	15.8	3,500

Qualities

Color: Excellent. Halogen lamps emit slightly whiter light than other incandescent lamps.

Light Output: Less lumen depreciation over the life span of the lamp.

Lamp Type	Rated Lamp Watts	Average Rated Lamp Life (hours)	Light Output (lumens)	CCT (K)	CRI	Typical Price per Lamp (S)
Halogen						
Halogen A-Lamp	42	3,500	665	3,050	95+	4.00
Halogen A-Lamp	52	3,500	885	3,050	95+	4.00
Halogen A-Lamp	60	3,000	960	3,050	95+	4.00
Halogen A-Lamp	72, 75	2,250–3,500	1,090–1,300	3,050	95+	4.00
Halogen A-Lamp	100	2,250–3,000	1,600–1,880	3,050	95+	4.00

CCT = Correlated Color Temperature   CRI = Color Rendering Index

Energy and Cost

Wattage: Typical halogen A-lamps are 42, 52, 60, 72, 75, and 100 watts.

Efficacy: Slightly more efficacious than common incandescent lamps; less efficacious than fluorescent lamps. The efficacy is reduced when lamps are dimmed.

Life: Longer than common lamps, reduced-wattage lamps, and most reduced-wattage, long-life lamps. Shorter life than fluorescent lamps.

Cost: About four times more expensive than common lamps. Electric utility company incentives may offer substantial savings.

Where to Buy: Lighting stores and utility promotions. Sometimes available at supermarkets, hardware stores, and drugstores.

Use

Installation: Easily replace common lamps. Due to their long life, they are ideal for luminaires where lamp replacement is inconvenient.

Luminaires: Can be screwed directly into any luminaire that is designed to operate common incandescent A-lamps.

Controls: Can be dimmed. Occasionally they should be operated at full output to retain the benefits of the halogen cycle.

For more information refer to

Designs: Small Kitchen, Large Kitchen, Small Dinette, Medium Dinette, Dining Room, Small Living Rooms, Medium Living Rooms, Large Living Rooms 1 and 3, Half Bath, Medium Bath 2, Small Bedroom, Children's Bedroom, Large Bedroom, Home Office, Multi-Family Fire Stair 1, Entry 1

Other Lamps: Reflector, Screwbase Compact and Circline Fluorescent

Incandescent: Reflector

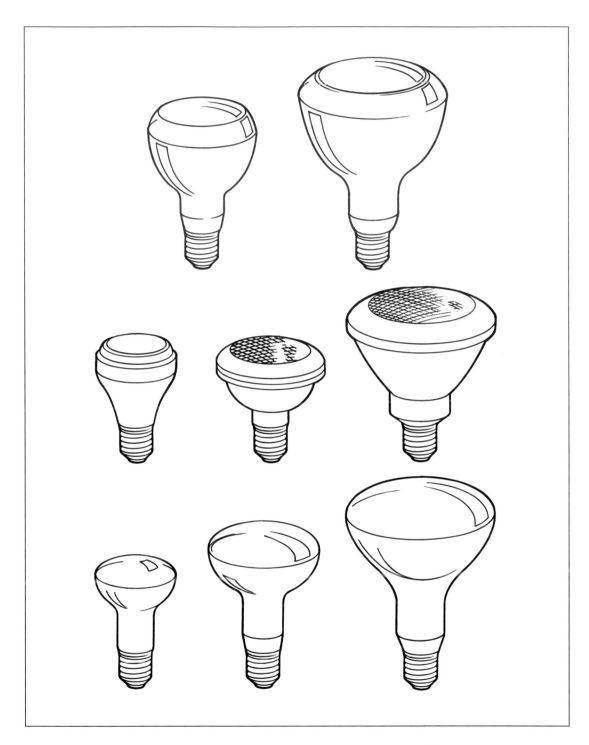

The bulbs of incandescent reflector lamps have reflective coatings, so they are directional light sources. Available in a number of bulb shapes, they typically operate on standard line voltage (120 V) and have medium screwbases. The shape of the light beam is cone-like, and can be specified in a range of beam spreads, from "narrow spot" to "wide flood." A "spot" lamp will have a narrower distribution, with greater intensity at the center of the beam, than a "flood" lamp with the same wattage and bulb shape. For this reason, candela distribution data, particularly "center beam candlepower" (CBCP), is more useful to the designer than light output when selecting reflector lamps. The major types, shown above from top to bottom, are: ellipsoidal reflector (ER), parabolic aluminized reflector (PAR), and common reflector (R).

The most common R-lamps found in homes are the 75-watt R30 and the 150-watt R40. Both offer opportunities for energy-efficient replacement, either with compact fluorescent reflector lamps or with halogen PAR-lamps. ER-lamps focus the beam approximately 2 inches in front of the bulb, thus making these lamps an efficient choice in deep, well-shielded luminaires. Both R- and ER-lamps are molded from "soft" soda lime glass and should not be used outdoors without an enclosure.

PAR-lamps provide better optical control than R30 or R40 lamps. Incandescent PAR-lamps, particularly the 75- and 150-watt PAR38, have been used extensively for residential outdoor area lighting. Newer products place halogen capsules within PAR enclosures in a wide variety of sizes and wattages, greatly improving the lamps' efficacies. Due to the relatively low efficacy of R-lamps and nonhalogen PAR-lamps, the Energy Policy Act of 1992 will restrict their use in the future. Among the most popular halogen PAR-lamps are the 45- to 75-watt PAR16 and the 50-watt PAR20 and PAR30, which provide good beam control, compact size, and efficient operation. A further variation is the halogen infrared (IR) PAR, which employs an IR-reflective coating to redirect infrared energy back onto the filament, thereby increasing efficacy.

The table compares the light output, efficacy, and lamp life of some common PAR-, halogen PAR-, and halogen IR PAR-lamps.

CONTINUED

Comparison of PAR38, Halogen PAR38, and Halogen IR PAR38 Flood Lamps

	Rated Lamp Watts	Light Output (lumens)	Efficacy (lumens/watt)	Lamp Life (hours)
PAR38	150	1,740	11.6	2,000
Halogen PAR38	90	1,270	14.1	2,000
Halogen IR PAR38	60	1,150	19.2	2,500

Qualities

Color: Excellent. Compared to an incandescent reflector lamp of the same wattage, a halogen reflector lamp has a slightly higher CCT. Usually, this causes the light that is produced by the halogen lamp to be slightly whiter in appearance than the light from the incandescent lamp.

Lamp Type	Rated Lamp Watts	Average Rated Lamp Life (hours)	Light Output (lumens)	Center Beam Candlepower (candelas)	Beam Spread (°)	CCT (K)	CRI	Typical Price per Lamp ($)
Reflector								
R20	50	2,000	410–420	510–550	38–43	2,800	95+	5.00
R30 Flood	75	2,000	830–900	430–470	65–130	2,800	95+	4.50
R40 Flood	150	2,000	1,900	1,300–1,400	59–76	2,800	95+	5.50
R40 Heat Lamp	250	5,000	—	—	—	—	—	15.00
ER30	75	2,000	850	1,200	42	2,800	95+	6.50
PAR38 Flood	75	2,000	750–765	1,750–1,800	30–37	2,800	95+	5.00
PAR38 Flood	150	2,000	1,740	3,100–4,000	30–36	2,800	95+	5.00
Halogen PAR16 Narrow Flood	55	2,000	—	1,300	30	3,050	95+	14.00
Halogen PAR20 Narrow Flood	50	2,000–2,500	560	1,250–1,400	30–32	3,050	95+	9.00
Halogen PAR30 Flood	50	2,000–2,500	670	1,100–1,600	36–42	3,050	95+	9.00
Halogen PAR38 Flood	45	2,000	540	1,600–1,800	32	3,050	95+	10.00
Halogen PAR38 Flood	90	2,000–2,500	1,270	3,500–4,000	30	3,050	95+	10.00
Halogen IR PAR38 Flood	60	2,000–2,500	1,150	3,300	32	3,050	95+	12.00

CCT = Correlated Color Temperature   CRI = Color Rendering Index

Energy and Cost

Efficacy: Halogen IR PAR-lamps are up to 65 percent more efficacious than common PAR-lamps of similar beam spread.

Life: Longer than common incandescent lamps. Halogen PAR-lamps have lower lumen depreciation over the life of the lamp.

Cost: Much more expensive than A-lamps. R-lamps are the least expensive reflector lamps; halogen IR PAR-lamps are the most expensive.

Where to Buy: Discount stores, supermarkets, hardware stores, and drugstores carry basic sizes. Lighting stores and electrical suppliers carry a larger selection of beam spreads and sizes for halogen PAR-lamps.

Lamps

Use

Installation: Use reflector lamps to replace A-lamps in applications such as track heads, recessed downlights, and wall wash, accent, and exterior flood luminaires. Reflector lamps of lower wattages than A-lamps can be used when directional light is needed. Reflector lamps fit into the same medium-based sockets as common incandescent lamps. Because diameters vary among the reflector lamps, however, check to be sure the lamp fits in the luminaire housing. For example, a PAR38 flood is 38 eighths of an inch (4¾ inches) in diameter, which may be too wide for some track heads or recessed downlights. The length of the lamp is also a factor. Some R-lamps may protrude below the ceiling plane in a recessed downlight, and some PAR-lamps may be too short for proper light distribution.

Luminaires: Ceiling- or Wall-Mounted Track or Adjustable Heads, Recessed, Exterior Large-Area Flood

Controls: Can be dimmed. Efficacy is reduced when lamps are dimmed.

Cautions: Do not use R- or ER-lamps in exposed exterior luminaires.

For more information refer to

Designs: Medium Kitchen 1, Dining Room, Large Living Rooms, Medium Bath 1, Large Bath, Closed Stair, Hallway, Floodlights

Other Lamps: Low-Voltage Halogen, Screwbase Compact Fluorescent with Integral Accessories

Incandescent: Tubular-Shaped Halogen

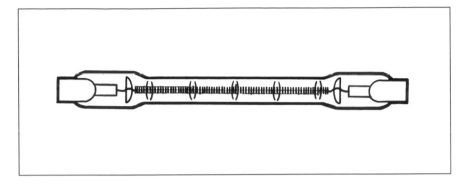

Tubular-shaped halogen lamps offer some of the same advantages as halogen A-lamps and halogen PAR-lamps. The halogen cycle provides greater efficacy, lower lumen depreciation over lamp life, and longer life than common incandescent lamp technology. The bulb wall of a tubular-shaped halogen lamp is made of quartz glass that can withstand high operating temperatures. Lamps should be handled carefully because the high temperatures may crack the quartz envelope if it has been etched with oils from hands and fingers.

Typical double-ended tubular-shaped halogen lamps are from 3 to 5 inches long and 100 to 1500 watts. Single-ended versions range from 75 to 500 watts. The single-ended lamps are available in line- and low-voltage varieties.

Tubular-shaped halogen lamps are nondirectional sources. Because of their high operating temperatures and different lamp bases, tubular-shaped halogen lamps are not direct replacements for common or halogen A-lamps. Thermal control and socket design within the luminaire are critical for the satisfactory performance of these lamps. For safety reasons, the lamps must be protected by a glass cover to prevent potential damage from lamp rupture.

Like the halogen IR PAR-lamps described in the Reflector Lamps section, some tubular-shaped halogen lamps have a special coating that directs infrared heat back to the filament, increasing efficacy. A 350-watt tubular-shaped IR-coated halogen lamp can replace a 500-watt tubular-shaped halogen lamp with similar light output, but at a higher lamp price.

Qualities

Color: Excellent color rendering characteristics.

Light Output: Less lumen depreciation over life than common incandescent lamps.

Lamp Type	Rated Lamp Watts	Average Rated Lamp Life (hours)	Light Output (lumens)	CCT (K)	CRI	Typical Price per Lamp ($)
Tubular-Shaped Halogen						
Tubular-Shaped, RSC Base	300	2,000	5,600–6,000	3,050	95+	10.00
Tubular-Shaped, RSC Base	500	2,000	10,500–11,100	3,050	95+	10.00
Tubular-Shaped IR, RSC Base	350	2,000	10,000	3,050	95+	30.00

CCT = Correlated Color Temperature   CRI = Color Rendering Index

Lamps

Energy and Cost

Wattage: Tubular-shaped halogen lamps often are high-wattage lamps.

Efficacy: Higher (16 to 29 lumens per watt) than other incandescent lamps. The tubular-shaped IR halogen lamps are more efficacious than those without an IR coating. Efficacy decreases when lamps are dimmed.

Life: Up to 2000 hours.

Cost: High compared with many other incandescent and some fluorescent lamps.

Where to Buy: In some geographic areas, the availability of tubular-shaped halogen lamps may be limited to lighting stores. Most luminaires purchased for residential use, however, are supplied with at least one lamp.

Use

Installation: Not direct replacements for common incandescent lamps. Tubular-shaped halogen lamps only fit into specific sockets.

Luminaires: Chandeliers, Recessed, Sconces, Desk Lamps, Floor Lamps, Exterior Large-Area Flood

Controls: Can be dimmed. Occasionally they should be operated at full light output to retain the benefits of the halogen cycle.

Cautions: Avoid using in locations where combustible materials could come in contact with the lamp. The lamps produce ultraviolet radiation that may be harmful if light is not first absorbed or filtered by a glass shield. Underwriters Laboratories now requires that all halogen lamps be shielded for safety reasons.

For more information refer to

Other Lamps: Reflector, Low-Voltage Halogen

Incandescent: Low-Voltage Halogen

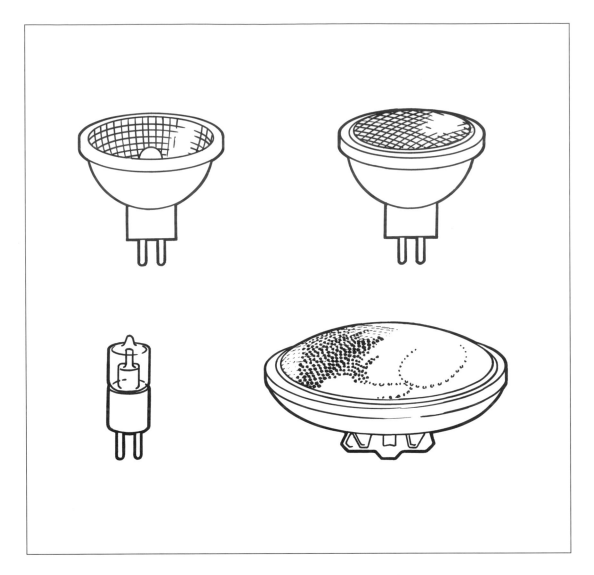

Low-voltage halogen lamps operate at less than 30 volts (typically 12 volts) and therefore require transformers to reduce the voltage supplied to the lamp. Their short, thick filaments allow compact lamp size, as shown above at lower left, and excellent optical control. Popular low-voltage halogen lamps include small multi-faceted reflector (MR) lamps, shown in the top row, and some PAR-lamps, lower right, commonly used in track lighting. Low-voltage halogen lamps are not a direct replacement for other types of incandescent lamps because they need a transformer and because their bases do not fit into the sockets that are designed for other incandescent lamps. Due to the initial investment required to install low-voltage lighting systems, they are better suited for accent lighting than ambient lighting. Their efficiency results from delivering light precisely where it is wanted and producing little wasted light. The number after the letter designation refers to the lamp's diameter in eighths of an inch. For example, an MR16 is 16 eighths of an inch, or 2 inches, in diameter. Low-voltage halogen lamps such as the MR16 and MR11 are directional sources.

Qualities

Color: Excellent.

Lamp Type	Rated Lamp Watts	Average Rated Lamp Life (hours)	Light Output (lumens)	Center Beam Candlepower (candelas)	Beam Spread (°)	CCT (K)	CRI	Typical Price per Lamp (S)
Low-Voltage Halogen								
PAR36 Narrow Spot	50	4,000	400	11,000	8	3,050	95+	14.00
MR11 (FTF)*	35	3,000	460	2,750–3,000	20	2,950	95+	14.00
MR16 Flood (BAB)*	20	2,000–4,000	280	460–850	36–40	2,925	95+	12.00
MR16 Flood (EXN)*	50	2,000–4,000	960	1,500–2,500	38–40	3,050	95+	12.00
Bi-pin Halogen	35	2,000	650	—	—	3,050	95+	15.00

CCT = Correlated Color Temperature   CRI = Color Rendering Index

* The three-letter code is an American National Standards Institute (ANSI) designation that identifies a lamp of a certain beam spread and wattage.

Energy and Cost

Wattage: Save energy by using low-voltage halogen lamps to replace higher-wattage lamps that do not deliver light effectively to the task.

Efficacy: Similar to other halogen reflector lamps.

Life: Up to 4000 hours.

Cost: High. Low-voltage operation requires a transformer, increasing the cost of the system.

Where to Buy: In some geographic areas, the availability of low-voltage lamps may be limited to lighting stores. Most low-voltage luminaires that are purchased for residential use are supplied with a lamp.

Use

Installation: Low-voltage lamps only fit into luminaires that are designed exclusively for their use. Low-voltage track lighting, recessed luminaires, and ceiling-mounted downlights are available. The size of the transformer may negate the advantage of the smaller luminaire size unless the transformer is remotely located. Compact lamp size permits flexible and inconspicuous lighting applications, such as in display cabinets. The lamp can be located close to the task, which increases illumination but reduces the area that is illuminated.

Luminaires: Track, Suspended Downlights, Accent, Shelf or Display Cabinet

Controls: Dimmable; use dimmers designed specifically for low-voltage lamps.

Cautions: As with line-voltage types, low-voltage halogen lamps may burst and therefore require shielding. They produce ultraviolet radiation that may be harmful if not filtered. Magnetic transformers may be noisy; electronic transformers are available and are quieter.

These lamps come in a variety of beam spreads, from "very narrow spot" to "flood." The lamps appear very much alike, so take care to use the manufacturers' information to select a lamp with the appropriate beam spread.

For more information refer to

Other Lamps: Reflector

Fluorescent

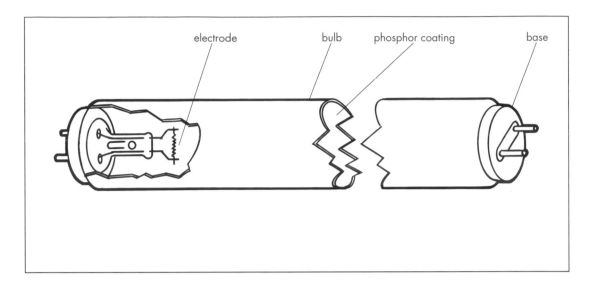

electrode   bulb   phosphor coating   base

Fluorescent lamps are cylindrical glass tubes that are coated on the inside with phosphors. They contain a small amount of mercury and are filled with a small quantity of argon, a combination of argon and neon, or krypton gases. During operation, an electrical current passes through the lamp and the mercury is vaporized, producing ultraviolet light. The phosphor coating absorbs the ultraviolet light and re-radiates it as visible light.

Fluorescent lamps require ballasts to provide the starting voltage and limit the electrical current during lamp operation. There are two types of ballasts commonly available for residential lighting: the energy-efficient magnetic ballast and the electronic ballast. The majority of ballasts sold today are energy-efficient magnetic types. Electronic ballasts are attractive because they are more energy-efficient than magnetic ballasts. They offer the advantages of lighter weight, quieter operation, and reduction of flicker, but they cost more than magnetic ballasts. For more information about ballasts, consult the Appendix.

Although fluorescent lamps all have tubular-shaped glass bulbs, the tubes can be bent into several shapes. The names for various shapes, and for shapes combined with ballasts and accessories, often are manufacturer-specific. This name variation can be confusing to consumers and specifiers. This book classifies compact fluorescent lamp shapes according to the 1992 National Electrical Manufacturers Association's system. Other names are adopted from the Illuminating Engineering Society of North America and the National Lighting Product Information Program.

A T12 or T8 tube bent in half is designated "U-shaped" and a tube bent to form a circle is designated "circline." Long twin-tube lamps, which consist of two parallel small-diameter tubes, are designated as "FT" for "fluorescent twin." The FT lamps are longer than most compact fluorescent lamps. "CFT" for "compact fluorescent twin" designates a shorter lamp composed of two parallel tubes. "CFQ" for "compact fluorescent quad" designates a lamp composed of four tubes in a quad formation. "CFM" designates other compact fluorescent shapes including the recently introduced triple loops or triple U's.

Compact and circline fluorescent lamps with an attached ballast that has a medium screwbase are designated "screwbase." Screwbase compact fluorescent lamp products can have one or two pieces; one-piece units are called "self-ballasted" and two-piece units are called "modular." Circline fluorescent lamp products are modular. When a self-ballasted screwbase lamp burns out, the ballast is discarded with the lamp; modular lamps allow replacement of just the lamp if the separate ballast is still operational. Some screwbase compact fluorescent lamps are made with glass or plastic globes, lenses, and reflectors that protect the lamp, may reduce glare, and may optimize the light distribution. These lamps are designated "screwbase compact fluorescent lamps with integral accessories."

All fluorescent lamps are nondirectional light sources, with the exception of compact fluorescent lamps with reflector accessories. These compact fluorescent reflector lamps are directional sources.

Qualities

Color: The color characteristics of the light, and to a large extent the efficacy, are determined by the chemical elements used to create the phosphor coating. By varying the proportions of different phosphors, it is possible to produce lamps with different color rendering properties and correlated color temperatures (CCT). Fluorescent lamp colors such as "cool white" and "warm white" are produced with a single coating of phosphors known as halophosphors. Other colors are produced by a coating of rare-earth phosphors, also called triphosphors, that may be added over a layer of halophosphors or used alone. The resulting rare-earth lamps are both more efficacious than halophosphor lamps and have better color properties. Rare-earth lamps are also more expensive than halophosphor lamps.

In 1992 the National Electrical Manufacturers Association adopted a new color rendering index (CRI) and CCT designation system for lamps containing rare-earth phosphors. This system is used throughout this book and is summarized below.

Generic Name	CRI Range	New Name
thin-coat rare-earth phosphor	70-79	RE70
thick-coat rare-earth phosphor	80-89	RE80

To specify CCT, the zero of the designation above is replaced by the first two digits of the CCT, given in Kelvin. For example, an RE70 lamp of 3000 K temperature is noted as RE730. This is the most commonly recommended fluorescent lamp in the Designs chapter. For living rooms, where color rendering may be especially important for aesthetic reasons, an RE830 lamp is recommended.

Light Output: Fluorescent lamps are available in a large range of light outputs, from 250 to 3800 lumens. See the tables for specific light output ranges.

CONTINUED

Energy and Cost

Wattage: A fluorescent lighting system usually uses more watts than the rated lamp wattage because the ballast also consumes power.

Efficacy: Fluorescent lamps are significantly more efficacious than incandescent lamps. Linear and U-shaped fluorescent lamps are more efficacious than compact fluorescent lamps.

Life: Fluorescent lamps have significantly longer lamp life than incandescent lamps. Average rated lamp life is based on 3 hours per start. Lamp life will be reduced when lamps are operated for fewer than 3 hours per start, but the lamps may last longer (have a longer service life) because they may be on for fewer hours per day than lamps that are operated for 3 hours per start or longer. Lamp life will be increased when lamps are operated for more than 3 hours per start, but the service life may be reduced because the lamps may be on for more hours per day than lamps that are operated for 3 hours per start or less.

Cost: Except for linear fluorescent lamps with poor color characteristics, some of which will soon be removed from the market in the United States, fluorescent lamps are more expensive than most incandescent lamps.

Where to Buy: Different types of fluorescent lamps have different availabilities. Refer to the sections on specific fluorescent lamp types for availability and purchasing information.

Use

Installation: With the large selection of fluorescent lamp sizes and types, many applications are possible in homes.

Luminaires: Except for those that use screwbase compact and circline fluorescent lamps, a luminaire using a fluorescent lamp must contain a ballast.

Controls: Most can be dimmed but at a higher cost than dimming incandescent lamps. Special dimming ballasts and dimming controls are required.

Cautions: Fluorescent lamps contain a small amount of mercury. Wear gloves if picking up broken fluorescent lamp fragments. Most fluorescent lamps operate poorly in extremely cold temperatures. Avoid exterior use in cold climates, unless an enclosed luminaire is used. Lamp ends may blacken and lamps may flicker as they reach the end of their useful life. Magnetic ballasts may produce an audible hum. Ballasts that have poor power quality characteristics may interfere with other household appliances. See the Appendix for more information.

For more information refer to

Designs: Fluorescent lamps commonly are used throughout a home.

Other Lamps: Incandescent, High-Intensity Discharge

Fluorescent: Linear

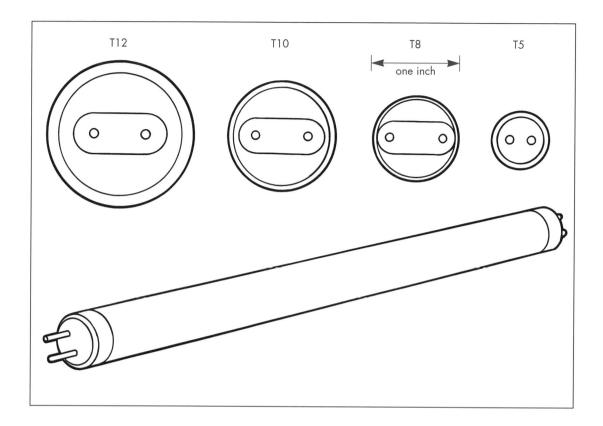

Linear fluorescent lamps are nondirectional light sources. The most common linear fluorescent lamps are 1½ inches in diameter and are designated as T12 for 12 eighths of an inch. Reduced-diameter fluorescent lamps, such as T10 (10 eighths or 1¼-inch diameter) lamps and T8 (8 eighths or 1-inch diameter) lamps with rare-earth phosphors, can provide improved system efficacy compared to conventional T12 lamps. Reduced-diameter lamps have created new opportunities for efficient luminaire designs that are better suited for focusing the light output from a fluorescent lamp. T5 (⅝-inch diameter) lamps are available in lower wattages for small spaces such as coves, furniture-integrated luminaires, and under-cabinet luminaires.

Rare-earth lamps of any size provide better color rendition and improved efficacy. Lamp efficacies associated with rare-earth phosphors are 5 to 15 percent better than those of conventional phosphors. Unfortunately, rare-earth phosphors are more expensive than conventional phosphors. However, because T10, T8, and T5 lamps have less surface area than T12 lamps, the cost of using rare-earth phosphors to coat these lamps is less than the cost to coat T12 lamps.

T10 lamps are used primarily to directly replace T12 lamps. They offer higher efficacies, increased light output, and longer life compared to common linear fluorescent lamps. Because of the higher light output of T10 lamps, fewer T10 lamps may be required in a design than T12 lamps. T10 lamps operate on the same ballasts as T12 lamps.

T8 lamps can fit in the same sockets as T12 lamps; however, they require a special ballast because they operate at a lower current. These lamps, like all four-pin fluorescent lamps, can be dimmed using dimming ballasts. T8 rare-earth lamps can have efficacies higher than T12 lamps. An excellent energy-saving system with good color rendering includes 4-foot T8 rare-earth phosphor lamps operating on electronic ballasts.

CONTINUED

Qualities

Color: Available in a variety of color characteristics. Good color is available that is compatible with incandescent lamps that are used in residences. To be compatible with incandescent lamps, select CCTs close to 3000 K. Higher CRI values indicate better color rendering for any given color temperature. For example, in areas where a warm color of light and colors are very important, such as a living room, an RE830 (rare-earth lamp with a color temperature of 3000 K and a CRI of 80+) is recommended. T8 lamps could be used for new installations.

Lamp Type	Rated Lamp Watts	Input Power per Lamp (Lamp + Ballast)*				Average Rated Lamp Life (hours)	Light Output (lumens)	CCT (K)	CRI	Typical Price per Lamp ($)
		Magnetic		Electronic						
		1 Lamp/ Ballast	2+ Lamps/ Ballast	1 Lamp/ Ballast	2+ Lamps/ Ballast					
Linear Fluorescent										
12" T5 Cool White	8	10				7,500	390–400	4,200	62	5.00
12" T5 Warm White	8	10				7,500	400	3,000	52	7.00
21" T5 Cool White	13	18				7,500	820–860	4,200	62	6.00
21" T5 Warm White	13	18				7,500	870–880	3,000	52	8.00
24" T12 Cool White	20	32	27			9,000	1,200–1,240	4,200	62	4.00
24" T12 RE730	20	32	27			9,000	1,275–1,300	3,000	70+	6.00
24" T12 RE830	20	32	27			9,000	1,300–1,350	3,000	80+	10.00
24" T8 RE730	17	24	22	22	17	20,000	1,325	3,000	70+	6.00
24" T8 RE830	17	24	22	22	17	20,000	1,400	3,000	80+	7.00
36" T12 Cool White	30	46	42	31	30	18,000	2,200–2,250	4,200	62	5.00
36" T12 Cool White, RW	25	41	37	26	25	18,000	1,925–2,000	4,200	62	6.00
36" T12 RE730, RW	25	41	37	26	25	18,000	2,025–2,350	3,000	70+	9.00
36" T8 RE730	25	33	33	30	24	20,000	2,125	3,000	70+	6.00
36" T8 RE830	25	33	33	30	24	20,000	2,250	3,000	80+	7.00
48" T12 Cool White	40	52	48	46	36	20,000	3,050	4,200	62	2.00
48" T12 Cool White, RW	34	46	42	38	30	20,000	2,650	4,200	62	3.00
48" T12 RE730, RW	34	46	42	38	30	20,000	2,800	3,000	70+	6.00
48" T12 RE830, RW	34	46	42	38	30	20,000	2,900	3,000	80+	10.00
48" T10 RE730	40	52	48	40	36	24,000	3,700	3,000	70+	7.00
48" T8 RE730	32	37	36	34	31	20,000	2,850	3,000	70+	5.50
48" T8 RE830	32	37	36	34	31	20,000	3,050	3,000	80+	7.00
60" T8 RE830	40	50	46	44	37	20,000	3,800	3,000	80+	8.50

CCT = Correlated Color Temperature   CRI = Color Rendering Index   RW = Reduced-wattage

* For two or more lamps, the number is the wattage consumed by one lamp plus its portion of the total ballast wattage. The total system wattage is the total number of lamps in the system multiplied by this number.

Lamps

Energy and Cost

Wattage: Require a ballast for operation, which consumes some power during lamp operation.

Efficacy: High (up to 90 lumens per watt, including the power consumed by the ballast). Ballasts are available that operate from one to four fluorescent lamps. Operating several lamps on a single ballast improves efficacy and reduces the initial cost because fewer ballasts are needed. Ask about ballast options when purchasing a luminaire.

Life: Long (up to 20,000 hours; 24,000 hours for T10 lamps), although inexpensive "shop light" lamps may have a much shorter lamp life.

Cost: Higher than common incandescent lamps, particularly for rare-earth lamps, but less expensive than many specialty incandescent lamps. Linear fluorescent lamps are less expensive than U-shaped lamps that are formed from straight tubes of the same length.

Where to Buy: Discount department stores and hardware stores carry various lengths of T12 lamps. Lighting stores, building and electrical supply stores, and utility promotions offer many color and size options for lamps and many ballast types.

Use

Installation: Linear fluorescent lamps usually are installed in workshops, kitchens, and family rooms, but they can provide light in all areas of the home. The use of linear fluorescent lamps is most successful when the CCT, CRI, and ballast are carefully selected for the intended purpose.

Luminaires: Many types are available, in many styles. Luminaires can be incorporated into architectural features such as cabinets, valances, soffits, or coves. In these applications, inexpensive strip luminaires can be used.

Controls: Dimmable with the proper dimming control and ballast.

Cautions: Magnetic ballasts may produce an audible hum. Lamp ends blacken and lamps may flicker as they reach the end of their useful life. Most fluorescent lamps operate poorly in extremely cold temperatures. Avoid exterior use in cold climates, unless an enclosed luminaire is used.

For more information refer to

Designs: Small Kitchen, Medium Kitchens 2 and 3, Large Kitchen, Small Dinette, Medium Dinette, Medium Living Rooms, Large Living Rooms 1 and 3, Half Bath, Small Bath, Large Bath, Small Bedroom, Children's Bedroom, Large Bedroom, Home Office, Foyer with Open Stair, Multi-Family Fire Stair 1

Other Lamps: U-Shaped and Long Twin-Tube Fluorescent, Compact and Circline Fluorescent, Screwbase Compact and Circline Fluorescent, High-Intensity Discharge

Fluorescent: U-Shaped and Long Twin-Tube

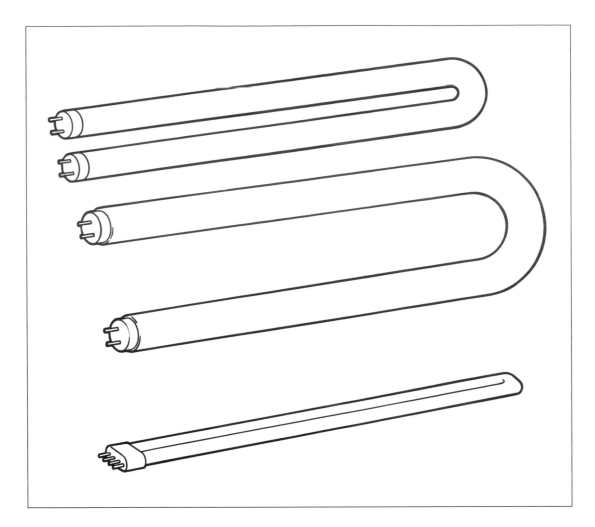

Fluorescent lamps are available not only in a linear shape but also in U shapes and long twin-tube shapes (FT designates fluorescent twin). U-shaped lamps offer the benefits of a linear lamp but can be contained in a smaller luminaire. FT lamps are available in 10.5-, 16.5-, and 22.5-inch lengths. The reduced overall width of an FT compared to a U-shaped lamp facilitates better optical control of the light within certain luminaires. Like linear fluorescent lamps, U-shaped and long twin-tube lamps are available with improved color rendering and are nondirectional light sources.

Qualities

Color: Available in a variety of color characteristics. Rare-earth lamps provide good color that is compatible with other lamps that are used in homes. To be compatible with incandescent lamps, select CCTs close to 3000 K. Select rare-earth lamps where good color rendering is important, such as in living rooms. In areas where CCT and CRI are less important, such as in garages or utility spaces, cool white or warm white lamps are acceptable and usually are less expensive.

Light Output: High compared to most incandescent lamps.

| Lamp Type | Rated Lamp Watts | Input Power per Lamp (Lamp + Ballast)* | | | | Average Rated Lamp Life (hours) | Light Output (lumens) | CCT (K) | CRI | Typical Price per Lamp ($) |
| | | Magnetic | | Electronic | | | | | | |
		1 Lamp/ Ballast	2+ Lamps/ Ballast	1 Lamp/ Ballast	2+ Lamps/ Ballast					
U-Shaped and Long Twin-Tube										
T12/U6 Cool White	40	52	48	46	36	12,000	2,600	4,200	62	10.00
T12/U6 Rare-Earth	34	52	48	46	36	12,000	2,400	3,000	70+	14.00
T8 U-Shaped Rare-Earth	31	36	35	37	30	20,000	2,800	3,100	80+	12.00
10.5″ FT18W Rare-Earth	18	22	20	21	18	20,000	1,250	3,000	80+	13.00
16.5″ FT36W Rare-Earth	36, 39	48	43	37	34	12,000	2,900	3,000	80+	15.00
22.5″ FT40W Rare-Earth	40	44	41	43	38	20,000	3,150	3,000	80+	15.00

CCT = Correlated Color Temperature   CRI = Color Rendering Index

* For two or more lamps, the number is the wattage consumed by one lamp plus its portion of the total ballast wattage. The total system wattage is the total number of lamps in the system multiplied by this number.

Energy and Cost

Wattage: Require a ballast, which draws a small amount of power during lamp operation.

Efficacy: High and similar to linear fluorescent lamps.

Life: Long (up to 20,000 hours).

Cost: Higher lamp cost than common incandescent and linear fluorescent lamps, particularly for rare-earth lamps.

Where to Buy: Lighting stores and building and electrical suppliers offer many color and size options for lamps and many ballast types.

Use

Installation: Smaller overall length than a linear fluorescent lamp of similar light output. The U-shaped fluorescent lamp can be used in many applications where reduced luminaire size is desired.

Luminaires: U-shaped lamps often are used in 2-foot by 2-foot luminaires. Fluorescent long twin-tube lamps are used in a variety of luminaires including wall wash luminaires and vanity lights.

Controls: Dimmable, with the proper dimming control and ballast.

Cautions: Magnetic ballasts may produce an audible hum. Lamp ends blacken and lamps may flicker as they reach the end of their useful life. These lamps operate poorly in extremely cold temperatures. Avoid exterior use in cold climates unless an enclosed luminaire is used.

For more information refer to

Designs: Large Kitchen, Small Bath, Large Bath, Home Office

Other Lamps: Linear Fluorescent, Compact and Circline Fluorescent

Fluorescent: Compact and Circline

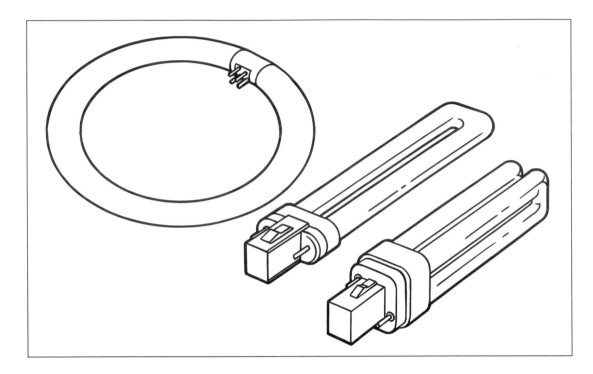

There are several types of compact fluorescent lamps. CFT or T4 twin-tube preheat lamps have starters in the base of the lamp and are available in 5, 7, 9, and 13 watts. CFQ or T4 or T5 quad-tube preheat lamps also have starters in the base and are most common in the 18- and 26-watt versions.

Circline fluorescent lamps are 6.5 to 16 inches in overall diameter and are available in wattages ranging from 20 to 40 watts. Compact fluorescent and circline lamps fit in even smaller spaces than U-shaped and FT lamps. Both energy-efficient magnetic ballasts and electronic ballasts are available for these lamps. Lamps with four-pin bases can be used with electronic ballasts or with dimming systems.

Although incandescent lamps cost less and can be more easily controlled optically, compact fluorescent lamps offer significantly greater efficacy and longer life than incandescent lamps. As a result, they are a relatively economical alternative to incandescent lamps. Both compact and circline fluorescent lamps are nondirectional light sources.

Compact lamp conversion kits for recessed luminaires containing incandescent lamps are available to modify the luminaire's optics and socket and to make room for compact fluorescent lamps.

Compact and circline fluorescent lamps can snap into screwbase ballasts and can directly replace many screwbase incandescent lamps. See Screwbase Compact and Circline Fluorescent Lamps for more information.

Qualities

Color: Compact fluorescent lamps use rare-earth phosphors and range from 2700 to 5000 K in correlated color temperature. Color appearance varies among manufacturers, but all render color well (CRI 80+). Select color temperatures of 2700 to 3000 K to approximate the color of incandescent lamps. Circline fluorescent lamps commonly are offered in warm white or cool white correlated color temperatures, with relatively poor color rendering. Rare-earth 3000 K circline fluorescent lamps are now available with good color rendering.

| Lamp Type | Rated Lamp Watts | Input Power per Lamp (Lamp + Ballast)* | | | | Average Rated Lamp Life (hours) | Light Output (lumens) | CCT (K) | CRI | Typical Price per Lamp (S) |
| | | Magnetic | | Electronic | | | | | | |
		1 Lamp/ Ballast	2+ Lamps/ Ballast	1 Lamp/ Ballast	2+ Lamps/ Ballast					
Compact Fluorescent and Circline										
CFT5W	5	7	6			10,000	250	2,700	82	6.00
CFT7W	7	9	8			10,000	400	2,700	82	6.00
CFT9W	9	11	10			10,000	600	2,700	82	6.00
CFT13W	13	15	14			10,000	825–900	2,700	82	7.00
CFQ9W	9	11	10			10,000	575	2,700	82	11.00
CFQ13W	13	15				10,000	860–900	2,700	82	11.00
CFQ18W	18	22				10,000	1,200	2,700	82	13.00
CFQ26W	26	30				10,000	1,800	2,700	82	14.00
6.5" Circline Cool White	20	25				12,000	800	4,200	62	8.00
6.5" Circline Warm White	20	25				12,000	825	3,000	52	8.50
8" Circline Cool White	22	27				12,000	1,025	4,200	62	7.00
8" Circline Warm White	22	27				12,000	1,000	3,000	52	9.00
8" Circline RE730	22	27		22		12,000	1,150	3,000	70+	11.00
12" Circline Cool White	32	42				12,000	1,800	4,200	62	8.00
12" Circline Warm White	32	42				12,000	1,500–2,100	3,000	52	10.00
12" Circline RE730	32	42		30		12,000	2,100	3,000	70+	11.00

CCT = Correlated Color Temperature   CRI = Color Rendering Index

* For two or more lamps, the number is the wattage consumed by one lamp plus its portion of the total ballast wattage. The total system wattage is the total number of lamps in the system multiplied by this number.

Energy and Cost

Efficacy: High (up to 84 lumens per watt for higher-wattage lamps with electronic ballasts). Require a ballast, which consumes a small amount of power during lamp operation.

Life: Long (up to 10,000 hours for T4 types and 20,000 hours for rapid-start T5 types).

Cost: Higher than common incandescent and most linear fluorescent lamps.

Where to Buy: Lighting stores, electrical suppliers, electric utility promotions, and lighting catalogs offer a wide variety of these lamps. Many luminaires that are designed for compact or circline fluorescent lamps come packaged with the appropriate lamps.

Use

Installation: Compact and circline fluorescent lamps frequently are used in "dedicated" luminaires that can accommodate only these lamps. Unlike screwbase compact or circline fluorescent lamps, lamps in dedicated luminaires cannot be replaced with incandescent lamps when the lamps burn out. Compact and circline fluorescent lamps also can be used with modular screwbase ballasts.

CONTINUED

Lamps

Luminaires: Some recessed luminaires, sconces, and table and desk lamps are designed for compact fluorescent and circline fluorescent lamps. In temperate climates, compact fluorescent lamps can be used for exterior lighting.

Controls: Most are not dimmable; however, dimming systems are available for compact fluorescent lamps that have four-pin bases.

Cautions: Magnetic ballasts may produce an audible hum. Magnetically ballasted compact fluorescent lamps may blink briefly when turned on. Avoid exterior use in cold climates.

For more information refer to

Designs: Medium Kitchen 1, Large Kitchen, Small Dinette, Medium Dinette, Dining Room, Small Living Room 2, Medium Living Rooms, Large Living Room 1, Medium Baths, Large Bath, Children's Bedroom, Large Bedroom, Home Office, Foyer with Open Stair, Closed Stair, Hallway, Multi-Family Lobby, Multi-Family Fire Stair 1

Other Lamps: Linear Fluorescent, U-Shaped and Long Twin-Tube Fluorescent, Screwbase Compact and Circline Fluorescent

Fluorescent: Screwbase Compact and Circline

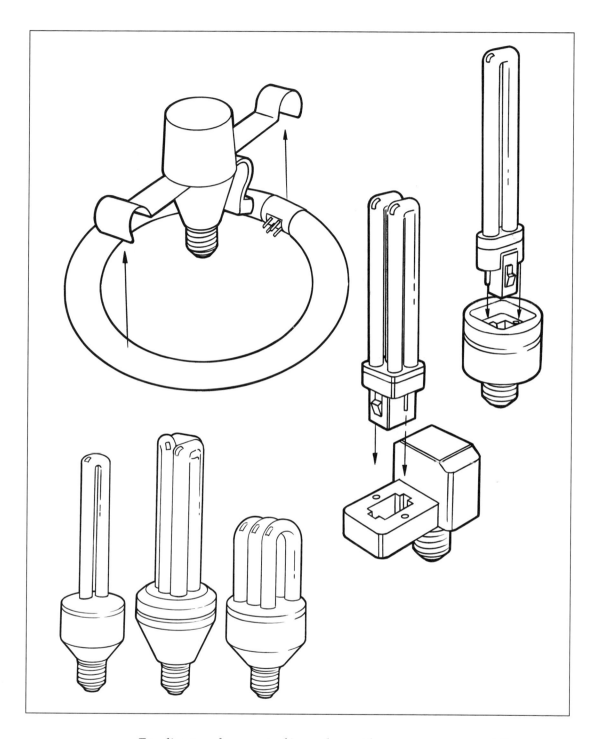

For direct replacement of incandescent lamps, some compact fluorescent lamp/ballast combinations are manufactured with medium screwbases. These may be two-piece (modular) units, shown above at the top and right, or one-piece (self-ballasted) units, lower left. The self-ballasted unit usually is smaller, and ensures that the lamp and ballast are compatible with each other. However, the entire unit must be replaced each time a new lamp is needed. Since ballasts can last three times longer than lamps, modular units with a lamp that separates from the ballast can be more economical. Compact and circline fluorescent lamps that were described in the previous section can also be used as screwbase units if they are snapped into a screwbase ballast.

CONTINUED

A 15-watt screwbase compact fluorescent lamp is rated at about the same light output as a 60-watt incandescent lamp. However, actual compact fluorescent light output is affected by lamp temperature, lamp position, and the luminaire's optical characteristics. Ongoing research will develop more-precise guidelines, but in the meantime, a reasonable rule of thumb is to divide the incandescent wattage by three to find the replacement compact fluorescent wattage. For example, replace a 75-watt incandescent lamp with one 26-watt or two 13-watt compact fluorescent lamps.

Like the common incandescent lamps they are designed to replace, screwbase compact and circline fluorescent lamps are nondirectional light sources. A screwbase compact or circline fluorescent lamp may easily be replaced by an incandescent lamp, which would negate the potential energy savings.

Qualities

Color: Choose a color temperature of 2700 to 3000 K to approximate the color of incandescent lamps. Circline fluorescent lamps commonly are offered in warm white or cool white color temperatures, with relatively poor color rendering, although some circline lamps use rare-earth phosphors and thus have good color rendering. Self-ballasted compact fluorescent lamps primarily are available in 2700 and 2800 K with good color rendering. Modular lamps are available in a variety of correlated color temperatures, from 2700 to 5000 K, all with good color rendering.

Lamp Type	Input Power (Lamp + Ballast Watts)*	Average Rated Lamp Life (hours)	Light Output (lumens)	CCT (K)	CRI	Typical Price per Lamp (S)
Self-Ballasted Compact Fluorescent**						
Ballast Type						
Electronic	15	10,000	900	2,700	82	17.00
Magnetic	18	10,000	700	2,800	82	20.00
Electronic	18	10,000	1,100	2,700	81	20.00
Electronic	20	10,000	1,200	2,700	82	20.00
Electronic	22	10,000	1,400	2,700	81	21.00
Electronic	23	10,000	1,550	2,700	82	20.00
Electronic	26, 27	10,000	1,550	2,800	84	22.00

CCT = Correlated Color Temperature   CRI = Color Rendering Index

* The wattage on the package for self-ballasted compact fluorescent lamps includes both the lamp wattage and the ballast wattage.

** For information on modular lamps, refer to the table in the previous section, Compact and Circline Fluorescent.

Energy and Cost

Wattage: Ballast draws a small amount of power during lamp operation. Self-ballasted units include ballast power in the wattage rating. Modular units do not.

Efficacy: High compared with incandescent lamps.

Life: Long (up to 10,000 hours).

Cost: Higher than common incandescent and linear fluorescent lamps. Electric utility company incentives may offer substantial savings.

Lamps

Where to Buy: Discount department stores and hardware stores may carry compact fluorescent lamps. Lighting stores, building and electrical supply stores, and utility promotions offer many color and size options for lamps and ballasts. Many mail-order catalogs offer screwbase compact fluorescent lamps.

Use

Installation: Screwbase compact and circline fluorescent lamps screw directly into medium-base lamp sockets that are used by incandescent lamps. A barrier to more widespread replacement of incandescent lamps with screwbase compact fluorescent lamps is luminaire compatibility. Screwbase compact fluorescent lamps are larger and heavier than the incandescent lamps that they replace. Check the available room in a luminaire before choosing a screwbase compact or circline fluorescent lamp and check to see if plug-in floor, table, or desk lamps would become unstable with the weight of the screwbase compact fluorescent lamp. It may be necessary to install a socket extender in luminaires with deeply recessed sockets or a harp extender to raise a table lamp shade to make more room for the compact fluorescent lamp. These adapters are available where the lamps are sold. Screwbase compact fluorescent lamps can be installed in a three-way incandescent lamp socket, but will only operate in two of the three settings and only at full light output.

Luminaires: In new construction, consider using luminaires that are designed for compact or circline fluorescent lamps instead of luminaires with sockets for screwbase lamps to prevent replacement with less-efficient incandescent lamps.

Controls: Most are not dimmable. Do not install screwbase compact or circline fluorescent lamps on dimmer circuits that are designed for incandescent lamps.

Cautions: Installation of compact or circline fluorescent lamps on an incandescent dimmer can cause overheating and possible loss of lamp life. Check lamp manufacturer's recommendations for maximum ambient temperature for rated life before installing a compact fluorescent lamp in an enclosed luminaire where ambient temperatures can be very high. Magnetically ballasted compact fluorescent lamps may blink briefly when turned on. Magnetic ballasts may produce an audible hum. Screwbase compact fluorescent lamps operate poorly in extreme temperatures. Electronic ballasts start lamps at 0°F and magnetic ballasts start lamps at 32°F. If the lamps are used outdoors in cold climates, however, they should only be used in enclosed luminaires. Most lamps provide less light output when operated in the base-down position. Ballasts that have poor power quality characteristics may interfere with television controls, timers, and other household appliances. See the Appendix for more information.

For more information refer to

Designs: Small Kitchen, Small Living Room 1, Large Living Rooms 1 and 3, Medium Bath 2, Small Bedroom, Large Bedroom, Home Office, Entry 1, Pole-Mounted Light

Other Lamps: Linear Fluorescent, U-Shaped and Long Twin-Tube Fluorescent, Compact and Circline Fluorescent, Screwbase Compact Fluorescent with Integral Accessories

Fluorescent: Screwbase Compact with Integral Accessories

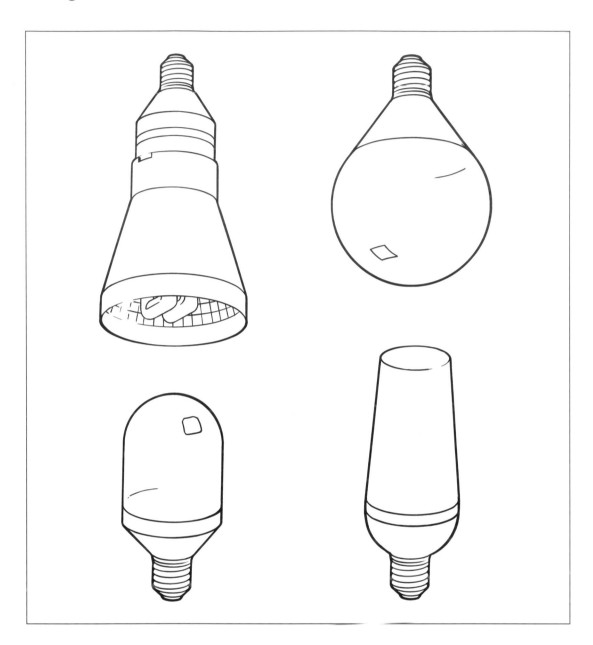

Screwbase compact fluorescent lamps are available with diffusers (top) and reflectors (bottom). A screwbase compact fluorescent lamp with a diffuser has its fluorescent lamp tubes covered by a cylindrical or spherical diffusing enclosure called a globe or capsule. The enclosure may be glass or breakage-resistant plastic. Screwbase compact fluorescent lamps with diffusers are nondirectional light sources.

Compact fluorescent reflector lamps are designed to aim light in a particular direction. There are two types. One contains a lensed, aluminized glass reflector, a screwbase ballast, and a compact fluorescent lamp; this can be a one-piece assembly or can be ordered in three pieces. The advantage of the three-piece units is that adapters are available in "short, normal, or narrow" sizes that allow the combination to fit a variety of sockets. For example, a "short" adapter is selected when the overall height of the combined assembly is a major concern. These units are offered to replace incandescent reflector lamps. The other type of compact fluorescent reflector lamp is a one-piece unit consisting of a screwbase ballast, a compact fluorescent lamp, and an attached reflector.

Both types of compact fluorescent reflector lamps are directional light sources; the reflector increases the efficiency of the luminaire in which the lamp is used by increasing the amount of light that reaches the task.

Screwbase compact fluorescent capsule, globe, and reflector lamps are designed so that they may be used alone in a simple socket. In some cases, such as some globe luminaires, a screwbase compact fluorescent globe lamp may replace an incandescent lamp and the existing diffuser.

Qualities

Color: Primarily available in 2700 and 2800 K with good color rendering.

Lamp Type		Input Power (Lamp + Ballast Watts)*	Average Rated Lamp Life (hours)	Light Output (lumens)	CCT (K)	CRI	Typical Price per Lamp ($)
Screwbase Compact Fluorescent with Integral Accessories							
Ballast Type	Accessory						
Electronic	Globe	11	10,000	450	2,700	82	23.00
Electronic	Globe	15	10,000	700	2,700	82	24.00
Electronic	Globe	18	10,000	1,100	2,700	82	24.00
Magnetic	Capsule	15	9,000	700	2,700	82	18.00
Magnetic	Capsule	18	9,000	750	2,700	82	20.00
Electronic	Capsule	18	10,000	1,100	2,700	82	20.00
Electronic	Reflector	15	10,000	900	2,700	82	23.00
Electronic	Reflector	18	10,000	800	2,700	82	23.00

CCT = Correlated Color Temperature   CRI = Color Rendering Index

* The wattage on the package for self-ballasted compact fluorescent lamps includes both the lamp wattage and the ballast wattage.

Energy and Cost

Wattage: Require a ballast, which consumes some power during lamp operation. The ballast wattage is included with the lamp wattage for self-ballasted units.

Efficacy: Higher than incandescent lamps, but not as high as linear or U-shaped fluorescent lamps. They emit less heat than incandescent lamps that provide equivalent light output.

Life: Long (up to 10,000 hours).

Cost: Higher than common incandescent R-, PAR-, and ER-lamps and other compact fluorescent lamps. Electric utility company incentives may offer substantial savings.

Where to Buy: Lighting stores, building and electrical supply stores, and utility promotions offer many options of lamps and ballasts. Many mail-order catalogs offer self-ballasted and modular compact fluorescent lamps with integral accessories.

CONTINUED

Use

Installation: Simple replacement for incandescent lamps. Globes and capsules are used primarily when the lamp will be seen. Compact fluorescent reflector lamps can replace R, PAR, or ER incandescent reflector lamps.

Luminaires: Screwbase compact fluorescent lamps with integral accessories are larger and heavier than the incandescent lamps they may replace. Some luminaires may not be able to accommodate the additional weight. Measure the dimensions of the luminaire before purchasing a compact fluorescent lamp to see if the lamp will fit. In new construction, consider using luminaires that are designed for compact fluorescent lamps, instead of those with screw sockets, to prevent replacement with less-efficient incandescent lamps.

Controls: Most are not dimmable. Do not install screwbase compact fluorescent lamps on dimmer circuits that are designed for incandescent lamps.

Cautions: Magnetically ballasted compact fluorescent lamps may blink briefly when turned on. Magnetic ballasts may produce an audible hum. Most screwbase compact fluorescent lamps operate poorly in extreme temperatures. Electronic ballasts start at 0°F, but if they are used outdoors in cold climates, lamps should be in enclosed luminaires. Lamps may provide less light output when in the base-down position. Ballasts that have poor power quality characteristics may interfere with television controls, timers, and other household appliances.

For more information refer to

Designs: Large Kitchen, Medium Dinette, Large Living Room 3, Small Bath, Hallway, Multi-Family Lobby, Multi-Family Corridor

Other Lamps: Halogen Incandescent, Reflector, Low-Voltage Halogen, Compact and Circline Fluorescent, Screwbase Compact and Circline Fluorescent

High-Intensity Discharge

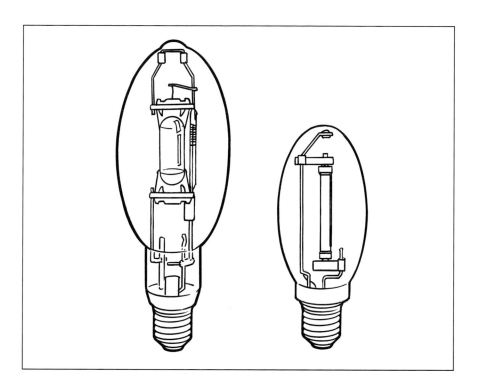

High-intensity discharge (HID) lamps include mercury vapor, metal halide, and high-pressure sodium lamps. This family of lamps contains some of the most efficacious lamps. All are nondirectional light sources, and all require a ballast for operation.

Some white mercury vapor lamps have phosphor coatings and have better color qualities than clear lamps. Although they are more efficacious than incandescent lamps and can be inexpensive, mercury vapor lamps are not as efficacious as most fluorescent lamps or other HID lamps of equivalent light output.

Metal halide lamps are more efficacious than mercury vapor lamps and have a higher CRI. Compact metal halide lamps come in lower wattages. Most metal halide lamps require an enclosed luminaire or other protective measure to guard against possible end-of-life rupture and to filter ultraviolet light, although some of the new low-wattage types are available for use in open fixtures.

High-pressure sodium lamps require a ballast with a high-voltage starter because, unlike mercury and metal halide lamps, they do not contain starting electrodes. High-pressure sodium lamps produce a yellow-white light and are not appropriate where good color rendering is important; however, there are two types of improved-color high-pressure sodium lamps: white and "improved color." White high-pressure sodium lamps have CCT ratings that approach those of incandescent lamps. In both types, efficacy is significantly reduced compared to standard high-pressure sodium lamps, but is still much greater than incandescent lamps.

Qualities

Color: Generally poor, although good color rendering is available from some metal halide and improved-color high-pressure sodium lamps. The color appearance of metal halide and improved-color high-pressure sodium lamps may shift over time.

Light Output: High.

CONTINUED

Lamp Type	Rated Lamp Watts	Input Power (Lamp + Ballast Watts)	Average Rated Lamp Life (hours)	Light Output (lumens)	CCT (K)	CRI	Typical Price per Lamp ($)
High-Intensity Discharge							
High-Pressure Sodium	35	53	16,000	2,250	2,100	22	18.00
High-Pressure Sodium	50	64	24,000	4,000	2,100	22	18.00
High-Pressure Sodium	70	95	24,000	6,300	2,100	22	18.50
High-Pressure Sodium	100	130	24,000	9,500	2,100	22	19.00
Metal Halide	70	95	10,000	5,000–5,200	3,700–4,000	65–70	27.00
Metal Halide	100	125	10,000	8,500–10,000	3,700–4,000	65–70	27.00
Mercury	75	93	16,000–24,000	2,800–3,150	5,700	22–50	23.00
Mercury	100	125	24,000	3,850–4,300	5,700	22–50	17.00
Mercury	175	200	24,000	7,850–7,950	5,700	22–50	17.00

CCT = Correlated Color Temperature   CRI = Color Rendering Index

Energy and Cost

Wattage: HID lamps require a compatible ballast, which consumes some power during lamp operation.

Efficacy: High.

Life: Very long (up to 24,000 hours).

Cost: Higher than incandescent and fluorescent lamps. Mercury vapor lamps are less expensive than high-pressure sodium or metal halide lamps, but are less efficacious. Electric utility company incentives may offer substantial savings.

Where to Buy: Builders and electrical supply stores, lighting stores, and manufacturer and mail-order catalogs offer HID lamps and luminaires.

Use

Installation: Interior applications include situations where lamps are used for extended periods of time. Compact HID lamps are sometimes used as an alternative to incandescent downlights, uplights, and accent luminaires. Potential users should note that the efficacies of low-wattage HID lamps, including compact types, are much lower than the higher-wattage HID lamps of the same type. HID applications for homes include lights that are left on for long periods of time for security or fire stairs in multi-family housing.

Luminaires: Metal halide lamps often require an enclosed luminaire or other protection. HID lamps are most frequently used in exterior lighting applications.

Controls: Not easily dimmed. Do not use motion detectors to operate high-intensity discharge lamps because of their warm-up and restart characteristics.

Cautions: Magnetic ballasts can have an audible hum. HID lamps require several minutes to reach full light output (warm-up time) and, once extinguished, may not be able to relight for several minutes; this period is called the restrike time. Manufacturers have developed several strategies to improve the lamps' warm-up and restrike times, but these strategies lower the efficacy of the lamps.

For more information refer to

Designs: Multi-Family Fire Stairs

Other Lamps: Incandescent, Fluorescent

Lamps

Luminaires

Luminaires, commonly called "lighting fixtures" or "fittings," hold one or more lamps and usually house the ballasts that operate fluorescent or high-intensity discharge lamps. When choosing luminaires for a lighting design, the most important feature is the luminaire's capacity to direct and distribute light to particular areas or objects. The style of the luminaire is an aesthetic consideration that of course is critical to the overall interior design of the home. The types of luminaires described in this chapter are available in many styles. Popular styles change with time, context, and the resident's taste; style is not discussed because this book focuses on generic and functional aspects of lighting. Luminaires are grouped by mounting type and location: Ceiling-Mounted, Suspended, Recessed, Architectural, Wall-Mounted, Furniture- or Cabinet-Integrated, Plug-In, and Exterior. Each mounting type is further grouped into two or more generic types of luminaires utilizing that mounting type. For any type of luminaire, read the introduction to the mounting type as well as the description of the luminaire. Luminaire descriptions include:

Techniques: Certain types of luminaires are best suited for each lighting technique. Consult the Techniques chapter for more details.

Price: Some typical price ranges for luminaires are listed in Table 6 of the Economics chapter; however, the price of luminaires varies widely, and depends on the cost of the materials used to construct the luminaire, the quality of construction, and the style. Both residential- and commercial-grade products are available; commercial-grade products will cost more, but will be made of higher-quality materials. Also, price varies greatly with both the number of luminaires purchased in one order and the source from which they are purchased. Durability of materials and quality of construction are important to consider for luminaires that receive frequent use in the home. Check the quality of any moving parts, such as switches, hinges, and springs. Make sure that any finishes, such as paint, reflective surfaces, and fabrics, will withstand wear and cleaning. For long-term use and for energy savings, consider the purchase of a luminaire as an investment in an appliance, rather than the purchase of a decorative item. Remember that most decorative items do not consume energy, but luminaires and the lamps within them do!

Where to buy: Luminaires can be purchased through retail or wholesale businesses. Purchase common luminaires at hardware, building supply, and discount department stores. For a larger variety, look in lighting stores or mail-order catalogs. For more-specialized luminaires, or luminaires most commonly found in commercial applications, contact electrical suppliers. Due to local variations in price, consumers and contractors should check several sources before buying a luminaire.

Luminaire characteristics are listed as follows:

Energy and Lamps

Lamps consume most of the energy that is used by luminaires; some energy is consumed by ballasts and transformers. Select the most efficacious lamp for the particular lighting need. Select fluorescent lamps with 2700 to 3000 K color temperature for best compatibility with incandescent lamps. Use rare-earth phosphor fluorescent lamps where good color is important. Consult the Lamps chapter for more details.

The efficiency of a luminaire indicates what percentage of the light that is emitted from the lamps actually leaves the luminaire. In an inefficient luminaire, lighting energy is wasted because the light is absorbed by the luminaire or is emitted into the ceiling cavity, or plenum. An efficient luminaire directs most of the light emitted by the lamp out of the luminaire, so it is very important to choose a lamp that is compatible with the luminaire. For example, the efficiency of a downlight luminaire designed for the optics of an incandescent lamp may be significantly decreased if a compact fluorescent lamp is used in place of the incandescent lamp. To maintain luminaire efficiency, globes, diffusers, reflectors, or shades require periodic cleaning because dust and insects can accumulate in or on them.

Installation

Locating a luminaire appropriately saves energy because light is directed only where it is needed. Also, proper location helps to achieve the technique(s) intended in the lighting design. See the Designs and Techniques chapters for examples of proper location of luminaires. Except for plug-in luminaires, installation usually involves wiring a luminaire to one or more controls and mounting the luminaire in or on a wall or ceiling. The room's structure and function must be considered before laying out the location of the luminaires.

Controls

The electricity that is supplied to the lamps and ballast in a luminaire must be controlled to permit switching on and off, and in some cases, dimming. Use dimming controls, especially for luminaires that contain incandescent lamps. Controls options include switches, dimmers, and automatic controls; consult the Controls chapter for more details.

The location of a control relative to the luminaire should be part of the lighting design. They should be logically related for the resident, so that the resident has easy access to the control, and can switch on the luminaires that are needed for particular activities. Easy access to controls also facilitates the energy-efficient behavior of switching lamps off when they are not needed. Locate switches near doorways, and consider three-way switches for rooms with more than one entrance.

Cautions

Some cautions must be noted for luminaires, particularly for safety and for compatibility with lamps and controls. Always read the manufacturer's instructions concerning installation and maximum lamp wattage.

For more information refer to

Techniques: Many luminaires can be used to achieve several of the techniques described in the Techniques chapter. Refer to the listed techniques for more information.

Lamps: Many luminaires can accommodate different types of lamps. Use the list of lamps as a general guide, and consult the manufacturer's information for the specific lamp types that a particular luminaire can accommodate. Refer to the Lamps chapter for more information about specific lamp types.

Designs: Most luminaire types are used in several of the designs in this book. Refer to the listed designs in the Designs chapter to see applications of the particular luminaire type.

Other Luminaires: If the luminaire described does not seem to be appropriate for a particular need or design, consider one of the other types in this chapter.

Ceiling-Mounted

10T-10T

Ceiling-mounted luminaires include diffusers and track and adjustable heads that attach directly to the ceiling. They are easy to install compared to recessed luminaires because they cover an outlet box in the ceiling, and do not require any cutting into the ceiling surface. Manufacturers offer many styles of ceiling-mounted luminaires that are available with many lamp types, including incandescent, halogen incandescent, compact fluorescent, and linear fluorescent. Nearly all lighting techniques except indirect lighting are possible with ceiling-mounted luminaires. Purchase ceiling mounted luminaires at lighting stores, electrical suppliers, and building supply stores.

Energy and Lamps

For energy savings select ceiling-mounted luminaires that use fluorescent lamps.

Installation

The ceiling may appear cluttered if different types of ceiling-mounted luminaires are used, or if they are not arranged attractively. Use ceiling-mounted luminaires when plenum space above the ceiling is limited or structural elements, pipes, or ducts prohibit the installation of recessed luminaires.

Controls

To achieve energy savings, increase lamp life, and reduce direct glare, use dimmers for luminaires that contain incandescent lamps and for fluorescent lighting systems with dimming ballasts.

Cautions

The potential for direct and reflected glare is high with many ceiling-mounted luminaires, so place luminaires carefully with regard to the occupants. For instance, one luminaire mounted in the center of a small or medium size living room would become a source of glare with typical arrangements of furniture. Large ceiling-mounted luminaires may extend too far below the ceiling in rooms with low ceiling heights. Ensure that the bottom of the luminaire will be at least 6 feet, 8 inches above the floor.

Luminaires

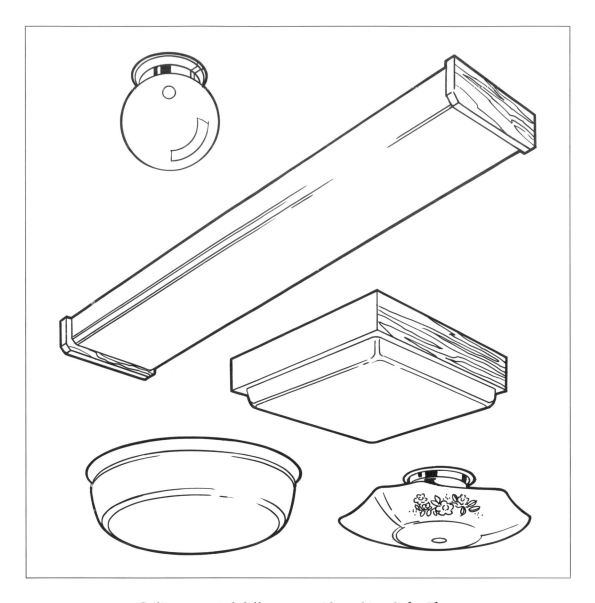

Ceiling-mounted diffusers provide ambient light. They are meant to distribute light uniformly throughout the room. Diffusers are made of clear or translucent glass or plastics, and are available in many sizes and shapes.

Energy and Lamps

For high luminaire efficiency, long lamp life, and low lamp replacement costs, consider diffuser luminaires containing linear or circline fluorescent lamps for kitchens, playrooms, home offices, and utility rooms.

Globe-shaped diffusers typically contain incandescent lamps, although some may accommodate compact fluorescent lamps. For "sparkle" use clear glass incandescent lamps in clear glass and crystalline luminaires. If replacing incandescent lamps in a globe diffuser, consider using screwbase globe compact fluorescent lamps: remove the original globe diffuser from the luminaire, and make sure that the replacement lamp is large enough in diameter to conceal any remaining mounting rings, clips, or screws.

Diffusers come in many other shapes and are designed for use with incandescent and compact, U-shaped, circline, and linear fluorescent lamps. Compact fluorescent lamps can be used in luminaires that have translucent or prismatic diffusers, but check to make sure that the light is evenly distributed and does not create "hot spots" on the diffuser.

Installation

Direct glare can be a problem, especially if a luminaire with a high light output is located in the center of the room. Use other luminaires in the room to provide task lighting to supplement low-level ambient lighting from the ceiling-mounted luminaire.

Cautions

Check the luminaire manufacturer's instructions for maximum lamp wattage, particularly for enclosed globes or diffusers. If you are considering using screwbase compact fluorescent lamps for use in an enclosed luminaire that was designed for incandescent lamps, check the lamp manufacturer's instructions.

For more information refer to

Techniques: Ambient

Lamps: Incandescent, Halogen A, Reflector, Fluorescent

Designs: Small Kitchen, Medium Kitchen 2, Large Kitchen, Small Dinette, Medium Dinette, Small Living Room 2, Medium Living Room 1, Half Bath, Medium Baths, Children's Bedroom, Large Bedroom, Home Office, Closed Stair, Multi-Family Lobby, Multi-Family Corridor, Multi-Family Fire Stair 1

Other luminaires: Ceiling-Mounted Track or Adjustable Heads, Suspended, Recessed, Architectural, Wall-Mounted

Ceiling-Mounted: Track or Adjustable Heads

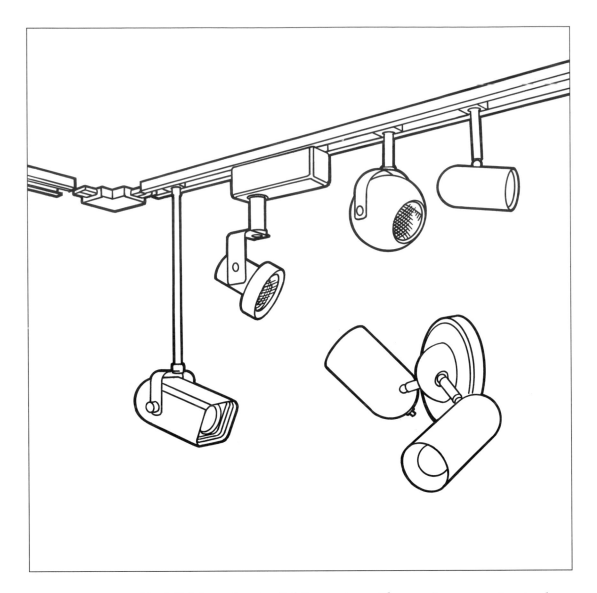

Track lighting refers to a lighting system with several components: a track, an electrical feed box, and one or more heads, each of which contains a lamp. The electrically fed linear track, strip, or rail of aluminum is usually mounted directly to the ceiling. It may also be recessed into the ceiling if it is specially designed for that purpose. Track heads can direct light in precise, controlled patterns. Some systems can be suspended from the ceiling or mounted on a wall for indirect lighting. Monopoint mounts allow a single track head to be mounted on an outlet box instead of a track. Track is available in lengths of 2, 4, or 8 feet, and with connectors that allow for a variety of configurations. Track heads are available in many shapes, styles, colors, and finishes; they house an array of lamp types from common and low-voltage incandescent to compact fluorescent.

Track lighting is most useful when flexibility is important because the heads can be repositioned on the track and aimed easily. Various types of heads can be installed to create different lighting designs. Purchase track lighting at lighting stores, electrical suppliers, and building supply stores.

Energy and Lamps

Track heads and lamps vary greatly, so use the minimum size and lamp wattage appropriate for lighting a surface or object. For higher luminaire efficiency, replace A-lamps with reflector lamps unless the track head

Luminaires

includes a reflector. For wall washing, several manufacturers make track heads that use energy-efficient long twin-tube fluorescent lamps. Other track heads use compact fluorescent lamps, but these are most effective when used for wall washing because most cannot achieve a tightly focused beam.

Installation

To achieve the desired light distribution pattern, follow the manufacturer's directions carefully to choose the appropriate number and type of track heads, to locate tracks and track heads, and to avoid direct and reflected glare. Low-voltage halogen lamps that are used in tracks require a transformer. The transformer can be used for individual heads and be located on the track or on the head itself. Alternatively, the transformer can be used for the entire length of track and located in the ceiling or wall cavity.

Controls

For energy savings, install dimming controls if incandescent lamps are used. Low-voltage halogen lamps require a special dimmer.

Cautions

Track heads from different manufacturers may not be compatible with all tracks, and combining different product lines may violate Underwriters Laboratories listings.

For more information refer to

Techniques: Indirect, Wall Washing, Accent, Task, Special Purposes

Lamps: Halogen A, Reflector, Low-Voltage Halogen, Long Twin-Tube Fluorescent, Compact Fluorescent

Designs: Large Kitchen, Large Living Room 3

Other luminaires: Wall Wash, Accent, Architectural

Suspended

A suspended luminaire hangs from the ceiling by a rod, cord, or chain. Suspended luminaires, also called pendants, include suspended downlights, uplights, diffusers or uplights/downlights, ceiling fans, and the most decorative suspended luminaires, chandeliers. Suspended luminaires provide ambient lighting, indirect lighting, and lighting for tasks and special purposes. Style is an important consideration because these luminaires are more visible than recessed or ceiling-mounted luminaires. Suspended luminaires contain incandescent, compact fluorescent, or fluorescent lamps. Purchase these luminaires from lighting stores, electrical suppliers, and some building supply stores.

Installation

Suspended luminaires are a good choice for rooms with high ceilings. Lamps in suspended luminaires should be shielded to reduce glare, so carefully adjust the height of the luminaire. To give the residents some flexibility in locating the luminaires, choose ones that have retractable cords or chains that allow the luminaires to be repositioned.

Suspended: Downlights

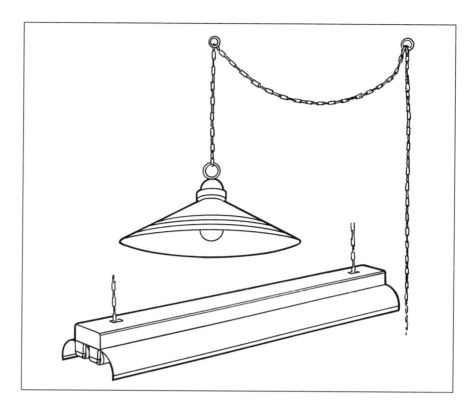

Suspended downlights direct most of the light downward. The lighting distribution patterns vary with the size and shape of the luminaire. To shield the lamps from view, luminaires that are used for ambient lighting typically have a translucent shade and those used for table lighting have an opaque metal or fabric shade. In most cases, suspended downlights used for task lighting should be supplemented with other luminaires that provide ambient lighting.

Energy and Lamps

Use halogen or compact fluorescent lamps to replace incandescent A-lamps. Use globe compact fluorescent lamps to replace globe incandescent lamps.

Installation

For lighting a dining table, place luminaires above the eye level of a seated person, approximately 24 inches above the horizontal surface. The luminaire should be properly shielded to avoid direct glare. Luminaires with a retractable cord are good for lighting a table or desk, because they allow the resident to adjust the height for comfort and to vary the amount of light on the table surface. For visually demanding tasks, place the downlight luminaire below eye level, approximately 15 inches above the horizontal surface. Chain-mounted luminaires can be relocated over important tasks if a long chain is used and the ceiling hook can be repositioned.

Controls

Use dimmers to control luminaires that contain incandescent lamps. Separately switch luminaires used for lighting for tasks or special purposes.

For more information refer to

Techniques: Ambient, Accent, Task, Special Purposes

Lamps: Incandescent, Compact Fluorescent

Designs: Large Kitchen, Medium Dinette, Dining Room, Large Living Room 3

Other luminaires: Ceiling-Mounted Diffusers, Suspended Uplight/Downlights, Recessed, Soffits

Suspended: Uplights

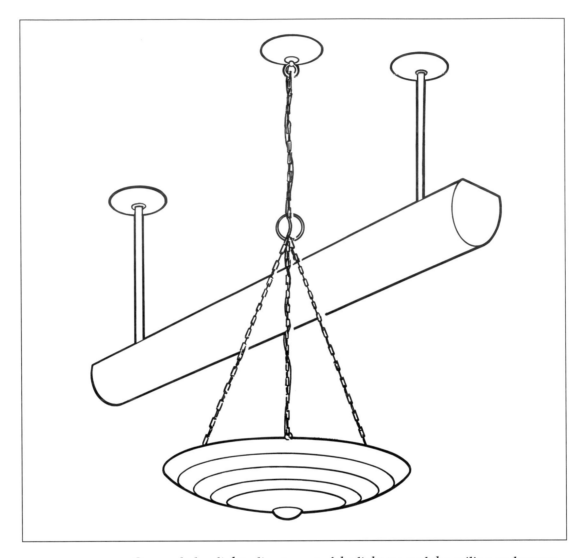

Suspended uplights direct most of the light toward the ceiling and upper portion of the walls so that these surfaces serve as reflectors. Uplights can create a soft, shadowless light in a room. Consider introducing a downlighting element to the design by using suspended uplights made of translucent materials.

Energy and Lamps

Use fluorescent lamps wherever possible. Paint the ceiling white for best reflectance and efficiency.

Installation

These luminaires are best used in rooms with high ceilings. For balconies or stair landings, locate luminaires so that the lamp will not be visible when the luminaire is viewed from above. Suspend the luminaire at least 18 inches below the ceiling because a luminaire mounted closer to the ceiling could create a "hot spot," an area of extreme brightness.

Cautions

Uplights emphasize any imperfections on poorly finished walls and ceilings.

For more information refer to

Techniques: Ambient, Indirect

Lamps: Reflector, Tubular-Shaped Halogen, Linear Fluorescent, Long Twin-Tube Fluorescent, Compact and Circline Fluorescent

Other luminaires: Coves, Valances, Wall-Mounted Track or Adjustable Heads (see Ceiling-Mounted Track or Adjustable Heads)

Luminaires

Suspended: Uplight/Downlights

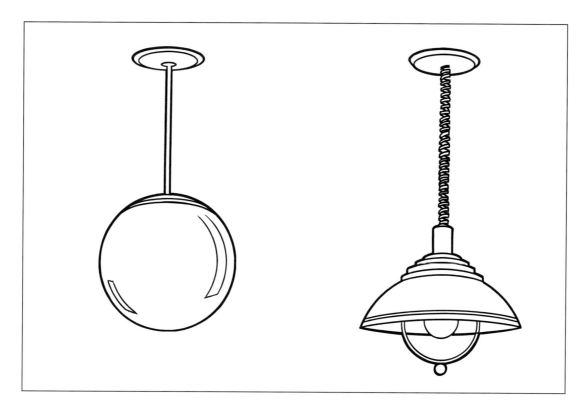

Suspended uplight/downlight luminaires provide ambient lighting. Some are made from clear or frosted glass or plastics. They are available in various sizes and shapes. They typically house incandescent lamps, although some may accommodate compact fluorescent lamps. Suspended uplight/downlight luminaires that house linear fluorescent lamps are common in commercial applications but also can be used attractively in homes.

Energy and Lamps

Consider using suspended luminaires that contain linear fluorescent lamps for best energy efficiency in rooms with high ceilings.

For ease in replacing lamps, choose luminaires with an opening in the bottom. Incandescent lamps can be replaced with compact fluorescent lamps in many luminaires, but check the lamp manufacturer's recommendations if you are installing a compact fluorescent lamp in an enclosed luminaire.

Installation

Suspended uplight/downlights are best used in rooms with high ceilings. Place them in the corner of a room, over a table or plant, to add interest and bring soft diffuse light into the room from the side. To reduce uneven "hot spots" on the ceiling, avoid mounting close to the ceiling.

Cautions

Diffusers, especially those with high-wattage lamps, can be a source of glare. Balance background brightness by using light colors with high reflectance values because diffusers may cause more discomfort when viewed against dark backgrounds.

For more information refer to

Techniques: Ambient, Task

Lamps: Incandescent, Linear Fluorescent, Compact Fluorescent

Other luminaires: Ceiling-Mounted Diffusers, Suspended Downlights, Chandeliers, Valances, Wall-Mounted Sconces or Diffusers

Suspended: Chandeliers

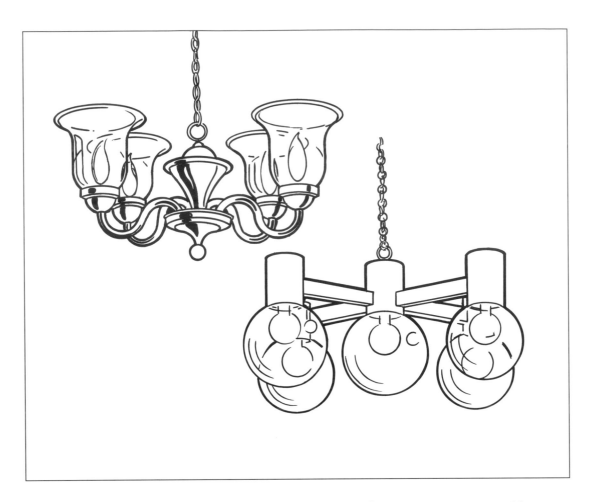

A chandelier is a suspended luminaire that incorporates exposed lamps as a decorative element. Chandeliers usually contain many low-wattage incandescent lamps, including decorative bent-tip, candle, or small globe types. A chandelier adds sparkle and visual interest to a room.

Energy and Lamps

Chandeliers that have diffusers or that use globe lamps may accommodate compact fluorescent lamps. Use halogen lamps to replace common A-lamps. Decorative candle lamps cannot be replaced with energy-efficient alternatives, so use a dimmer to control the chandelier and save energy.

Installation

Select a chandelier that is in scale with the room. For use over tables, a chandelier should be 12 inches smaller in diameter than the smallest table dimension and mounted 2.5 feet above the table. For lighting a table surface, choose a chandelier that has a downlighting component and consider coordinating sconces or accent luminaires in the same room to enhance the overall effect.

Controls

Chandeliers frequently use dimmers to create various light levels and to save energy.

For more information refer to

Techniques: Ambient, Task

Lamps: Incandescent

Designs: Dining Room, Foyer with Open Stair

Other luminaires: Ceiling-Mounted Diffusers, Other Suspended, Wall-Mounted Sconces or Diffusers

Luminaires

Suspended: Ceiling Fans

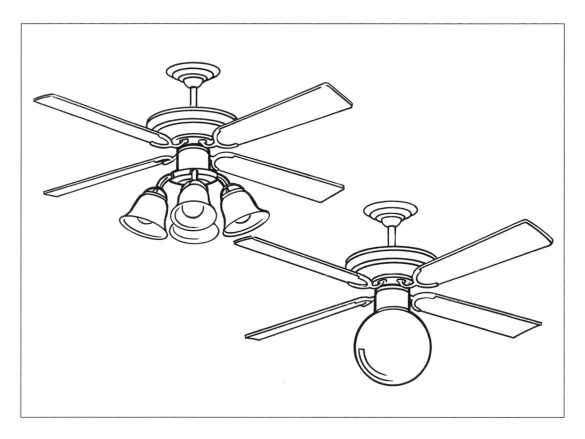

Ceiling paddle fans may include a luminaire. Many have a single globe or multiple decorative shades on arms located below the fan. Uplights are also offered with some fans. Some manufacturers offer a removable "light kit" option, which usually contains incandescent lamps.

Energy and Lamps

Replace common incandescent A-lamps with halogen A-lamps or compact fluorescent lamps if they fit in the luminaire.

Installation

Ceiling fans are best used in rooms with high ceilings.

Controls

Choose products that have the fan and luminaire switched separately, and that have a dimmer for the luminaire.

Cautions

Ceiling fan luminaires can be a source of glare. When using ceiling fans, avoid locating other luminaires in positions that would direct light through the blades because a stroboscopic effect may occur. This is a problem if a strong uplight, such as a torchiere or wall-mounted track head, is mounted below the fan or if a ceiling-mounted downlight is mounted above the fan.

For more information refer to

Techniques: Ambient, Indirect

Lamps: Halogen A, Tubular-Shaped Halogen, Compact Fluorescent

Designs: Medium Living Room 2, Large Living Room 3

Other luminaires: Ceiling-Mounted Diffusers, Other Suspended

Recessed

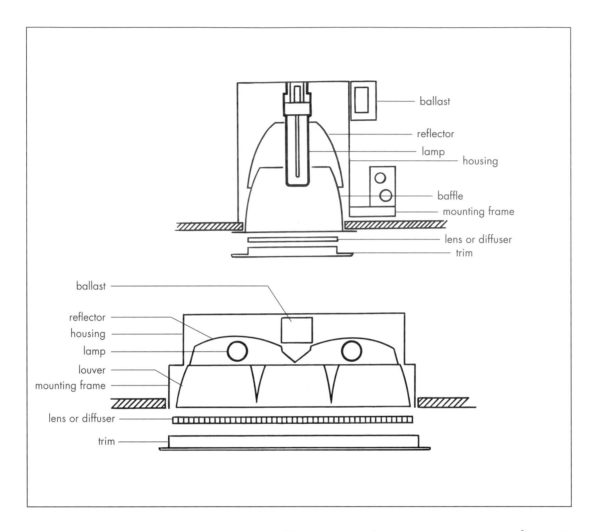

In a recessed luminaire all electrical and optical components are housed above the ceiling line. Recessed luminaires direct light downward, or downward and toward a wall. The light distribution pattern can be narrow or broad, intense or diffuse, and provide ambient light, wall washing, or accent lighting. Recessed luminaires include troffers and "luminous ceiling," downlight, wall wash, and accent types. These luminaires differ in size and shape, mounting, and trim choices. Many types of lamps, both incandescent and fluorescent, can be used in recessed luminaires. Purchase recessed luminaires from lighting stores, electrical suppliers, and building supply stores.

Both commodity and specification grades are available. While commodity-grade luminaires are generally less expensive, specification-grade luminaires are better quality and offer many reflector and trim options that fit into the same mounting frame. Recessed luminaires for homes have some or all of the following components.

Components

Housing: The housing surrounds the luminaire and usually is made of steel or aluminum. For some recessed luminaires, the reflector serves as the housing. The depth of the housing limits the ceilings into which the luminaire will fit. Many recessed luminaires need at least 8 inches of clearance in the ceiling cavity, or plenum. Some housings restrict air leakage through the luminaire to meet energy code air infiltration requirements. Luminaires that are rated "IC" (insulated ceiling) can be covered by insulating materials.

Lamp socket or lamp holder: The lamp socket is the electrical fitting into which the lamp base is inserted. Socket adapters are needed when a replacement lamp does not have the same type or size base as the original lamp.

Mounting frame: The mounting frame is a flanged, metal support that is used to attach the luminaire to the ceiling structure. Special frames can be obtained for mounting recessed luminaires in sloped ceilings. Mounting frames may also be different for plaster or T-bar dropped ceilings.

Ballast: A ballast is an electrical device that is used to start and operate fluorescent and high-intensity discharge lamps. In recessed lighting, the ballast is hidden from view and typically is attached to the housing or mounting frame. Ballasts usually last for many years of service and can be replaced when they fail. See the Appendix for more details on types of ballasts.

Aperture: The aperture is the opening at the bottom of the recessed luminaire through which light is directed into the room. Recessed luminaires are available in a variety of aperture shapes including round, square and rectangular. Aperture sizes and typical ceiling openings can be as small as 2 inches in diameter and as large as 2 feet by 4 feet.

Baffle: A baffle is a series of light-absorbing ridges that ring the lower inside portion of the luminaire's aperture. The baffle shields the luminaire's brightness from the occupant's normal field of view. Deep or dark-color baffles reduce a luminaire's efficiency.

Reflector: The reflector is a component that is optically designed and shaped to maximize the efficiency of the luminaire for a particular type of lamp by directing light out of the luminaire. The reflector typically is made of specular aluminum or white-painted steel. Reflectors are available in several colors, including silver, gold, bronze, and white. Light color reflectors make a luminaire more efficient than dark-color reflectors do. Some recessed luminaires that do not have separate reflector components have reflective surfaces on the interior of the housing. Recessed luminaires that have no reflector at all should incorporate a reflector lamp.

Lens or diffuser: Lenses and diffusers are optically designed to create specific light distribution patterns. They are formed from glass or plastics and are positioned in the aperture, or opening, of the luminaire. Several choices may be offered by the manufacturer for each luminaire. The use of a lens reduces a luminaire's efficiency.

Louver: A louver is a device that is inserted into a recessed luminaire that does not have a lens or diffuser. The louver shields the lamps in the luminaire from the direct view of the resident. Louvers are made of thin metal or plastic, and consist of vertically oriented parallel strips, hollow cubes, honeycomb, or parabolic shapes.

Trim: Trim commonly refers to a reflector and shielding package that fits into the housing and mounting frame of a recessed luminaire. For example, trims could include lenses, open reflectors, or black, grooved baffles, each offering a different appearance, efficiency, and level of comfort. A plastic or metal trim ring is often used to cover and seal the edges of holes cut in the ceiling for round recessed luminaires.

CONTINUED

Energy and Lamps

Often one type of luminaire is offered with the option of several types of lamps. For energy efficiency, choose the most efficacious lamp available for each luminaire.

Installation

Recessed lighting is a good design choice for low ceilings and situations where a clean ceiling line is desired. Too many recessed luminaires in the same ceiling give a cluttered appearance, especially if they have different trims; coordinate trim selection and install the minimum number of luminaires required for the design. Locate luminaires near important visual tasks because the closer the luminaire is to the area that needs to be illuminated, the lower the required wattage of the lamp will be. Generally, luminaires mounted to the side and slightly in front of or slightly behind the task minimize glare and shadows.

It is easiest to install recessed luminaires in new construction or during major remodeling. Unlike many surface-mounted or suspended luminaires, which can be purchased late in the construction process, the mounting frame and housing of the recessed luminaire must be on the job site prior to the enclosure of the ceiling. Joists of nominal 8-inch depth accommodate many recessed luminaires. Coordinate the location of recessed luminaires with joists, ducts, or plumbing that may also be located in the ceiling. Recessed luminaires that install from below, sometimes called "remodel housings," are available for retrofit jobs where there is no above-the-ceiling access. Low-profile downlights and troffers are available for use in plenums of minimal depth. Check the manufacturer's data carefully for recessed depth dimensions and for required clearances around the housing.

Cautions

If the lamp in an existing luminaire is replaced with a different type of lamp, the reflector may also need to be replaced to maintain luminaire efficiency. Some ceiling types, such as concrete or stress-skin panels, leave no room for recessed luminaires. Always check the manufacturer's directions concerning installation in insulated spaces, because the heat from an improperly selected or installed recessed luminaire can be a fire hazard. The directions for installing recessed luminaires in insulated ceilings usually specify a minimum size air space to be left around the housing, unless the luminaire is specially designed for contact with insulation; if so, it will be labeled "IC" for insulated ceilings.

Recessed: Troffers and "Luminous Ceilings"

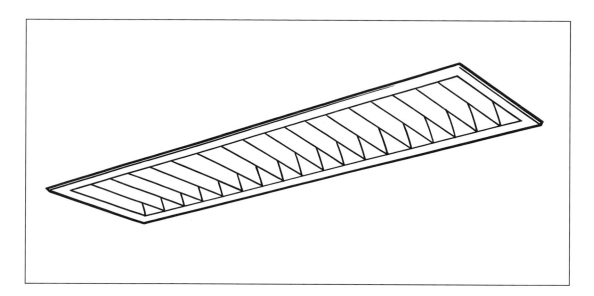

A recessed troffer is usually 2 feet by 2 feet, 1 foot by 4 feet, or 2 feet by 4 feet, and houses fluorescent lamps. A "luminous ceiling" may be recessed or attached to the ceiling and is constructed of multiple fluorescent lamp strip luminaires behind diffusing lenses. Recessed troffers distribute light downward, but vary greatly in the spread of the light distribution pattern. Troffers with diffusers have the widest spread; troffers with deeply recessed parabolic louvers have a very narrow spread. Luminous ceilings have a uniformly broad and diffuse light distribution pattern.

Energy and Lamps

Reflectors or highly reflective housings that are properly designed for the type of lamp that is used in the luminaire ensure efficiency.

Installation

Use where high light levels are needed throughout the room. Recessed troffers fit easily in suspended ceilings. One-foot by 4-foot troffers fit between ceiling joists if run parallel to the joists.

For more information refer to

Techniques: Ambient, Task

Lamps: Linear Fluorescent, U-Shaped and Long Twin-Tube Fluorescent

Designs: Medium Kitchen 3

Other luminaires: Ceiling-Mounted Diffusers, Suspended, Recessed Downlights, Architectural

Luminaires

Recessed: Downlights

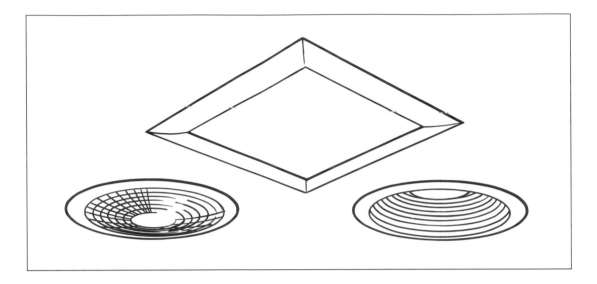

Recessed downlights direct light down, usually in a symmetrical distribution. Common names for recessed downlights include "cans" and "high-hats." They are used for many lighting techniques, including ambient and accent.

Energy and Lamps

Incandescent, halogen, and compact fluorescent lamps can all be appropriate for use in recessed downlights. If an existing room has recessed downlights that contain incandescent A-lamps, consider several more-efficient alternatives: replacing them with halogen lamps; replacing them with R-, ER-, or PAR-lamps if the luminaire does not have a reflector; replacing them with compact fluorescent reflector lamps if they will fit into the housing; or, using compact fluorescent lamp conversion kits as shown below. Select downlights with high efficiencies for new construction or remodeling.

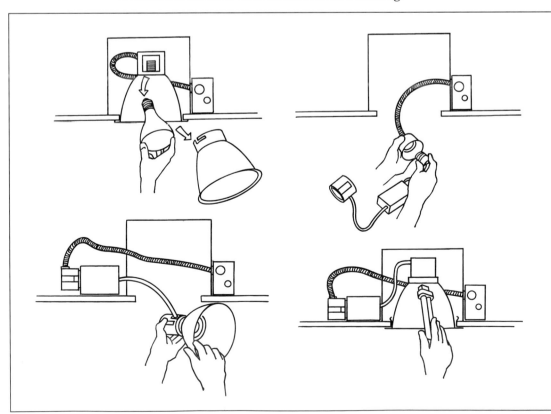

Installation

Downlights mounted to the side and slightly forward of or behind the task minimize glare and shadows. Locate downlights near important visual tasks to allow lower-wattage lamps to be used. Downlights placed near a wall produce vertical scallops. If they are placed very close to the wall, the intense downlight will accentuate any texture on the wall surface. When this effect is planned, it adds visual interest to a room; when unplanned, it can be distracting. For instance, downlights placed near a brick or stone wall create dramatic shadows but downlights near a gypsum board surface will reveal any taping or sanding irregularities.

Controls

In a room with many recessed luminaires, wire the luminaires in several groups so that residents can choose to use only the luminaires that they need.

Cautions

Where recessed downlights are the only source of light in a room, the ceiling may appear dark.

For more information refer to

Techniques: Ambient, Task, Special Purpose

Lamps: Halogen A, Reflector, Compact Fluorescent

Designs: Medium Kitchen 1, Dining Room, Large Living Rooms 1 and 2, Medium Bath 1, Large Bath, Large Bedroom, Home Office, Closed Stair, Hallway

Other luminaires: Ceiling-Mounted, Suspended, Recessed Wall Wash, Recessed Accent

Recessed: Wall Wash

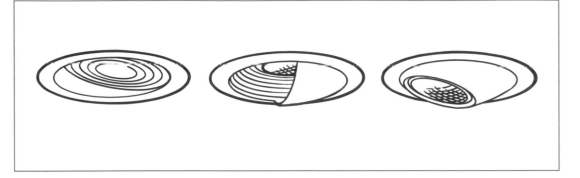

Wall wash luminaires direct light asymmetrically downward to create an area of light on a wall. How evenly the wall is "washed" depends upon three factors: the quality of the luminaire design, how far the luminaire is located from the wall, and the spacing between luminaires. The intensity of light from a wall wash luminaire decreases as it nears the bottom of the wall. One type of wall wash luminaire has a lens in the aperture that provides a diffuse light distribution pattern. Others are designed without lenses, and may have a plate partially covering the aperture to conceal the internal reflector from the occupant's view

Energy and Lamps

Select new wall wash luminaires with high efficiencies. For existing luminaires, replace the lamp with lower-wattage lamps when light output is excessive. For example, where R-lamps are used, replace the lamps with halogen PAR-lamps. Some wall wash luminaires are designed optically for A-lamps. Replace the A-lamps with halogen A-lamps for energy savings and longer life.

Installation

Most wall wash luminaires should be spaced the same distance from each other as they are from the wall; this is known as a one-to-one spacing ratio. It usually is not necessary to place a downlight near a wall wash luminaire, since the wall wash luminaire also has a downlighting component.

Controls

Switch wall wash luminaires separately if they are used only for dramatic or architectural effect and are not needed for everyday use.

Cautions

Most wall wash luminaires should not be placed closer than 2.5 feet from the wall, or "hot spots" will result. Glossy surfaces, such as oiled wood or polished marble, will produce a mirror image of the luminaire, and should not be illuminated by wall wash luminaires. Wall wash luminaires should not be directed toward doors, because someone entering the room could be bothered by the direct glare of the lamp. Wall wash luminaires should not be directed toward windows, because lamp images can be reflected in the window glass, and those outside can be offended by direct glare.

For more information refer to

Techniques: Wall Washing, Special Purpose

Lamps: Halogen A, Reflector, Compact Fluorescent

Designs: Home Office

Other luminaires: Ceiling-Mounted Track and Adjustable Heads, Recessed Troffers, Recessed Accent, Soffits, Valances, Wall-Mounted

Luminaires

Recessed: Accent

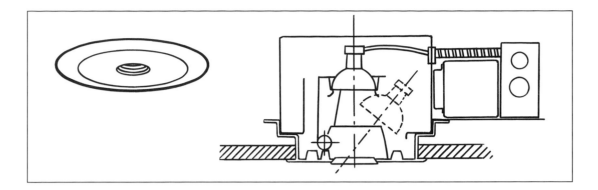

Recessed accent luminaires are used to accentuate works of art, architectural features, plantings, and other items of interest. "Eyeballs" are recessed accent luminaires with a partially recessed sphere that can be rotated to provide directional lighting. Most recessed accent luminaires can be positioned to aim light where it is needed for emphasis and have an adjustable range of 35° from the vertical, and rotation of approximately 350°. An accent luminaire should be able to use a variety of lamp types so that changes in placement of artwork and furniture can be accommodated.

Recessed accent luminaires typically use incandescent or halogen reflector lamps. Accent luminaires that accommodate color filters, spread lenses, and framing shutters offer unique design choices. Direct glare can be a problem with accent luminaires; however, louvers or baffles fitted into the luminaire can reduce direct glare. An alternative to recessed accent luminaires is a specially designed track lighting system recessed into narrow openings between ceiling joists.

Energy and Lamps

If existing luminaires use R-lamps, replace the lamps with halogen PAR-lamps. When using reflector lamps of any kind, choose a beam spread to match the size of the object being illuminated.

Installation

Accent luminaires should be used sparingly, with only the most important features of a room being highlighted. Unless low-voltage lamps are used, the apertures of recessed accent luminaires can be quite large. To avoid reflected glare from glossy artwork, position the lamp inside the luminaire so that it is tilted up 30° from the vertical position. Recessed accent luminaires can be used effectively as downlights in sloped ceilings, provided the slope does not exceed 35°.

For more information refer to

Techniques: Accent, Special Purpose

Lamps: Reflector, Low-Voltage Halogen

Designs: Dining Room, Large Living Room 1

Other luminaires: Ceiling-Mounted Track or Adjustable Heads, Recessed Wall Wash, Artwork

Luminaires

163

Architectural

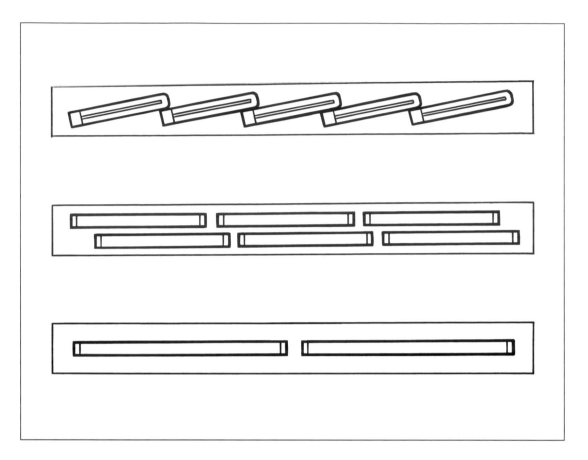

Architectural luminaires are mounted horizontally on the wall, ceiling, or on top of cabinets. They include coves, soffits, and valances. Coves distribute light upwards; soffits distribute light downwards; valances distribute light up and down. These luminaires usually contain linear fluorescent lamps, lamp sockets or holders, and ballasts. Architectural luminaires can also contain incandescent and compact fluorescent lamps. Some architectural luminaires contain reflectors to increase the efficiency of the luminaire. A shield positioned vertically or at a slight angle hides the lamps from view. Shields can be constructed of metal, wood, plywood, or gypsum board. Optional baffles, louvers, or diffusers can be incorporated to direct light and to reduce glare.

Architectural luminaires provide soft, diffuse ambient light that may need to be supplemented by luminaires in other parts of the room. They can unobtrusively emphasize the architectural design of the space, and can be attractively incorporated into the interior design of a room if they are painted or decorated with moldings, trims, or fabrics.

Purchase architectural luminaires from lighting stores or electrical distributors or build them on-site using materials that are available at building supply and hardware stores.

Energy and Lamps

Manufacturers offer cove, valance, and soffit lights that produce higher luminaire efficiencies and better light distribution patterns than do most site-built luminaires; nevertheless, a well-designed room with site-built luminaires can be far more efficient than many typical designs that use incandescent lamps.

Installation

For greatest efficiency, lowest cost, and an even distribution of light on walls, use linear fluorescent lamps. Use T8 fluorescent lamps with electronic ballasts to achieve lowest operating costs. In rooms where color appearance of the furnishings is important, such as living rooms and bedrooms, choose lamps that have good color qualities. See Fluorescent Lamps in the Lamps chapter and see the People, Energy, and Light chapter for more information on color rendering and correlated color temperature.

Use architectural luminaires in rooms with white or light-colored walls and ceilings. Use coves and valances in rooms with ceiling heights of at least 8 feet. Shield lamps that can be seen from normal viewing positions with baffles, louvers, or diffusers to limit discomfort glare. Paint the inside surface of the shielding boards of site-built luminaires white for highest reflectance. Arrange the lamps inside site-built architectural luminaires so that the light is distributed evenly. If using linear or compact fluorescent lamps, consider mounting them so that their ends overlap slightly, thus avoiding gaps in the light distribution, or "socket-shadows." If two rows of linear fluorescent lamps are used, stagger the ends of the lamps.

Simple architectural luminaires can be economical, especially in remodeling or new construction, and particularly for multi-family housing, if many luminaires are purchased or built at once. For lowest cost when building architectural luminaires, use inexpensive strip luminaires that contain linear fluorescent lamps. Note that 4-foot T12 linear fluorescent lamps are readily available, relatively inexpensive, last a long time, and are not difficult to replace; these are factors that benefit residents, especially those with low and fixed incomes.

Controls

Switch the luminaires on each wall separately for the resident's convenience and for energy savings. If each luminaire contains two rows of lamps, wire them for separate row switching to achieve two levels of light output. Use dimmers for luminaires containing incandescent lamps. Also consider dimmers for linear fluorescent lamps: special ballasts must be used.

Cautions

Use only where wall and ceiling surface textures are finely finished or interesting, because the grazing light from these luminaires will accentuate imperfections and any other textures.

Architectural: Coves

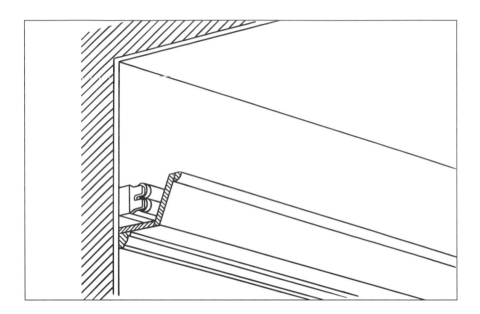

Coves are architectural luminaires that direct light upward to the ceiling and use the ceiling as a reflector to distribute light indirectly throughout the room.

Energy and Lamps

Consider using T5 linear fluorescent lamps rather than larger diameter lamps for above-cabinet cove lighting because lower light output may be sufficient for this area of the room. Alternatively, use T8 or T12 lamps operating on reduced-light-output (50 percent) ballasts.

Installation

Consider coves for rooms with high ceilings, including vaulted or cathedral ceilings, and rooms where the ceiling height abruptly changes. Use coves to emphasize decorative ceilings. To prevent hot spots or excessive brightness on the ceiling, place the top of the cove at least 18 inches from the ceiling; position the base of the cove at least 6 feet, 8 inches above the floor. For kitchens without soffit enclosures above the upper wall cabinets, simple fluorescent lamp holders can be mounted on top of the cabinets and concealed from direct view with a trim board. This provides ambient lighting for the kitchen and it can be supplemented with under-cabinet luminaires or other task lighting. To reduce glare, the cove shielding board should hide the lamp from the eye of the resident while allowing the lamps to light the ceiling directly.

Controls

If a cove has two rows of lamps, switch them individually to achieve two light levels. Use dimming controls and dimming ballasts for further variations in light output.

Cautions

If a landing or balcony overlooks a room with coves, shield the cove lamps from view from above.

For more information refer to

Techniques: Ambient, Indirect, Special Purpose

Lamps: Fluorescent

Designs: Medium Kitchen 2

Other luminaires: Suspended Uplights, Valances, Wall-Mounted Track or Adjustable Heads (see Ceiling-Mounted Track of Adjustable Heads), Floor Lamps

Architectural: Soffits

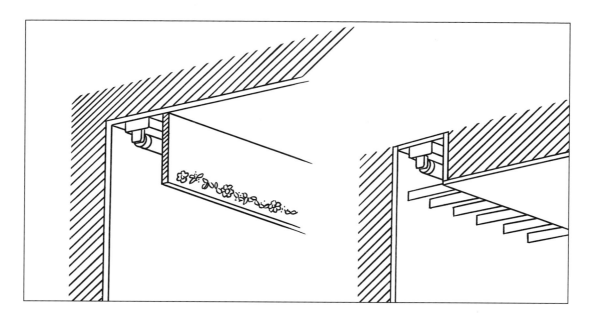

Soffits, sometimes referred to as cornices, are architectural luminaires that provide downlighting only. They can produce dramatic lighting effects on walls, draperies, and murals. Soffit lighting produces a grazing effect that enhances textured surfaces such as wood, brick, and stucco.

Energy and Lamps

Use linear fluorescent lamps in soffits.

Installation

Soffits can be used in rooms with low ceilings, and can be integrated into cabinetry, particularly in kitchens and bathrooms where light is needed on countertops. Where joists run parallel to the wall, recessed soffits can be inserted; these are also called "wall slots."

Controls

If a soffit has two rows of lamps, switch them individually to achieve two light levels. Use dimming controls and dimming ballasts for further variations in light output.

For more information refer to

Techniques: Ambient, Wall Washing, Task, Special Purpose

Lamps: Fluorescent

Designs: Small Dinette, Large Living Room 1, Small Bath, Medium Bath 1, Large Bath, Large Bedroom, Home Office

Other luminaires: Suspended Downlights, Recessed, Valances, Wall-Mounted Track or Adjustable Heads (see Ceiling-Mounted Track of Adjustable Heads), Floor Lamps

Luminaires

167

Architectural: Valances

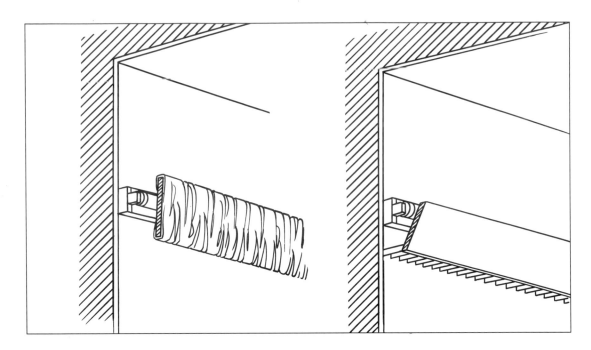

Valances are architectural luminaires that direct light both upwards and downwards. The upper portion acts as a cove and the lower portion acts as a soffit.

Energy and Lamps

Use linear fluorescent lamps in valances.

Installation

Valance lighting can be used with ceiling heights of at least 8 feet. Consider valance lighting for rooms with high ceilings, including vaulted or cathedral ceilings. Valance lighting is a good choice for living rooms, bedrooms, and kitchens, where general lighting and lighting for special purposes is required. Consider a lower valance mounting height for lighting specific tasks such as reading in bed. The downlight component of a valance light is used to wall wash and can be used effectively above draperies.

Mounting height will vary according to window and door height. Consider aligning the valance height with the top of the doors and windows, typically at 6 feet, 8 inches. Valances can run continuously along a wall. A combination of 4-foot and 3-foot fluorescent lamps may be used to span the full length of the valance. Try to use the same length lamp throughout a room. Lamps of different lengths may appear slightly different in color, even though they have the same correlated color temperature.

Cautions

If a valance has two rows of lamps, switch them individually to achieve two light levels. Use dimming controls and dimming ballasts for further variations in light output.

For more information refer to

Techniques: Ambient, Indirect, Wall Washing, Task, Special Purpose

Lamps: Fluorescent

Designs: Medium Kitchen 2, Medium Dinette, Medium Living Rooms, Large Living Rooms 1 and 3, Small Bedroom, Home Office, Foyer with Open Stair, Multi-Family Fire Stair 1

Other luminaires: Suspended Uplight/Downlights, Coves, Soffits, Wall-Mounted Track or Adjustable Heads (see Ceiling-Mounted Track of Adjustable Heads), Floor Lamps

Luminaires

Wall-Mounted

Wall-mounted luminaires are mounted directly to a wall surface. This type includes sconces, diffusers, and vanity lights. Track lighting can be also be mounted to the wall. Refer to Ceiling-Mounted Track or Adjustable Heads for more information.

Wall-mounted luminaires are commonly used in homes because they are easy to install, are available in a wide variety of styles, and accommodate many lamp types. They can be used for most lighting techniques, particularly ambient, indirect, task, and special purposes. Purchase them from lighting stores, electrical suppliers, and building supply stores.

Energy and Lamps

Select wall-mounted luminaires with fluorescent lamps for energy savings.

Installation

Wall-mounted luminaires are an appropriate choice for rooms with low ceilings. Direct glare potential is increased since wall-mounted luminaires are often directly in the field of view. Consider mounting heights, aiming angles, and shielding of the luminaire. Also, wall-mounted luminaires can limit the wall space that is available for furniture and artwork, so plan accordingly.

Use wall-mounted luminaires when plenum space is limited or structural elements, pipes, or ducts prohibit installing recessed luminaires.

For high-rise multi-family housing, wall-mounted luminaires can be used where electrical distribution through the ceiling is limited or not available, such as in hallways and stairwells. Also, for public spaces such as multi-family corridors, note that the Americans with Disabilities Act limits the outward extension of wall-mounted luminaires that are mounted below 80 inches (6 feet, 8 inches) above the floor. They may not extend beyond 4 inches from the wall; make sure that the luminaire does not protrude beyond this limit. If a landing or balcony overlooks a room with wall-mounted luminaires, shield the lamps from view from above.

Cautions

Be careful with mounting heights and location to avoid physical contact. Surfaces may be hot and some luminaires can be damaged.

Wall-Mounted: Sconces or Diffusers

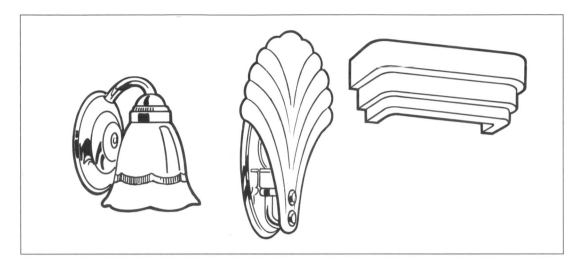

Wall-mounted sconces or diffusers typically are decorative as well as functional. Some sconces are referred to as wall brackets. They may contain exposed lamps, or the lamps may be concealed by opaque or translucent glass or plastics, or other opaque materials. Light distribution varies according to type and style. Wall sconces can provide indirect lighting and/or downlighting or general, diffuse lighting.

Energy and Lamps

Many wall sconces and diffusers contain incandescent lamps, but also may accommodate compact fluorescent lamps. For maximum efficiency, select sconces and diffusers that use fluorescent lamps. Luminaires designed solely for compact fluorescent lamps are available, too. Avoid the excessive brightness that may occur when high-wattage lamps are used. Direct glare occurs when lamps are poorly shielded.

Installation

Luminaires that provide diffuse light are appropriate for use in hallways, dining rooms, living rooms, and bedrooms, but they cannot be relied upon to light areas where people sit to read or sew. Avoid using sconces or diffusers near visual tasks such as television viewing and the use of computers because these shiny screens may reflect the image of the luminaire.

Mounting height is critical: for sconces with an indirect lighting component, mounting height should always be high enough that the lamp is concealed from view to prevent direct glare. Install the outlet box for the luminaire at least 5.5 feet above the floor.

Controls

Switch sconces or diffusers separately to provide flexibility, create visual interest, and achieve energy savings. Use dimmers for luminaires that contain incandescent lamps.

Cautions

Heat from incandescent lamps may damage or ignite sensitive wall coverings.

For more information refer to

Techniques: Ambient, Indirect, Special Purpose

Lamps: Incandescent, Compact Fluorescent

Designs: Dining Room, Medium Bath 2, Large Bedroom, Foyer with Open Stair, Hallway, Multi-Family Lobby, Multi-Family Corridor, Multi-Family Fire Stair 2

Other luminaires: Ceiling-Mounted Diffusers, Architectural, Vanity Lights, Night Lights

Luminaires

Wall-Mounted: Vanity Lights

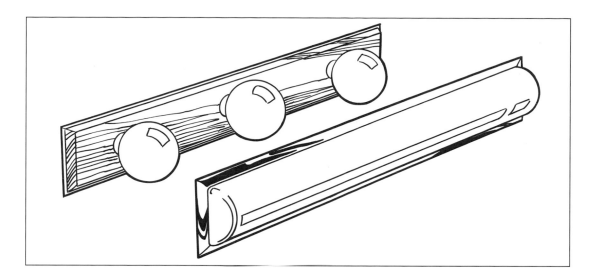

The two most common types of wall-mounted vanity lights are "Hollywood lights" and translucent diffusers. Hollywood lights are strips of globe lamps next to the mirror on one, two, or three sides. The globe lamps vary in wattage from 15 to 60 watts. The translucent diffusers are also located above or beside the mirror. They are available in several lengths and typically use incandescent A-lamps or linear fluorescent lamps.

Energy and Lamps

For luminaires that are on for many hours a day, fluorescent lamps are a good choice. Install a plug-in night light with a photocell to discourage the use of the vanity lights for night-time orientation.

Lamp color and color rendering are critical for vanity lights because people are sensitive to the appearance of their skin and clothing. If using fluorescent lamps, choose those that have a CCT of 2700 to 3500 K and contain rare-earth phosphors. To reduce glare when using incandescent lamps, use frosted or coated lamps instead of clear lamps and also use more lamps of lower wattage rather than a few high-wattage lamps. Consider compact fluorescent globe lamps as replacements for incandescent lamps; note that the compact fluorescent lamps are more costly to replace, but they should last much longer than the incandescent lamps.

Installation

Locate luminaires to the sides of the mirror to help eliminate facial shadows, and use light colors on countertops for maximum light reflectance to the underside of the chin. If installed above the mirror, locate vanity lights 6.5 feet above the floor.

Controls

Switch vanity lights separately from other luminaires in the room. If incandescent vanity lights are the sole light source, consider a dimmer to increase comfort when residents enter from a dark room, such as during the middle of the night. Consider installing an interval timer.

For more information refer to

Techniques: Special Purpose

Lamps: Incandescent, Linear Fluorescent, Long Twin-Tube Fluorescent, Compact Fluorescent

Designs: Half Bath, Small Bath, Large Bath

Other luminaires: Soffits, Valances, Wall-Mounted Sconces or Diffusers, Medicine Cabinet, Night Lights

Furniture or Cabinet-Integrated

Many times, furniture, cabinetry, and appliances for homes include lighting elements. Included are lighting for medicine cabinets, shelves or display cabinets, under-cabinet, artwork, and stove/appliances. Typically, low-wattage incandescent or linear fluorescent lamps are incorporated to provide task or accent lighting. Purchase luminaires at department stores, appliance stores, building supply stores, and with the furniture at furniture stores. Lamps, sockets, and strip luminaires for fluorescent lamps are available at lighting stores and electrical suppliers and can be built into furniture such as shelves or cabinets.

Energy and Lamps
Choose or build luminaires that use fluorescent lamps for highest efficiency. Replace incandescent lamps in existing luminaires with fluorescent lamps wherever possible.

Installation
Luminaires can be purchased as manufactured units and added to furniture or cabinets, or may be offered as an option by the maker of the furniture, cabinets, or appliances.

Controls
Some built-in luminaires are provided with switches that are located in awkward places, so the resident frequently leaves the luminaire on. Choose luminaires with controls in an easily accessible position for the resident's convenience and for energy savings. Switch furniture- and cabinet-integrated luminaires separately from other luminaires in the room so that the lighting is used only when needed.

Cautions
Glare can be a problem with furniture- or cabinet-integrated lighting for people in seated positions, so conceal or shield the lamps. As a safety precaution, choose luminaires and lamps that are intended for use in enclosed areas.

Furniture or Cabinet-Integrated:
Medicine Cabinet

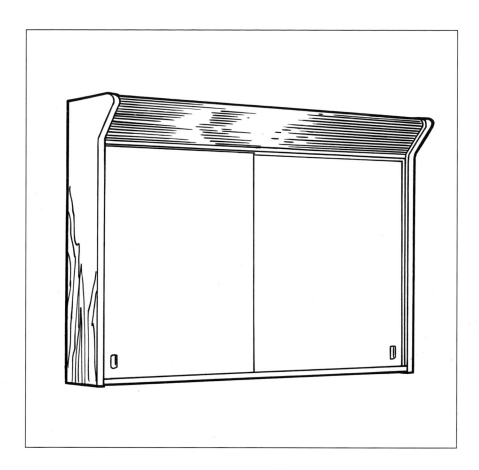

Medicine cabinets often include luminaires that provide diffuse lighting for the sink area. The luminaires may contain two to four 40- to 60-watt incandescent A-lamps. Luminaires with linear and compact fluorescent lamps are also available. Some medicine cabinets position the luminaires on either side of the mirror; others position the luminaire above the mirror. The resident's face will be more evenly illuminated with side-mounted luminaires.

Energy and Lamps
Select medicine cabinets with fluorescent lamps for highest efficiency. If an existing medicine cabinet contains common incandescent A-lamps, replace them with halogen A-lamps or screwbase compact fluorescent lamps, if the latter will fit in the luminaire.

Installation
For fewer shadows, select medicine cabinets with lighting mounted vertically on both sides.

Controls
Consider using timers or motion detectors, which can reduce wasted lighting energy in bathrooms.

For more information refer to
Techniques: Special Purpose

Lamps: Halogen A, Linear Fluorescent, Compact Fluorescent

Designs: Medium Bath 2

Other luminaires: Soffits, Valances, Wall-Mounted, Night Lights

Furniture or Cabinet-Integrated:
Shelf or Display Cabinet

Shelf and display cabinet luminaires accent books, plants, glassware, and collections of other objects and art. They can also be used to light shelves in storage areas. The "spill light" from these luminaires in a living room can provide a soft, ambient light for watching television or relaxing.

Energy and Lamps

Consider linear fluorescent lamps, including small-diameter T5 lamps, to wash shelves with light and save energy. Incandescent lamps, especially low-voltage MR-lamps, are best for lighting crystal and glass objects because they create a sparkling effect. Linear fluorescent lamps mounted near the front of the shelves and concealed behind the trim are appropriate for lighting books and other matte-surface objects.

Controls

Switch shelf and display cabinet lighting separately from other luminaires in the room. Use a timer for utility shelves. Place controls on or near the luminaires, or in a convenient location for residents.

Cautions

Ventilate shelf units and cabinets properly to dissipate heat from the lamps. Light fades many colors of paper and fabric, so use the luminaires only when needed for viewing the display.

For more information refer to

Techniques: Ambient, Accent, Special Purpose

Lamps: Common Incandescent, Low-Voltage Halogen, Linear Fluorescent, Compact Fluorescent

Designs: Large Living Room 3

Other luminaires: Ceiling-Mounted Track or Adjustable Heads, Recessed Wall Wash, Recessed Accent, Soffits, Under-Cabinet

Luminaires

Furniture or Cabinet-Integrated: Under-Cabinet

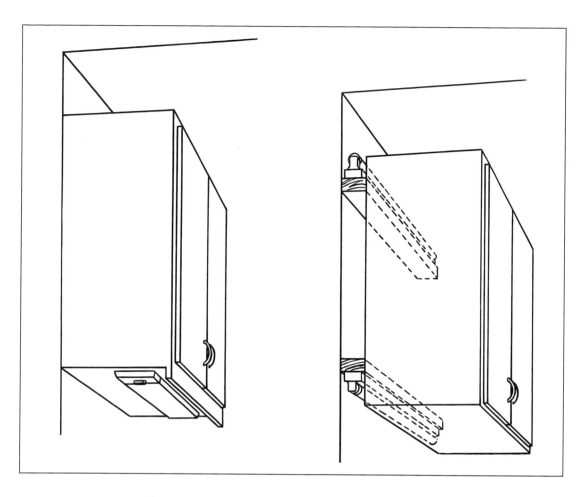

Lighting for areas such as countertops and desks is efficiently provided by under-cabinet luminaires. Under-cabinet luminaires use incandescent or fluorescent lamps installed below the upper cabinet to direct light down to the work surface. Manufactured units with small-diameter, low-wattage fluorescent lamps such as the 8- and 13-watt T5 linear fluorescent lamps are readily available in lengths of 12 to 42 inches and fit easily under many cabinets. Various diffusers are also offered to spread the light uniformly over the work area.

Energy and Lamps

Use the longest linear fluorescent lamp that will fill at least two-thirds of the cabinet width.

Installation

Mount lamps as close to the front of the cabinet as possible without exposing the lamps to view. Check that the lamp is properly concealed to avoid glare from a seated position, such as someone sitting at the counter. A shielding board may be added to extend the depth of the recess under some cabinets.

Cautions

Shield the lamps to avoid direct glare and to prevent breakage or burns.

For more information refer to

Techniques: Task, Special Purpose

Lamps: Linear Fluorescent

Designs: Medium Kitchen 2, Large Kitchen

Other luminaires: Ceiling-Mounted Track or Adjustable Heads, Recessed Downlights, Soffits, Desk Lamps

Furniture or Cabinet-Integrated: Artwork

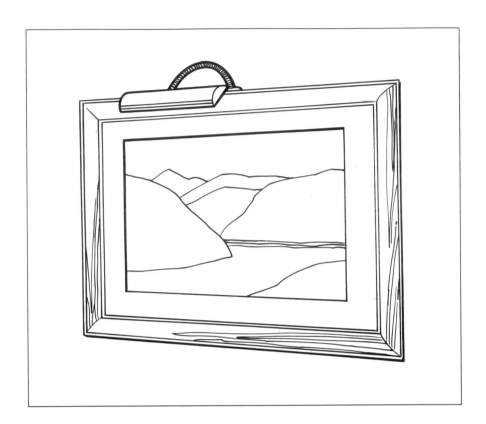

Artwork luminaires can be an integral part of a frame or may be attached to an existing frame by clips or brackets. Typically, artwork luminaires have a 7- to 14-inch linear housing that contains one or two low-wattage incandescent lamps. Luminaires containing low-voltage halogen lamps with remote transformers also are available. Linear fluorescent lamps in 2-foot housings may be furnished with filters to screen ultraviolet radiation.

Installation

Many of these lamps have adjustable arms so that the angle may be changed to decrease glare.

Controls

Switch each artwork luminaire separately to avoid excessive exposure of the artwork to light.

Energy and Lamps

Often tubular incandescent lamps are used. Consider low-voltage halogen lamps. A series of low-wattage (3 to 7 watts) halogen lamps spaced about 8 inches apart are used in some artwork luminaires. For larger artwork, consider using wall washing or accent techniques. These luminaires can use high-color-rendering linear or compact fluorescent lamps with higher efficacy than incandescent lamps.

Cautions

These luminaires may cause reflected glare on glass surfaces. Light fades many colors of paper and fabric, so use the luminaires only when needed for viewing the display.

For more information refer to

Techniques: Accent, Special Purpose

Lamps: Common Incandescent, Low-Voltage Halogen, Linear Fluorescent, Compact Fluorescent

Other luminaires: Ceiling-Mounted Track or Adjustable Heads, Recessed Wall Wash, Recessed Accent, Soffits

Luminaires

Furniture or Cabinet-Integrated: Stove and Appliance

Luminaires are commonly provided with range hoods. Many other kitchen appliances, including conventional and microwave ovens and refrigerators, also contain luminaires. Many use 25-watt clear incandescent lamps.

Energy and Lamps

Follow the appliance manufacturer's recommendation for permissible lamp types and sizes. Incandescent A-lamps can be replaced with halogen A-lamps. Some luminaires may be large enough to accommodate screwbase compact fluorescent lamps.

Installation

Consider appliance lighting when designing kitchens. For example, an additional ceiling-mounted or recessed luminaire over the stove may be unnecessary if a range hood with a luminaire is chosen. A range hood containing a low-wattage lamp can serve as a night light.

Controls

Refrigerators incorporate door switches. Most other appliances have switches on the luminaire.

For more information refer to

Techniques: Task

Lamps: Common Incandescent, Compact Fluorescent

Designs: Small Kitchen, Medium Kitchen 2

Other luminaires: Under-Cabinet

Plug-In

Plug-in luminaires or "lamps" as they are often called, are portable luminaires that plug into an electrical outlet. They include table lamps, desk lamps, floor lamps, and night lights. These luminaires are both decorative and functional. They give a room sparkle or visual interest while providing additional light to areas of the room. Many styles are available and prices range widely. Plug-in luminaires use many types of lamps, particularly A-lamps, tubular-shaped halogen lamps, and compact fluorescent lamps. These luminaires offer flexibility to the resident because they can be moved when furniture is rearranged and they can be positioned close to critical tasks such as reading or sewing.

Light can be distributed in many directions; the size, shape, and materials of the shade determine the light distribution. Most plug-in luminaires can be adjusted to positions and angles that reduce glare. Also, they allow a resident to add more light to a room without the effort and expense of installing a hard-wired luminaire.

Purchase plug-in luminaires from department and furniture stores, office supply stores, lighting stores, and catalogs.

Energy and Lamps

Although many plug-in luminaires are purchased as decorative elements, consumers should be aware that they consume energy and should be considered an appliance. Choose luminaires that contain fluorescent lamps or that will accommodate screwbase compact fluorescent lamps if the luminaire will be used frequently or for long periods of time. Operate three-way incandescent lamps at the lowest comfortable level to save energy.

Replace existing lamps of any type with lower-wattage lamps if lower light output is acceptable. If luminaires contain incandescent A-lamps, consider replacing them with halogen lamps or screwbase compact fluorescent lamps of equivalent light output.

Installation

Avoid placing the luminaire directly over a task, especially over tasks with glossy surfaces. Generally the best location is to the side and slightly behind the viewer. Use a plug-in luminaire to balance brightness within a space from other luminaires or from daylight. Decreasing the distance between the luminaire and the task allows lower-wattage lamps to be used.

Controls

Many controls are available for plug-in lamps; some are inserted into the lamp socket, some into the electrical socket, and some can be spliced into the cord. Use dimmers, photocells, or timers for plug-in lamps that contain incandescent lamps. Two popular control options for people with limited dexterity are the touch switch and touch dimmer.

Choose plug-in luminaires that allow multiple-level switching. For instance, luminaires that contain two lamps may offer the choice of switching only one of the two lamps on.

Cautions

For safety, consider the weight and balance of luminaires, especially those containing compact fluorescent lamps. Make sure that luminaires and cords are located and secured so that people will not trip on them and young children will not overturn the luminaire. Luminaires that contain high-wattage lamps, particularly tubular-shaped halogen lamps, can be a fire and burn hazard. Locate them a safe distance from flammable materials, and away from possible skin contact.

To prevent glare, the lamp should not be exposed to view. Do not use compact fluorescent lamps in a table lamp that is controlled by a dimmer because fluorescent lamps are not compatible with dimmers designed for incandescent lamps. If incandescent A-lamps are replaced with screwbase compact fluorescent lamps, which are heavier, check the stability of the plug-in lamp.

Plug-In: Table Lamps

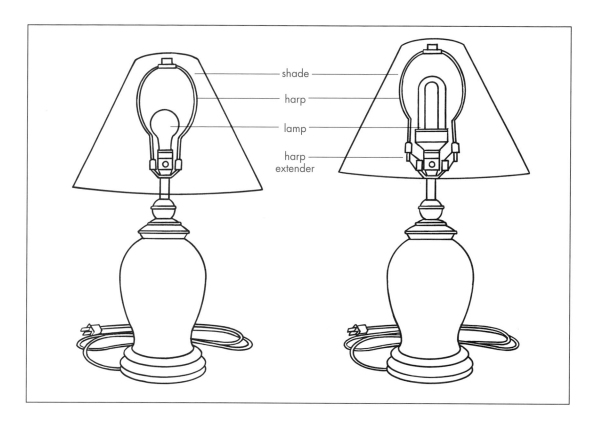

Table lamps are plug-in luminaires that sit on a table or desk. They incorporate diffusers, reflectors, and shades that direct the light to suit various needs.

Energy and Lamps

Replace incandescent A-lamps with screwbase compact fluorescent lamps if the luminaire does not have a dimmer. If compact fluorescent lamps are used to replace incandescent lamps, a harp extender may be required.

Avoid using a three-way incandescent lamp in a table lamp that does not have three-way switching, because the lamp will operate only at the highest wattage.

Installation

The appropriate location of the table lamp depends on the size of the shade, position of the lamp within the shade, aperture diameter, base height, eye position, and desired light distribution. The bottom of the shade should be located at eye level to reduce glare and maximize light distribution.

Controls

Three-way switching is a common option for table lamps. If a single wattage lamp is used in a table lamp designed for a three-way lamp, the single wattage lamp will operate only at two switch settings.

For more information refer to

Techniques: Ambient, Task

Lamps: Halogen A, Tubular-Shaped Halogen, Compact and Circline Fluorescent

Designs: Small Living Rooms, Medium Living Rooms, Large Living Rooms 1 and 3, Small Bedroom, Large Bedroom

Other luminaires: Suspended Downlights, Recessed, Desk Lamps, Floor Lamps

Plug-In: Desk Lamps

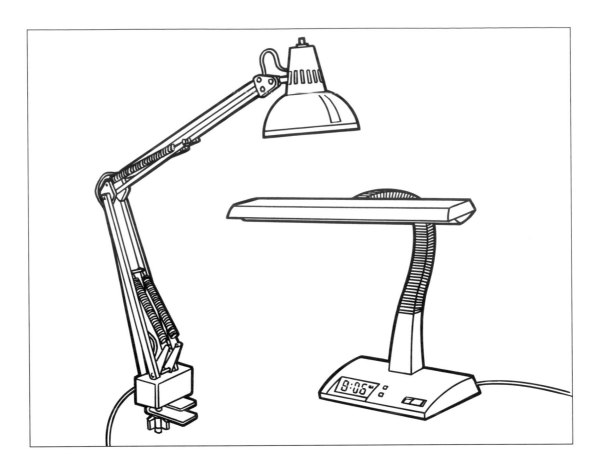

Desk lamps provide light for demanding visual tasks such as reading and writing. These tasks require higher levels of light than do most other activities. Preventing shadows and glare is very important to avoid discomfort and distraction. The placement, shade design, socket location, shielding, and choice of lamp are the primary factors that determine the quantity and quality of the light at the task.

Energy and Lamps

Use desk lamps to supplement ambient lighting when high illuminance is needed on the desk surface. Well-designed desk lamps deliver light efficiently because they are close to the task.

Incandescent lamps are common in desk lamps. In existing luminaires, replace incandescent A-lamps with halogen A-lamps, or with screwbase compact fluorescent lamps if they will fit in the luminaire; harp or socket extenders may be needed. "High-intensity" desk lamps use low-voltage halogen lamps; the transformer typically is housed in the base.

For energy savings, select one of many new models of desk lamps that are designed for compact fluorescent lamps or linear fluorescent lamps; look for them in office supply stores or catalogs.

Installation

Shadows can be an annoying problem when using a desk lamp for writing tasks. Place the desk lamp to the left for a right-handed person, and to the right for a left-handed person. Locate the desk lamp carefully to avoid reflections in a computer screen, but to provide enough light for reading documents. Also locate a desk lamp so that it provides some ambient light near a computer screen; this will help balance the contrast between the screen and the surrounding area.

Cautions

Some desk lamps are packaged with hard-to-find tubular-shaped halogen lamps; ask the retailer if they stock replacement lamps.

For more information refer to

Techniques: Task

Lamps: Halogen A, Tubular-Shaped Halogen, Low-Voltage Halogen, Linear Fluorescent, Compact Fluorescent

Designs: Small Bedroom, Children's Bedroom, Home Office

Other luminaires: Suspended Downlights, Recessed Downlights, Soffits, Under-Cabinet, Table Lamps, Floor Lamps

Plug-In: Floor Lamps

Floor lamps complement the lighting from other luminaires and can balance brightness in a room or provide additional light for an area of the room. A typical floor lamp is approximately 4 to 5 feet tall and adds a vertical emphasis in a room. Like table lamps, floor lamps are decorative, available in many styles, and range widely in price. A torchiere is a floor lamp that directs all light upwards.

Energy and Lamps

Choose floor lamps that are designed for compact fluorescent lamps. In existing luminaires, replace incandescent A-lamps with halogen A-lamps, or with screwbase compact fluorescent lamps if they will fit in the luminaire; harp or socket extenders may be needed. The 500-watt tubular-shaped halogen lamps in some floor lamps can be replaced with 350-watt IR tubular-shaped halogen lamps, and the 300-watt lamps can be replaced with 225-watt IR tubular-shaped halogen lamps. Check the manufacturer's instructions. Use dimmers on these lamps.

Installation

Torchieres work well in rooms with high ceilings, but avoid placing them in rooms with very low ceilings. For other types of floor lamps, use a shade to shield the lamp from direct view. Locate the luminaire so that there is no view of an exposed lamp from stairs, landings and balconies. Floor lamps can create distracting light distribution patterns if located too close to a wall.

Cautions

Do not place an uplight floor lamp or torchiere beneath ceiling fan blades because a stroboscopic effect may occur. Never place a torchiere or any floor lamp with an indirect lighting component under flammable materials such as drapes. Check the balance of floor lamps, especially those that contain screwbase compact fluorescent lamps: make sure that they are not top-heavy.

For more information refer to

Techniques: Ambient, Indirect, Task

Lamps: Halogen A, Tubular-Shaped Halogen, Compact and Circline Fluorescent

Designs: Medium Living Room 2, Large Bedroom

Other luminaires: Ceiling-Mounted, Suspended, Recessed, Architectural, Table Lamps

Luminaires

Plug-In: Night Lights

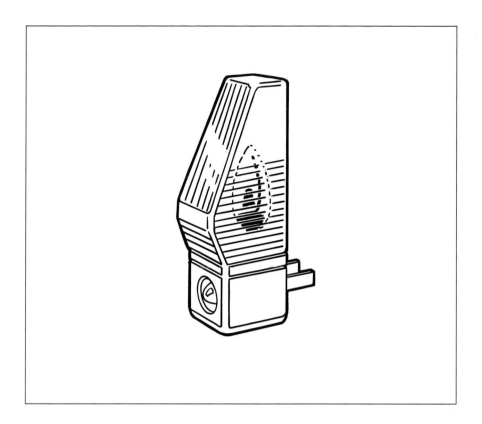

Night lights may be hard-wired or plug-in units; they use low-wattage lamps to provide lighting for finding your way in the dark. Night lights may have a diffuser to shield the lamp. Plug-in night lights may be switched by removing them from the outlet, by an on-off switch, or by a photocell that turns the night light off when light from other luminaires or daylight illuminates the space. Plug-in night lights can be purchased at discount stores, supermarkets, hardware stores, and through electric utility company promotions.

Energy and Lamps

If luminaires are left on all night for orientation, adding and using night lights is a simple way to reduce waste. They present a good opportunity to explain to family members that using the night lights rather than other luminaires saves energy. Use the lowest-wattage lamp available that will provide sufficient light for orientation. Typically, 7-, 4-, and ¼-watt incandescent lamps are used, but some luminaires of this type use fluorescent lamps.

Installation

Night lights typically are used in bedrooms, hallways, and bathrooms, but they may also be useful in basements, attics, garages, and other utility rooms.

Controls

Choose night lights with both a photocell and a manual switch for greatest efficiency and convenience. As an alternative to night lights, consider using light switches with dim, illuminated handles which can be located easily in the dark.

For more information refer to

Designs: Children's Bedroom

Other luminaires: Stove/Appliance

Exterior

Exterior luminaires include large-area flood and small-area, landscape, and accent luminaires. They illuminate building facades, pathways, and landscapes and can provide lighting for safety, security, and decoration. Exterior lighting also extends the hours that residents can enjoy their outdoor living spaces. Exterior luminaires are most effective in a design if they are considered along with the form and materials of the building, plantings, and other landscape features. Purchase them at lighting stores, electrical suppliers, and building supply stores.

Incandescent, fluorescent, and high-intensity discharge lamps can be used in exterior luminaires. Exterior luminaires are available in many styles and may be mounted on posts, bollards, the building, or on or in the ground.

Energy and Lamps

If incandescent lamps are used, select reflector lamps of the highest efficacy and lowest wattage possible for the desired illuminance, and of the appropriate beam spread. Fluorescent lamps may be appropriate energy-efficient lamps for exterior use in warm-to-moderate climates. High-intensity discharge lamps such as high-pressure sodium and metal halide lamps may be appropriate energy-efficient lamps for exterior use, especially for long hours of operation, for large areas, and for security lighting.

Installation

To extend the view from the interior to exterior, the light must be balanced on both sides of the windows. If the light is much brighter on the inside than the outside, the view is diminished. Exterior night-time scenes are best viewed from interiors with low levels of ambient light. Exterior lighting should never be aimed directly at windows. To avoid direct glare, choose luminaires in which the lamp is properly shielded from view. Aim the light only on the objects or areas to be viewed. Stray light is wasted and interferes with seeing the stars!

Follow the National Electrical Manufacturers Association's guidelines and the National Electrical Code and local code requirements.

Controls

Use timers, motion detectors, remote controls, and photocells to reduce waste.

Cautions

Exterior luminaires must be weatherproof, and the housings should be Underwriters Laboratories listed for either "wet location" (fully exposed to weather) or for "damp location" (sheltered areas such as enclosed porches). Fluorescent lamps may not start well in cold weather. Check manufacturers' recommendations for starting temperatures. Avoid light trespass: light that strays onto a neighbor's property may be annoying and illegal. Shadows can be an advantage as well as a disadvantage: they can create dramatic effects, but they provide areas where intruders may pass undetected.

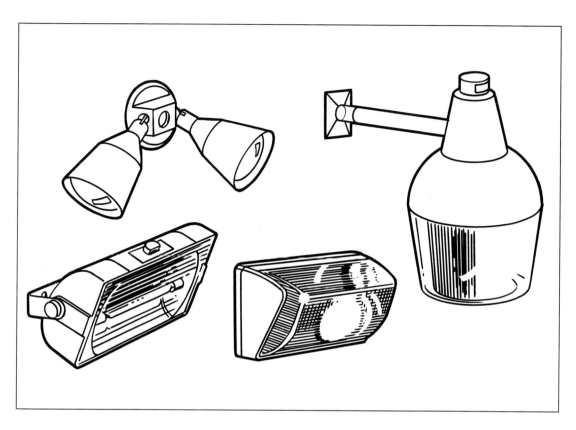

Lighting of large areas such as building facades, driveways, pools, and decks may be accomplished in a variety of ways. One technique floods the area with a low level and uniform distribution of light. Floodlights typically have one or two lamps mounted in a simple housing. Some floodlights protect the lamps and alter the light distribution with a glass or plastic lens or diffuser.

Energy and Lamps

Replace incandescent PAR-lamps with halogen PAR-, IR PAR-, or compact fluorescent reflector lamps. The compact fluorescent reflector lamps are best applied where lower light outputs are acceptable and the weather is not excessively cold. Luminaires that are designed to incorporate compact fluorescent lamps are also available. Use high-pressure sodium lamps only if color in the landscape is not critical; these lamps produce a yellowish-white light. Metal halide lamps are also efficient and long-lasting. Inexpensive luminaires that contain mercury vapor lamps are commonly available, but they are less efficient than luminaires that use high-pressure sodium or metal halide lamps.

CONTINUED

Luminaires

Installation

Avoid direct glare by carefully adjusting the angle of proximity and the distance from residents.

The simplest installation is to mount the luminaire on a pole or on the eave or side of the building. Increasing the mounting height of the luminaire increases the area that will be lit, but lowers the illuminance over the area. Higher mounting heights often make replacing the lamps more difficult. Floodlight luminaires throw light in a fairly symmetrical and uniform distribution over a large area. Refer to manufacturers' data for mounting heights and distance of throw.

Controls

Use luminaires with an integrated photocell for lamps that are operated all night. When floodlighting is used for security, consider using motion detectors that switch lamps on only when motion is sensed.

Cautions

High-intensity discharge lamps take several minutes to come to full brightness and do not restart immediately after they are turned off. Avoid using high-intensity discharge lamps with motion detectors or where light is needed quickly or will be turned on and off frequently. Also avoid using poorly shielded luminaires that contain HID lamps in areas where glare would pose problems for residents.

For more information refer to

Techniques: Ambient, Special Purposes

Lamps: Halogen A, Reflector, Linear Fluorescent, Compact Fluorescent, High-Intensity Discharge

Designs: Floodlights

Other luminaires: Small-Area, Landscape, and Accent

Luminaires

Exterior: Small-Area, Landscape, and Accent

Accent lighting is used to define or emphasize an area or objects of special interest, such as entries and porches, fountains, pools, sculpture, trees, and plantings. Small-area lighting also allows residents to perform tasks such as finding the key at an entry.

Energy and Lamps

Consider the use of fluorescent lamps for moderate climates. Low-voltage and solar-powered systems can be installed for landscape or walk lighting; they do not require a building permit for underground installations. In luminaires that are powered by integral photovoltaic cells, the sun charges a battery for night-time use. These luminaires can be particularly useful where power is not readily available. If a large area of the landscape must be lit for many hours, consider using luminaires that contain mercury vapor, metal halide, or high-pressure sodium lamps, but note that the color characteristics of some of these lamps may not be acceptable to some residents.

CONTINUED

Installation

Lighting a small area such as an entry or porch allows guests safe passage and intruders to be easily identified. To light objects, use spot lighting with luminaires designed for a narrow beam distribution. Shield the lamps from view and conceal them with shrubbery if mounted on the ground. Use spread-lighting luminaires to create circular patterns of light for illuminating ground cover, low plantings, walkways, and pathways. Spread luminaires are fully shielded on the top and direct all light downwards.

Controls

Consider the use of timers to control exterior lighting that is used on a regular schedule. Use motion detectors to illuminate areas only when people approach. Photocells can be used to turn off exterior luminaires automatically during daylight.

For more information refer to

Techniques: Ambient, Wall Washing, Accent, Special Purposes

Lamps: Halogen A, Reflector, Linear Fluorescent, Compact Fluorescent, High-Intensity Discharge

Designs: Entries, Pole-Mounted Light

Other luminaires: Ceiling-Mounted Diffusers, Suspended Downlights, Suspended Uplight/Downlights, Downlights, Recessed Wall Wash, Recessed Accent, Recessed Wall-Mounted Sconces or Diffusers, Large-Area Floodlights

Luminaires

Controls

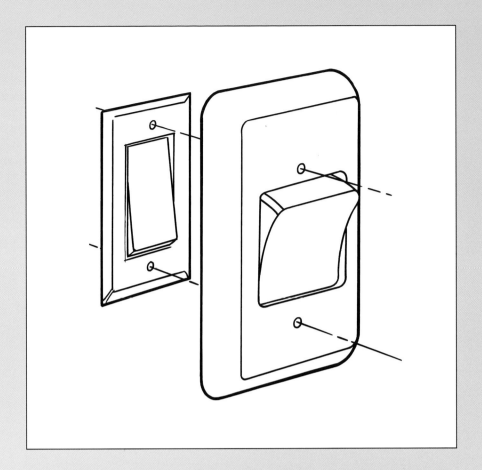

Lighting controls include switches, dimmers, timers, motion detectors, photosensors, and central controls. Lighting controls operate the lamps within luminaires. In most applications, the greatest opportunity to avoid wasted lighting energy is the proper use of controls.

Lighting controls appropriate for use in homes can be operated manually or automatically. Manual controls include switches and dimmers. Switches turn the lamps on and off and dimmers vary the light output of some lamps. Automatic controls include timers, motion detectors, and photosensors. Timers can be used to turn lamps on either manually or automatically, but they always turn lamps off automatically after a designated time period. Motion detectors operate the lamps in response to motion, so they can be used to turn lamps off or dim lamps when no one is present. Photosensors switch or dim lamps in response to other sources of light, particularly daylight. Central controls can switch or dim lamps in many locations. They can be operated manually from a single location or automatically using timers, motion detectors, photosensors, or a programmable pattern of operation.

Controls vary in complexity and price. Use this chapter to identify controls that will be appropriate for your lighting needs. Typical price ranges for common controls are listed in Table 6 of the Economics chapter; however, the prices of these controls vary widely and depend upon the quality of construction, quantity purchased, and style. Controls can be purchased through retail or wholesale businesses. Purchase common controls at hardware, building supply, and discount department stores. For a wider variety, look in lighting stores. For more specialized controls, contact electrical suppliers. Due to variations in quality and price, consumers and contractors should check several sources before buying a control.

The following characteristics are described for each type of control.

Energy

Energy can be saved by turning off or dimming lamps. Controls make this energy savings more convenient and predictable. All lighting designs have at least a single switch control. Consider a greater investment in controls for rooms with high-wattage lamps or rooms where the lamps are likely to be left on when not needed. Table 1 of the Economics chapter gives some estimates of the impact of dimmers on power and lamp life; Table 2 gives typical hours of lamp operation and motion detector factors for several rooms in the home.

Installation

Controls must be appropriately located to make it convenient for residents to turn off lamps. Also, not all controls are appropriate for all rooms or lamps. Consider the accessibility of controls for people in wheelchairs and others who may have difficulty reaching a control. For residents with limited finger dexterity, choose controls that are large and easy to operate. Some manufacturers produce adaptive devices that attach to common switches to make them easier to grasp, or to operate without using hands. Some types of controls are not compatible with some compact fluorescent lamps; check the lamp and control manufacturers' recommendations for compatibility.

Cautions

Some cautions are noted for controls, particularly for safety and for compatibility with lamps and luminaires. Always read the manufacturer's instructions concerning installation and maximum lamp wattage. A qualified electrician should install hard-wired lighting controls.

For more information refer to

Designs: Most of the controls described in this chapter are used in the Designs chapter. Refer to the listed designs to see an application of the control.

Switches

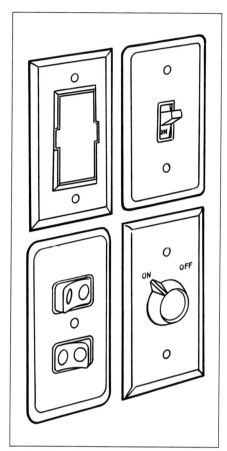

Switches are manual controls that turn lamps on and off. These controls are usually located on a wall or on the luminaire. Wall-mounted toggle switches, pull-cords, and luminaire-mounted switches are all examples of switches. These are the most inexpensive and popular means of operating lamps.

Wall switches are used widely in homes and are available in different types. The most common is called a single-pole switch, which operates one or more luminaires from a single location. To operate a luminaire from two locations, use three-way switches. To operate a luminaire from three locations, use four-way switches.

The operating handles of switches are available in toggle, push, rocker, rotary, and tap-plate types. Adaptive devices that are attached to wall switches facilitate operation by disabled persons and children. The cover plates for switches are usually available in white, ivory, brown, or black finishes. Some manufacturers offer special "designer" colors. To avoid wasting energy, people must use switches to turn off lamps when light is not needed. A "switch sticker" is a simple message affixed to a switch plate to remind residents to save energy. Switch stickers are an easy way to encourage children (and forgetful adults) to develop energy-conserving behavior.

Switches also can be located on the luminaire. Fluorescent lamp strip luminaires and porcelain sockets located in basements, storage spaces, and garages often have pull-cord switches. Pull-cords are a length of rope or chain that switches the light on or off when pulled. They are an inexpensive method of lighting control because no additional electrical wiring to the switch is needed. Attach a card or decorative ball to the end of pull-cords so that they can be found in the dark and easily grasped.

Door switches automatically turn lamps on when the door is opened. A small switch is mounted on the inside face of the door jamb and wired to the luminaire; it is similar to the switch on a refrigerator or car door. Use door switches in closets and pantries where supplemental lighting is needed, where luminaires are likely to be left on after use, or where the door is likely to be closed after use. Door switches can save energy and extend the service life of lamps.

Purchase switches from lighting stores, electrical suppliers, building supply stores, and hardware stores. Switches are the least-expensive type of lighting control, but other controls may result in greater energy savings and thus have lower life-cycle costs.

Energy

Manual switches only save energy if the lamps are turned off when the space is unoccupied or light is not needed. Locate switches in convenient locations so that people will be more likely to turn off lamps when they are not needed. Consider adding additional switches if people enter the space from multiple locations.

CONTINUED

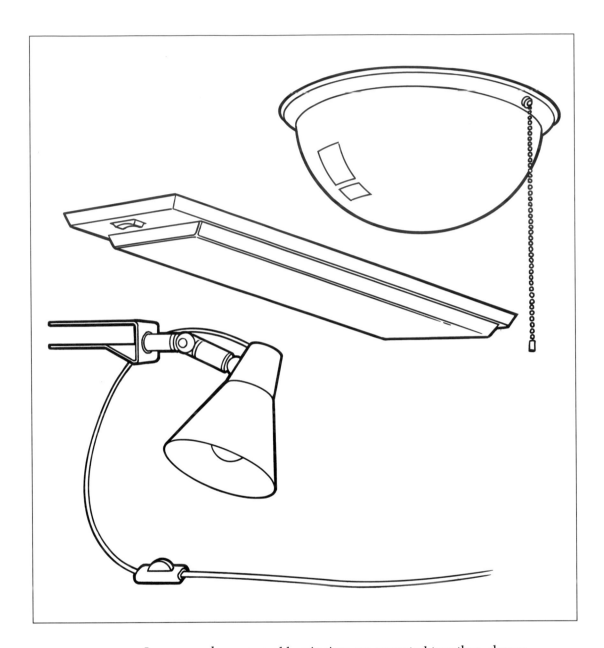

In rooms where several luminaires are operated together, choose
luminaires that are designed with pull-cords or other luminaire-mounted
switches. For example, if a basement has four porcelain lamp holders
that are controlled by the same switch, pull-cord lamp holders will allow
three of these lamps to be left off when light is needed in only one area of
the basement.

Switch accent and task luminaires separately from the luminaires that
provide ambient light so that only the luminaires that are needed at a
given time are operated. Many of these luminaires are available with
luminaire-mounted switches.

If a luminaire contains more than one lamp, as in an architectural
luminaire, use two or more switches wired to separate rows or sections
of lamps to provide multiple levels of light output.

Consider using wall switches with dim, illuminated toggles for switch identification in the dark. These switches may replace the need for leaving other luminaires on at night. Also consider using switches with a pilot light, which is illuminated whenever the luminaires are on, in applications where the luminaire(s) that is operated by the switch cannot be seen from the switch location. For example, a pilot light on the switch to luminaires in the basement or on the porch may remind the resident that the luminaires have been left on inadvertently.

Installation

Use three-way switches or four way-switches in spaces where it is desirable to control a luminaire from two or more locations in the room, such as hallways, stairs, garages, and any room entered from two or more locations. Special three-way or four-way switches and wiring configurations are required.

Switches are often located on the wall beside doors that are used to enter rooms and are usually mounted 4 feet above the floor to the center of the switch. This mounting height is the maximum acceptable height for people in wheelchairs. Lower mounting heights are also more easily reached by children and avoid interference with the 4-foot horizontal drywall seam that is common in new construction. The switch is mounted in a switch box that is recessed in the wall. When one switch is used, it is mounted in a "single-gang" box. A cover plate is used to conceal the wiring and provide a finished appearance to the switch. Where multiple switches are required to operate different luminaires from the same location, a "multi-gang" switch box and cover plate are required.

Recessed retrofit wall switch boxes are available that can be installed in existing plaster and drywall walls. Switches can also be added using surface-mounted switch boxes and wire raceways.

Recessed wall switches can be wired to operate a receptacle or receptacles instead of a luminaire. These "switched plugs" can be used for controlling plug-in luminaires. Receptacles can be split-wired so that only one receptacle in a duplex outlet is operated by the switch, leaving the other receptacle available for other electrical devices.

For more information refer to

Designs: Switches are used throughout the Designs chapter.

Dimmers

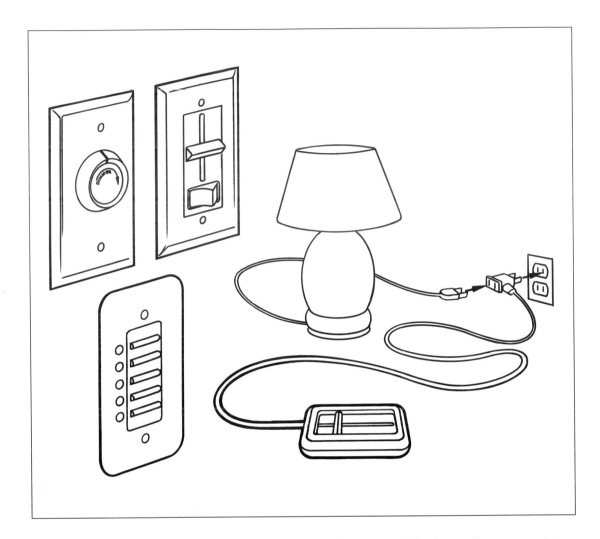

Dimmers are used to vary the light output of the lamps that are used in a space. Use dimmers in rooms where a range of light outputs is desirable. Dimmers can be used to control incandescent lamps, including low-voltage halogen lamps, and many fluorescent lamps. Different lamp types may require different electronic circuitry for proper dimming.

Ideally, dimmers should have the capability of "full-range" dimming. Full-range dimming refers to the continuous variation of light output from a minimum to a maximum level. Efficient dimmers, commonly referred to as "solid-state" dimmers, incorporate electronic circuitry into their design. Purchase dimmers from lighting stores, electrical suppliers, building supply stores, and hardware stores.

Wall-mounted dimmers include four styles: toggle dimmers, rotary dimmers, linear slide dimmers, and touch dimmers. Most of these are available in single-pole and three-way models to allow dimming from two locations. The four styles differ in their appearance and operating complexity.

Toggle dimmers look like a toggle switch, except that they provide full-range dimming control. They can match standard toggle switches or toggle fan-speed controls in the same multi-gang switch box. Some are available with an illuminated toggle that serves as a switch locator in dark rooms.

Rotary dimmers use a knob to adjust light output. Some models are available with a push/on and push/off rotary knob. Pushing the knob turns the lamps on, turning the knob alters the light output, and pushing the knob again turns the lamps off. Ivory or white knob finishes are the most common, although other colors can be ordered.

Linear slide dimmers provide full-range dimming using a slide element to adjust the lighting. These models range in complexity. The simplest type has a linear slide to control the lighting. Sliding up increases light output; sliding down decreases light output. Some linear slides are available with "preset" buttons and on/off switches. With these types, the linear slide is used to adjust the lighting to a desired level, then the "preset" button is pushed, programming the preset level in memory. The on/off switch is then used to turn the lamps on to this preset level.

Touch dimmers provide full-range dimming control using touch-sensitive solid-state circuitry. A person taps the touch-sensitive panel to turn the lamps on, continuously presses the panel to dim the lamps to the desired level, and taps again to turn off the lamps.

Some dimmers are combined with a motion detector to dim lamps to a preset level when no motion is detected in a space. See Motion Detectors for more information. Preset dimmers can control several luminaires. Multiple "scenes" can be programmed, so that several lamps are dimmed to preset levels by touching a single control button. A specific "scene" is switched on for a different atmosphere or set of tasks.

Socket and cord dimmers provide full-range dimming and are used for dimming incandescent table lamps, floor lamps, or other plug-in lamps that are not manufactured with a dimming switch. The system is made up of a plug-and-adapter combination that is wired to a dimmer. The luminaire plugs into the adapter which in turn plugs into the wall. The dimmer can then be used to dim the lamp.

Energy

Operating lamps at less than full output saves energy. If lower light outputs are acceptable only some of the time, use dimming. If lower light outputs are consistently desired, consider using lower-wattage or fewer lamps.

Dimming incandescent lamps decreases the light output, decreases energy use, and extends the life of the lamp. See Table 1 in the Economics chapter for more information. Consider a simple replacement of a switch with a dimmer to save energy by dimming incandescent lamps. Replace switches with dimmers that control many lamps in an over-lit area for energy savings.

Dimming fluorescent lamps decreases light output and energy use, but does not extend lamp life. Both magnetic and electronic ballasts are available with dimming capabilities. Electronic ballasts offer quieter operation, dimming over a wider range, and greater energy savings. High-quality fluorescent lamp dimmers can dim to as low as 1 percent of full light output. Check manufacturers' specifications for ballast dimming capabilities for fluorescent lamps. Only four-pin compact fluorescent lamps with special dimming ballasts and controls can be dimmed. Compact fluorescent lamp dimming systems are just being introduced to the market, but are not yet available for screwbase compact fluorescent lamps.

Installation

Most residential-grade dimmers are designed to control up to 600 watts of lighting load. Loads greater than 600 watts require commercial-grade dimmers, which are significantly more expensive than residential-grade dimmers. Incandescent lamp dimmers are available for 120-volt applications. Fluorescent lamp dimmers are available for 120-volt (most common in homes) and 277-volt applications; thus it is important to

CONTINUED

order the appropriate voltage. Dimmers are usually recessed into the wall in a switch box in the same manner as switches. See Switches for more information.

An incandescent lamp dimmer has three wires: a hot, a common, and a ground. Rapid-start fluorescent lamps have a total of four pins on their bases and can be dimmed. Use a fluorescent lamp dimmer or dimming control to operate a dimming ballast located in the housing of the luminaire. The fluorescent lamp dimmer requires more wiring to send the dimming signal to the dimming ballast than does a dimmer for incandescent lamps.

Cautions

Install dimmers according to the manufacturer's instructions. Verify the maximum load that the dimmer can accommodate with the manufacturer's instructions.

Occasionally operate halogen lamps at full output to retain the benefits of the halogen cycle.

Use dimmers that are designed for low-voltage lamps to control these lamps.

Do not install a compact fluorescent lamp in a luminaire that is controlled by a dimmer that is designed for incandescent lamps.

Dimmers should incorporate electromagnetic interference (EMI) and radio frequency interference (RFI) filters to prevent causing static on radios or on audio equipment.

Do not use dimmers to control receptacles, fluorescent lamp luminaires, motor-operated appliances such as ceiling fans, or transformer-operated appliances, unless the dimmers are specifically designed for these applications. The dimmer could overheat and become damaged or cause a fire if used incorrectly.

Make sure dimmers click when turned off; otherwise, the lamps will still draw current which wastes energy and may shorten lamp life.

For more information refer to

Designs: Large Kitchen, Small Living Room 2, Large Living Rooms 2 and 3, Multi-Family Lobby

Timers

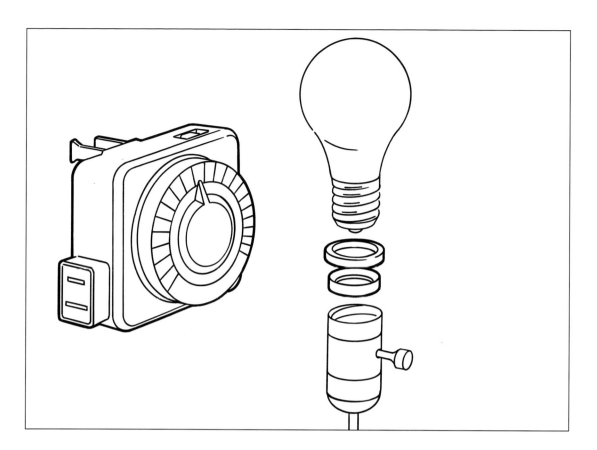

Timers turn lamps on either manually or automatically, but turn lamps off automatically after a designated time period. Three types of timers for lighting are interval timers, plug-located timers, and socket-located timers.

Interval timers often are used in place of wall switches in areas that are used for short or predictable amounts of time, such as bathrooms, utility areas, and storage closets. These devices are equipped with a mechanical spring-winding system that turns the lamps off automatically as soon as the set time interval has elapsed. Various time intervals are available, including 5, 15, or 30 minutes, to 4, 6, or 12 hours. Interval timers are a low-cost alternative to motion detectors. Interval timers also are available in solid-state models that fit directly into a standard switch box. Some interval timers are designed for use in multi-level stairwells.

Plug-located timers are used to turn table or floor lamps off and on at various times of the day or night, often while a house is empty. The system is made up of a plug and a timer. The table or floor lamp plugs into the timer which in turn plugs into the receptacle. The timer is set for the desired time to turn on the lamps. These devices are available with spring-wound or electronic components. The electronic versions can be programmed to turn the lamps on and off at different times and on different days. Lights controlled by these timers give the impression of occupancy for an unoccupied home. Hard-wired timers, which often are used for exterior luminaires, can be used to switch lights automatically.

A socket-located timer is a small button that fits in a medium-base socket before an incandescent lamp is inserted. The timer has a fixed duration, usually of ten to thirty minutes. When the switch is turned on, the lamp comes on, but the socket-located timer will turn the lamp off automatically after the designated time has elapsed. These are inexpensive and easy to install.

CONTINUED

Purchase timers from lighting, building supply, and hardware stores, electrical suppliers, and catalogs featuring energy-saving products.

Energy

Interval timers save energy and may extend the service life of lamps by turning lamps off when light is no longer needed. Use plug-located timers for security when the home will not be occupied for an extended period of time. Operate low-wattage and / or fluorescent lamps to save energy. Use socket-located timers on luminaires that have incandescent lamps and are in spaces occupied for short periods of time such as closets or pantries where the lamps are likely to be left on.

Installation

Use interval timers in rooms that are occupied infrequently or on luminaires that are operated for short periods of time, including vanity lights, bathroom heat lamps, or closet or pantry lamps. Mount interval timers in standard switch boxes. An electrician should install hard-wired interval timers. Plug- or socket-located timers do not require an electrician's services.

Cautions

Install interval timers according to manufacturers' recommendations. Avoid using timers in rooms where the resident could be stranded away from the switch when the lamps turn off. Spring-wound interval timers may produce noise, so use a solid-state electronic interval timer if quiet operation is preferred. Some screwbase compact fluorescent lamps are not compatible with timing devices. Follow the lamp manufacturer's directions for use.

Although socket-located timers can be installed without an electrician, care must be taken to avoid electric shock. Some socket-located timers have an insulating ring to reduce risk of shock. Follow manufacturers' recommendations.

For more information refer to

Designs: Large Bath, Children's Bedroom, Closed Stair, Multi-Family Fire Stairs, Entry 2

Controls

Motion Detectors

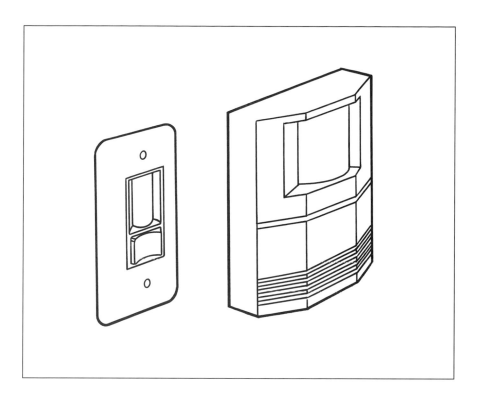

Motion detectors, often called occupancy sensors, automatically turn lamps on when motion is detected and off when no motion is detected. They are used for interior and exterior applications. There are two primary types of motion detectors, infrared and ultrasonic. Infrared sensors respond to a change in infrared heat motion in a space, and ultrasonic sensors respond to a change in ultrasonic frequencies caused by motion in the space.

In homes, motion detectors are used in place of a standard wall switch. They are mounted and wired in a manner similar to standard switches. Options include dimming, manual on and/or manual off switching, and three-way switching. A manual on/automatic off motion detector does not turn the lamps on unless someone touches the switch, but will turn the lamps off automatically when no motion is sensed.

Combination motion detector and dimmer units are available that dim lamps instead of turning lamps off when no motion is detected. Also available are motion detector and photosensor combinations, which only turn lamps on when motion is detected and the surrounding light levels are below a preset level.

Purchase motion detectors from lighting stores, electrical suppliers, or electric utility promotions. Some luminaires with built-in motion detectors for exterior applications are available at building supply and hardware stores. Conversion kits containing a photosensor and a motion detector are available for luminaires that contain incandescent lamps but are not manufactured with an automatic control.

Energy

Motion detectors save energy and can extend the service life of lamps by turning lamps off when a room is unoccupied. Frequent switching of fluorescent lamps will shorten lamp burning life, but may increase actual lamp service life since the lamps are turned off during periods when they might have been left on. See the Economics chapter for a procedure to estimate the economic impact of switching fluorescent lamps.

CONTINUED

Controls

Installation

Use motion detectors in rooms where occupancy is infrequent or of short duration and the lamps are likely to be left on, such as basements, bathrooms, bedrooms, and exterior applications. Use manual on/automatic off motion detectors for rooms with windows, so the lamps will not operate when daylight is sufficient for the resident's needs. Manual on/automatic off motion detectors also decrease the likelihood of lamps being activated by motion caused by pets or moving objects. Use motion detectors with a manual off override in any space where the resident may want the lamps off during occupancy, such as bedrooms.

Use either infrared or ultrasonic sensors for detecting large body motions such as walking. Use ultrasonic sensors for detecting small body movements in a room such as writing, typing, or turning pages in a book. Follow manufacturers' instructions for mounting sensors.

Cautions

Do not switch high-intensity discharge lamps with motion detectors because these lamps have a delay before they will relight. If a motion detector switches a fluorescent lamp frequently, the life of the lamp will be reduced. Some compact fluorescent lamps are not compatible with motion detectors; check the lamp manufacturer's recommendations for compatibility.

For more information refer to

Designs: Medium Kitchen 1, Medium Living Room 1, Large Living Room 1, Small Bath, Children's Bedroom, Multi-Family Lobby, Multi-Family Corridor, Entry 2, Floodlight 2

Controls

Photosensors

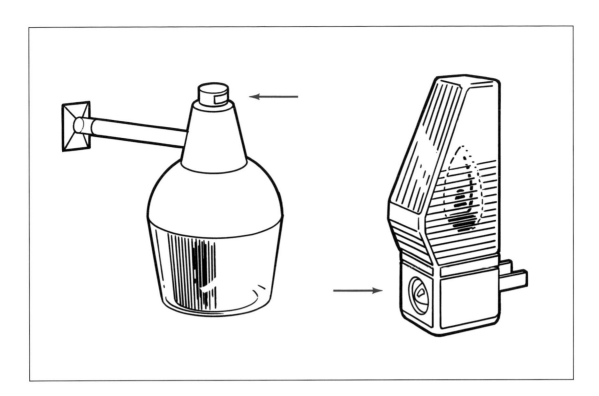

A photosensor is a light-detecting device that operates a luminaire when the surrounding light level drops below a specified level. Typically, photosensors operate exterior luminaires that are on all night and are off in the daytime. Photosensors can also operate interior luminaires that are intended to operate all night, such as security lighting in a daylit lobby or a night light.

Luminaires with photosensors are available at lighting stores and electrical suppliers. Conversion kits containing a photosensor and a motion detector are available for luminaires that contain incandescent lamps but are not manufactured with an automatic control.

Energy

Use photosensors only for luminaires that are operated all night, but do not need to be on in the daytime. Consider timers or motion detectors instead of photocells if the luminaire does not need to be operated all night long. Use a photosensor integrated into a night light to automatically switch off the night light in the morning or when other luminaires are used.

Installation

Position luminaires with photosensors so that the photosensor is not obstructed.

Cautions

Some compact fluorescent lamps are not compatible with photosensors; check the lamp manufacturer's recommendations for compatibility.

For more information refer to

Designs: Children's Bedroom, Floodlight 2

Central Controls

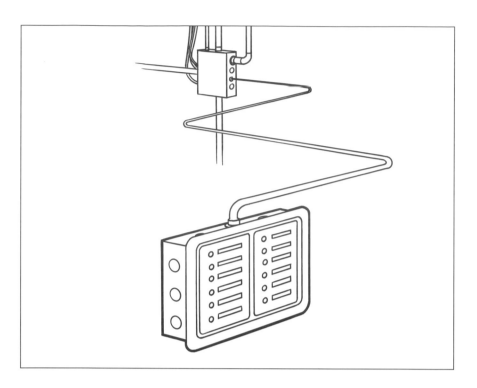

Central lighting controls allow a person to control switches and dimmers located throughout a home from a central location. These systems can be used to monitor the lighting in a house, turn lamps off that have been left on unnecessarily, and turn lamps on remotely as needed for security. Light-emitting diode (LED) indicator lamps sometimes are used to indicate that certain elements in the lighting system are on or off. Central systems can be used to create a path of light through the house, or can be used as a security measure to monitor outdoor lighting. Security systems, receptacles, telephone jacks, and cable television jacks also can interface with these types of controls. Some of these systems are expensive, especially the sophisticated systems that allow for programmable switching and the switching of groups of lamps for pre-defined functions or scenes.

Power-line carrier control systems are a type of central control system that controls luminaires by transmitting signals over existing household wiring. This type of control system allows switching and dimming from multiple locations without the added cost of running control wiring. A transmitter sends coded signals through the house wiring to receivers located at strategic points throughout the home. The receivers then send an on, off, or dim signal to the luminaires. The receivers are used in place of standard wall switches or dimmers. Luminaires can be wired to one or more receivers. Any number of transmitters can control one receiver.

Purchase central controls at lighting stores and electrical suppliers.

Energy

Central controls may save energy because the master control can monitor the status of lighting in each room of the house and detect lamps that have been left on unnecessarily.

Installation

Use central controls when master control of multiple areas in the home is desired. Use power-line carrier control systems when dimming and switching from multiple locations is desired and/or the added costs of new wiring are prohibitive. Install central controls according to the manufacturer's recommendations.

Appendix

Ballasts

The ballast for any fluorescent lamp has two main functions: it provides the high voltage required to start the lamp, and it controls the current provided to the lamp during operation. Magnetic ballasts have a transformer that consists of a magnetic core with copper or aluminum wire wound around it. Electronic ballasts transform voltage by using solid-state circuitry rather than magnetic components. Electronic ballasts operate lamps at high frequency (20,000 hertz (Hz) or higher compared to 60 Hz for magnetic ballasts), resulting in a 10 to 12 percent increase in lamp efficacy over magnetic ballasts.

Ballasts start fluorescent lamps in one of three ways: preheat start, rapid start, or instant start. For preheat starting, the starter is a component separate from the ballast. Preheat starting is characterized by the lamp flashing on and off a few times before it starts. For screwbase compact fluorescent lamps, the starter is actually built into the base of the lamp, whereas for other fluorescent lamp systems, the starter is a separate component.

A rapid-start mode usually is used to operate 4-foot linear fluorescent lamps. In rapid-start systems, the starter is an integral part of the ballast. A 1- to 2-second delay occurs before the lamps start, but the lamps do not flash on and off. Rapid-start ballasts are presently not available for screwbase compact fluorescent lamps.

For the instant-start method, a very high voltage is applied to the lamps while they are cold. No preheating is required, and the lamps start instantly. Most electronic ballasts are instant start. In some cases, instant start operation reduces the life of the lamp.

For remodeling projects, contractors and residents should note that ballasts that were manufactured prior to 1978 may contain polychlorinated biphenyls (PCBs), which are toxic and must be disposed of with caution. The label "No PCBs" should appear on all ballasts manufactured after 1978; assume that all others contain PCBs. Consult your state's department of environmental conservation for more information.

Power Quality

In a residential electrical system, the current and voltage supplied to electrical equipment should be sinusoidal in wave shape and should be in phase with one another. Any technology that causes variations in the shape of the current and voltage waves or in the phase relationship between current and voltage raises power quality concerns. Many electrical devices used in residences, including some efficient lighting technologies, affect power quality. Poor power quality can cause inefficient operation or failure of other electrical equipment on the same supply line, and it can result in excessive current in electrical distribution systems. The total impact of poor power quality from lighting products on other residential appliances and on the utility distribution grid is not yet fully understood.

One measure used to evaluate the power quality of electrical devices is power factor. Power factor is defined as a ratio: power (watts) divided by root-mean-square (rms) volt-amps (the product of the rms voltage and rms current). The rms of any wave shape expresses the effective average value of the wave shape. The power factor indicates the amount of current and voltage that a utility must supply with respect to the power that produces useful work. Power factor is a measure of the efficiency with which an electrical device converts input current and voltage into useful electric power. Power factor may range from zero to one, with one being the ideal. Power factor is lowered by devices that shift the phase of the voltage and current and by devices that distort the sinusoidal wave shapes of the input voltage and current. The figure illustrates possible relationships between voltage and current and their impact on power factor.

In fluorescent lighting systems, magnetic ballasts usually cause the current to be out of phase with the voltage. Reductions in power factor that are caused by a phase shift may be corrected by including a capacitor in the ballast design. This correction is commonly included in ballasts for 4-foot linear fluorescent lamps, resulting in a high power factor (0.95 and higher). However, many compact fluorescent magnetic ballasts do not use a capacitor to correct the phase shifts, and thus they have low power factors (some as low as 0.50). Newer magnetic ballasts for compact fluorescent lamps are available that include power factor correction.

Electronic ballasts for fluorescent lighting systems seldom affect the voltage-current phase relationship, but they often distort the voltage and current wave shapes. Distorted wave shapes contain components with frequencies that are multiples of the fundamental frequency, which usually is 60 Hz. As in music, these higher-frequency components are known as harmonics. Total harmonic distortion (THD) is a measure of the degree by which a sinusoidal wave shape is distorted by harmonics. THD expresses the harmonic components as a percentage of the fundamental component.

Electronic ballasts for 4-foot linear fluorescent lamps often are designed to minimize THD; some ballasts are available with THD less than 10 percent. Many utilities have established a limit of 20 percent maximum THD for ballasts that are approved for incentive programs. However, compact fluorescent devices for residential use may have THD greater than 100 percent. Techniques for minimizing THD and improving power factor are available but increase the cost of manufacturing ballasts.

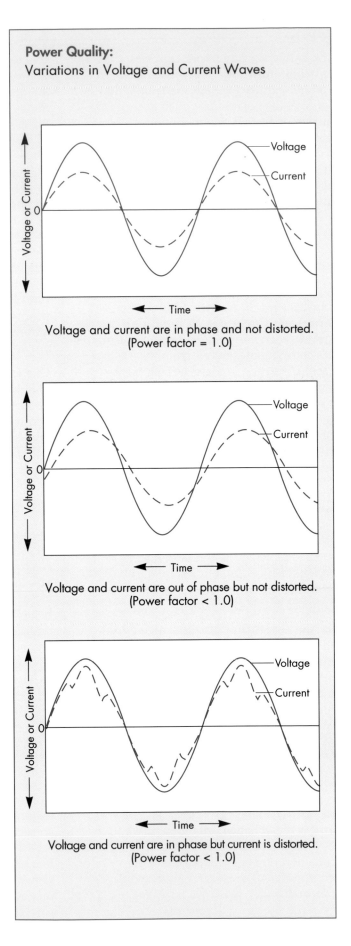

Power Quality:
Variations in Voltage and Current Waves

Voltage and current are in phase and not distorted.
(Power factor = 1.0)

Voltage and current are out of phase but not distorted.
(Power factor < 1.0)

Voltage and current are in phase but current is distorted.
(Power factor < 1.0)

Glossary

A-lamp: Common incandescent "light bulb" used throughout most homes in North America. An A-lamp can have a clear glass bulb or a white coating or an etched frost on the inside of the glass bulb.

accent lighting: A technique that emphasizes a particular object or draws attention to a particular area. Accent lighting usually utilizes the tight beam control of PAR-lamps and MR-lamps. Also called highlighting.

accent luminaire: A type of luminaire that includes ceiling-mounted track and directional luminaires and recessed accent luminaires. Accent luminaires provide directional lighting to accent an object or an area within a space.

adjustable head: An adjustable luminaire that is surface-mounted, or that inserts into a linear track and provides directional lighting.

ambient lighting: Lighting that is designed to provide a substantially uniform light level throughout an area, exclusive of any provision for special local requirements.

annual energy savings: A term used in the Economics chapter to refer to the difference per year in kWh between the energy used for lighting Design 1 and Design 2.

annual energy use: A term used in the Economics chapter to refer to the energy used per year in kWh by a lighting system.

annual lamp replacement costs: A term used in the Economics chapter to refer to the cost per year of replacement lamps, excluding labor.

annual operating cost savings: A term used in the Economics chapter to refer to the difference between the annual operating cost of Design 1 and that of Design 2.

annual operating cost: A term used in the Economics chapter to refer to the cost per year of electricity and replacement lamps.

aperture: An opening, usually in a recessed luminaire, through which light enters a space.

architectural luminaire: A luminaire that is integrated into the structure of the room. Architectural luminaires are mounted horizontally on a wall or ceiling with a shield to hide the lamp(s) from view. See also cove, soffit, and valance luminaires.

average rated lamp life: The average rated life of a lamp is the number of hours when 50 percent of a large group of lamps have failed. For fluorescent lamps, the operating conditions include operation at nominal line voltage at 3 hours per start. For high-intensity discharge lamps, the lamps are operated at 10 hours per start. The average rated life of an electric lamp is a median value of life expectancy. Any individual lamp, or group of lamps, may vary from the published average rated life.

baffle: A single opaque or translucent element that shields a light source from direct view at certain angles or that absorbs unwanted light.

ballast: A device that is used with a fluorescent or high-intensity discharge lamp to provide the necessary circuit conditions (voltage, current, and wave form) for starting and operating the lamp.

beam spread: The width of a light beam, expressed in degrees. The beam of light from a reflector-type lamp (PAR, R, ER, or MR) can be thought of as a cone. The beam spread is the angular width of the cone. The edge of the beam is defined as "50 percent of center beam intensity (candlepower)" or "10 percent of center beam intensity," depending upon the lamp type.

bi-pin base: A base with two pins that is used for some tungsten-halogen reflector lamps, low-voltage tungsten-halogen lamps, and fluorescent lamps.

bollard: A low, pole-mounted luminaire, usually for outdoor use. Bollards commonly are used to light pathways.

brightness: Subjective impression of light reaching the eye. Subjective brightness does not correlate exactly with luminance, which is measured with an instrument.

bulb: The outer envelope of a light source, usually quartz glass or other varieties of glass.

candle lamp: A decorative incandescent lamp with a bulb shaped like a flame. The lamp designation is usually "F" or "C."

candlepower: See luminous intensity.

cans: Square or round recessed downlight luminaires. These are also called "high-hats." Also, a surface-mounted luminaire, usually a downlight, that has a cylindrical shape.

capsule compact fluorescent lamp: A screwbase compact fluorescent lamp product whose lamp(s) is covered by a diffusing glass or acrylic lens. Capsule compact fluorescent lamps commonly are available in three shapes: globe, bullet, or jar.

ceiling-mounted luminaire: See surface-mounted luminaire.

center beam candlepower (CBCP): The luminous intensity (in candelas) of a reflector lamp measured at the center of its beam.

central controls: Lighting controls systems that control many luminaires from one or two locations.

chandelier: A decorative, often branched, luminaire suspended from the ceiling.

circline lamp: A fluorescent lamp bent in a circle so that the ends meet at the socket.

color: The color appearance of a lamp, and how the lamp makes other colors appear. See correlated color temperature and color rendering index.

color rendering index (CRI): A technique for describing the effect of a light source on the color appearance of objects being illuminated, with a CRI of 100 representing the reference condition (and thus the maximum CRI possible). In general, a lower CRI indicates that some colors may appear unnatural when illuminated by the lamp. CRIs of two or more lamps should only be compared if the lamps have the same correlated color temperature. See also correlated color temperature.

color temperature: See correlated color temperature.

commodity-grade luminaire: A commonly available luminaire that is constructed of less-expensive materials, with lower-quality construction standards. It is usually lower in price than a specification-grade luminaire. Commodity-grade luminaires commonly are used in homes and are available at discount stores and some electrical suppliers.

common incandescent lamp: See A-lamp.

compact fluorescent lamp: A small fluorescent lamp, usually with one or more bends in the tube.

contrast: The relative brightness (luminance) of an object against its immediate background.

control: A mechanism to turn lamps on and off, or dim lamps. Controls include switches, dimmers, timing devices, motion detectors, photosensors, and central control systems.

cornice luminaire: See soffit luminaire.

correlated color temperature (CCT): Describes the color appearance of the light that is produced, in terms of its warmth or coolness. The CCT relates the color appearance of the lamp to the color appearance of a reference source when the reference source is heated to a particular temperature, measured on the Kelvin (K) temperature scale. A low color temperature (3000 K and lower) describes a warm source, such as a typical incandescent lamp and a warm fluorescent lamp. A high color temperature (4000 K and higher) describes a cool source, such as a cool white fluorescent lamp.

cove luminaire: An architectural luminaire that directs light from sources that are mounted in a cove to the ceiling or upper wall. A cove is a ledge or shelf on the wall, or a recess in the wall.

current: A flow of electric charge, measured in amperes or amps.

daylight: Light produced by solar radiation. Daylight includes direct sunlight, sunlight scattered by the atmosphere, and sunlight reflected from clouds or other surfaces.

Design 1: A term used in the Economics chapter to refer to an existing lighting system, a common-practice lighting system, or any other lighting design that serves as a point of reference for comparison to another lighting design, Design 2.

Design 2: A term used in the Economics chapter to refer to a new lighting system that is being compared to Design 1.

diffuse lighting: Lighting provided on the work plane or on an object that does not come from any particular direction. Diffuse lighting produces less-distinct shadows than directional lighting.

diffuser: A device to redirect or scatter the light from a source, primarily by the process of diffuse transmission.

dimmer: A device used to control the intensity of light emitted by a luminaire by controlling the voltage or current available to it.

dimming power reduction factor: See power reduction factor.

direct glare: Glare resulting from very bright sources of light in the field of view. It usually is associated with bright light from luminaires and windows. A direct glare source may also affect performance by reducing the apparent contrast of objects in the field of view, especially those near the source of light.

directional lighting: The lighting produced by luminaires that distribute all, or nearly all, of the light in one direction.

directional luminaire: A luminaire that provides directional lighting, including downlights, accent luminaires, and the like.

distribution: See light distribution.

downlight: A directional luminaire that directs light downward.

efficacy (of a light source): The total light output of a light source divided by the total power input. Efficacy is expressed in lumens per watt.

efficiency (of a luminaire): The ratio of luminous flux (lumens) emitted by a luminaire to that emitted by the lamp or lamps used therein. Luminous efficiency is a dimensionless measure, expressing the percentage of initial lamp lumens that ultimately are emitted by the luminaire.

electromagnetic interference (EMI): The impairment of a wanted electromagnetic signal by an electromagnetic disturbance.

electronic ballast: A ballast that uses electronic circuitry to provide the voltage and current that are needed to start the lamp(s) and to maintain its operation. Electronic ballasts weigh less than magnetic ballasts and operate more quietly. Electronic ballasts operate lamps at a higher frequency than magnetic ballasts (20,000 to 60,000 hertz compared to 60 hertz), which eliminates flicker and increases efficacy. See also ballast.

ellipsoidal reflector lamp (ER-lamp): An incandescent lamp with an internal reflector that has a focal point a few inches in front of the lamp face. ER-lamps are used in grooved-baffle recessed downlights or track heads to reduce the amount of light absorbed by the baffle trim.

energy: The product of power (watts) and time (hours). Energy used for lighting can be saved either by reducing the amount of power required or by reducing the amount of time lighting is used.

ER-lamp: An ellipsoidal reflector lamp.

exterior lighting: Lighting for the outside of a building, including decorative and functional lighting.

"eyeball" luminaire: A recessed luminaire with a partially recessed sphere that can be rotated to provide adjustable, directional lighting.

facade lighting: Floodlighting the exterior of a structure for security or for illuminating architectural features.

filament: A fine wire heated electrically to incandescence in an electric lamp.

fitting: See luminaire.

fixture: See luminaire.

flood lamp: A lamp that produces a relatively wide beam of light.

fluorescence: The ability of some materials, such as phosphors, to convert ultraviolet energy into visible light.

fluorescent lamp: A lamp containing mercury under low pressure, relative to high-intensity discharge lamps. The mercury is ionized by an electric arc, producing ultraviolet energy which, in turn, excites phosphors coating the inside of the lamp to fluoresce.

footcandle: Imperial unit of illuminance equal to one lumen per square foot. One footcandle equals 10.76 lux.

footlambert: Imperial unit of luminance equal to $1/\pi$ candelas per square foot. One footlambert equals 3.426 candelas/m^2 (nits).

four-way switch: One of three switches that controls the same luminaire or group of luminaires. The luminaire(s) may be turned on or off from any of the three switches. It is called a four-way switch because it contains four contact points: the luminaire and the three switches.

G-lamp: A globe-shaped incandescent lamp, usually having a spherical bulb.

general lighting: See ambient lighting.

glare: The loss of visibility and/or the sensation of discomfort associated with bright light within the field of view. See also direct glare and reflected glare.

globe: A spherical transparent or diffusing enclosure that is intended to protect a lamp, to diffuse its light, or to change the color of the light.

globe lamp: An incandescent lamp with a globe-shaped bulb or a compact fluorescent lamp with a globe-shaped diffusing cover. See also capsule compact fluorescent lamp.

globe luminaire: A luminaire with a spherical diffuser, typically used for ambient lighting.

grazing light: Directional, usually downward, light that emphasizes the texture of surfaces by creating contrast between highlights on raised portions and shadows beyond them. Heavily textured surfaces, such as stucco, are complemented by grazing light.

halogen incandescent lamp: An incandescent lamp whose filament is encapsulated; the capsule contains a halogen gas that reacts with

tungsten evaporated from the filament to redeposit it on the filament. Halogen incandescent lamps have higher efficacies than common incandescent lamps. They are sometimes referred to as quartz lamps because the capsule is made from quartz glass.

halophosphates: The class of phosphors that commonly are used in fluorescent lamps. Halophosphates are limited in their ability to provide a high color rendering index without sacrificing light output. See also rare-earth phosphors.

HID lamps: High-intensity discharge lamps.

"high-hat" luminaire: A square or round recessed downlight luminaire. Also called a "can."

high-intensity discharge (HID) lamps: A group of electric discharge lamps operating at relatively high pressures (compared to fluorescent lamps). This group includes the lamp types known as mercury vapor, metal halide, and high-pressure sodium.

highlighting: See accent lighting.

high-pressure sodium lamp: HID light source in which radiation from sodium vapor under high pressure produces visible light. High-pressure sodium lamps are orangish in color appearance, take a few minutes to achieve full light output on lamp startup, and require several minutes to restart if power to the lamp is interrupted, even briefly.

"Hollywood" lights: A luminaire that uses a strip of multiple globe lamps mounted on one or more sides of a mirror. They are common in bathrooms.

"hot spot": An area of higher illumination than that on the immediate surrounding area, often resulting from a lamp being placed close to a surface. Hot spots also can occur due to improper optical design of a luminaire.

human factors: The study of the interaction of people and lighting.

illuminance: The density of luminous flux incident on a surface. Illuminance is the luminous flux divided by the area of the surface when the surface is uniformly illuminated. Illuminance is calculated as the amount of lumens per unit area. Two common units used to measure illuminance are footcandles (lumens/square feet) and lux (lumens/square meter). For conversion purposes, 1 footcandle is equal to 10.76 lux. The IESNA recommends illuminance levels for a variety of lighting applications in which visual performance (for example, speed and accuracy) is important. These recommendations are a function of the visual task being performed, the adaptation level of the observer, and the age of the observer.

incandescent lamp: A lamp producing visible radiant energy by electrical resistance heating of a filament.

incentive: A reimbursement of a portion of the cost of a product. Incentives commonly are offered by electric utilities and manufacturers on some energy-saving lighting products. Also known as rebates.

incremental cost: The difference between the cost of two items that perform similar functions.

indirect lighting: Light arriving at a point or surface after reflection from one or more surfaces (usually walls and/or ceilings) that are not part of the luminaire.

infrared-reflecting lamp (IR-lamp): A halogen lamp with an infrared-reflecting coating on the capsule that surrounds the filament. The coating redirects infrared energy onto the filament, which increases the temperature of the filament without additional input power, thereby increasing efficacy.

initial cost: The original cost of equipment, lamps, and installation, exclusive of operating costs such as energy, maintenance, and lamp replacement.

input power: The active power that is used by a lamp or lamp/ballast combination, measured in watts.

intensity: See luminous intensity.

interval timer: A lighting control that automatically switches the luminaire off after a selected time interval. An interval timer can be either electronic or mechanical.

IR-lamp: See infrared-reflecting lamp.

IR PAR-lamp: An infrared-reflecting PAR-lamp. See infrared-reflecting lamp.

kelvin (K): The standard unit of temperature that is used in the Système Internationale d'Unités (SI) system of measurements. The Kelvin temperature scale is used to describe the correlated color temperature of a light source.

kilowatt (kW): One thousand watts. See also watt and watt-hour.

kilowatt-hour (kWh): Measure of electrical energy consumed; 1 kilowatt-hour is equal to 1000 watts used for 1 hour. See also watt and watt-hour.

lamp: A manufactured light source. For electric lamps, it includes the bulb, the base, and the internal structure that produces light, either a filament or an arc tube. Lamps are often referred to as light bulbs. The term lamp also is commonly used to refer to plug-in luminaires (see desk, floor, and table lamps).

lamp life multiplier: A factor used in the economic analyses in this book to adjust the average rated lamp life to reflect the effects of hours per start and dimming of lamps.

lamp life: See average rated lamp life and service life of a lamp.

LED: See light-emitting diode.

lens: A glass or plastic element used in luminaires to refract, that is, to control, the distribution of light. Lenses can be flat and fitted into the aperture, or cup-shaped or spherical to fit over a lamp.

light: Radiant energy that is capable of producing a visual sensation. The visible portion of the electromagnetic spectrum extends from about 380 to 770 nanometers.

light distribution: The pattern of light that is produced by a lamp or a luminaire, or the patterns of light created in a room.

light-emitting diode (LED): A semiconductor diode that radiates in the visible region of the spectrum. LEDs are used as indicator lamps on some lighting controls, and are used in some emergency exit signs.

light output: Luminous flux, measured in lumens. The light output rating of a lamp is a measure of its total integrated light output. See also lumen.

light source: The object that produces the light. For electric lighting, a lamp; for daylighting, the sun.

lighting design: The planned application of lighting systems to an indoor or outdoor space.

lighting system: The set of equipment that is used to produce light, including a luminaire and control.

lighting technique: A way to light a space to achieve a desired effect.

linear fluorescent lamp: Any of the family of straight tubular fluorescent lamps. Lamps are available in 6-inch to 8-foot lengths, with the most-common length being 4 feet.

louver: A series of baffles or reflectors that is used to shield a light source from view at certain angles, absorb unwanted light, or reflect light.

low-voltage lamp: A lamp that nominally operates at 6, 12, or 24 volts. A transformer must be used to convert the 120-volt line voltage to the lower voltage.

lumen: The unit of luminous flux. The lumen is the time rate of flow of light.

lumens per watt (LPW): See efficacy.

luminaire: A complete lighting unit consisting of a lamp or lamps, together with the parts designed to distribute the light, to position and protect the lamps, and to connect the lamps to the power supply. Also referred to as a light fixture, fitting, or unit.

luminance: (footlamberts, candelas/m², or nits) The luminous intensity of a surface of a given projected area. Luminance is closely related to the brightness of an object. One candela/m² = 1 nit = 0.2919 footlamberts.

luminance ratio: See brightness ratio.

luminous ceiling: A dropped ceiling containing lamps above translucent panels. Luminous ceilings provide bright, diffuse lighting.

luminous flux: The time rate of flow of light, measured in lumens.

luminous intensity: Total luminous flux within a given solid angle, in units of candelas, or lumens/steradian.

luminous intensity distribution data: Curve, generally plotted on polar or rectilinear coordinates, which represents variation in luminous intensity (in candelas) from a bare lamp or from a luminaire. Distribution data can also be presented in tabular format.

lux: Standard international unit of illuminance equal to 1 lumen per square meter. One lux equals 0.0929 footcandles.

magnetic ballast: A ballast that uses a magnetic core and coil to provide the voltage and current that are needed to start the lamp(s) and to maintain its operation. Magnetic ballasts are heavier than electronic ballasts. See also ballast.

matte surface: A surface from which the reflection is predominantly diffuse.

mercury vapor lamp: HID light source in which radiation from mercury vapor produces visible light.

metal halide lamp: HID light source in which radiation from a mixture of metallic vapor and additives of halides (e.g., sodium, thallium, indium) produces visible light.

modular compact fluorescent lamp: In this book, the replaceable lamp in a two-piece compact fluorescent lamp product. It is a single-ended fluorescent lamp with a two- or four-pin base. When used with a modular compact fluorescent lamp ballast, the combination can replace an incandescent lamp.

modular compact fluorescent lamp ballast: In this book, the ballast in a two-piece compact fluorescent lamp product. It has a medium screwbase with a socket for the modular compact fluorescent lamp. The ballast and lamp connect together using a socket-and-base design that ensures compatibility of lamps and ballasts.

motion detector: Also called an occupancy sensor, a device that detects the movement of people, animals, and objects using a passive infrared and/or ultrasonic sensor. Motion detectors are used to control other devices, such as alarm systems and luminaires, so that these devices are activated when motion is detected. Some motion detectors offer manual on and/or manual off override capabilities. See also passive infrared and ultrasonic.

motion detector factor: A factor that is used in the economic analyses of this book to adjust the hours of lighting use to account for a motion detector that turns off lamps when no motion is detected.

mounting height: The distance from the floor to the lamp center of the luminaire or to the plane of the ceiling for recessed equipment. Motion detectors also have a recommended mounting height.

MR-lamp: A multi-faceted reflector lamp.

multi-faceted reflector lamp (MR-lamp): A low-voltage halogen reflector lamp that is used in lighting applications where precise beam control is required, such as accent lighting. Some MR-lamps, such as projection lamps, are designed for line-voltage operation.

multiple-level switching: A switching technique wherein the individual lamps, or groups of lamps, in a luminaire are switched independently to achieve multiple light outputs. For example, an architectural luminaire that

contains two rows of lamps may have each row controlled by a separate switch, so that the two rows of lamps may be turned on and off independently.

occupancy sensor: See motion detector.

operating cost: See annual operating cost.

PAR-lamp: A parabolic aluminized reflector lamp.

parabolic aluminized reflector lamp (PAR-lamp): An incandescent or tungsten-halogen incandescent lamp with a hard glass bulb and an interior reflecting surface, a precisely placed filament, and a lens to control beam spread. The lens is hermetically sealed to the reflector. Metal halide PAR-lamps are also now available.

parabolic reflector: A reflector with a parabolic shape that usually is used to concentrate the light in the direction parallel to the axis of the reflector. The location of the light source relative to the reflector is crucial to the design of the reflector.

passive infrared (type of motion detector): Passive infrared motion detectors sense the motion of infrared energy (heat) within a space. A detector is located behind an infrared-transmitting lens, which is usually vertically segmented with multiple smaller lenses etched within each segment. This lens design results in horizontal and vertical "fan" pattern detection zones. When a passive infrared sensor detects motion from one zone to another, it activates whatever device it controls (usually an alarm system or one or more luminaires). See also motion detector.

pendant luminaire: See suspended luminaire.

phosphors: Chemical compounds that are used to coat the inside of fluorescent and some HID lamps. See also fluorescence.

photosensor: A device that converts light to electrical current. Based on the amount of incident light, a photosensor can switch a lamp on or off or regulate a lamp's light output to maintain a preset light level.

plenum: The space between the ceiling and the floor or roof above.

point source: A source of radiation, the dimensions of which are small enough, compared with the distance between the source and the lighted surface, for them to be neglected in calculations and measurements.

power reduction factor: A factor used in the Economics chapter that accounts for the reduction in power that is drawn by lamps when they are dimmed to a specified level (expressed as a fraction of full power), or when they are operated by multiple-level switching. The power reduction factor also accounts for the use of multiple-level lamps (e.g., 50-100-150 watts) at various levels.

pull-cord: A string or chain that is attached to a switch that is mounted in a luminaire. Pull cords typically are used to control individual ceiling-mounted luminaires, as in an attic or basement.

quartz-halogen lamp: See halogen incandescent lamp.

R-lamp: A common reflector lamp.

radio frequency interference (RFI): Direct radiation from lamps or wiring, or conducted interference through wiring, that can affect the operation of other electrical devices.

rare-earth phosphors: A group of phosphors containing rare-earth elements. Rare-earth phosphors are used in fluorescent lamps to achieve higher efficacy and better color rendering than can be achieved with halophosphates. Rare-earth phosphors each produce light in a very narrow wavelength band. Although collectively they are more efficacious than halophosphates, they are more expensive. Thus, to reduce manufacturing costs, lamps often are coated first with halophosphates and then with a thin layer of rare-earth phosphors. RE designates a lamp containing rare-earth phosphors.

rated life: See average rated life.

receptacle: An electrical outlet.

recessed luminaire: A luminaire that is mounted above the ceiling (or behind a wall or other surface) with the opening of the luminaire flush with the surface.

reduced-wattage lamp: A lamp that is of slightly lower wattage than the lamp it is intended to replace. A reduced-wattage lamp also provides less light.

reflectance: A measure of how effectively a surface will reflect light, that is, the ratio of lumens reflected off a surface to lumens falling on it. Pale surfaces have a higher reflectance than dark ones.

reflected glare: Glare resulting from bright reflections from polished or glossy surfaces in the field of view. Reflected glare usually is associated with reflections from within a visual task or areas in close proximity to the region being viewed.

reflector: A surface of mirrored glass, painted metal, polished metal, or metalized plastic that is shaped to project the beam from a light source in a particular direction. Reflectors may be an integral part of a lamp or they may be part of the luminaire.

reflector lamp (R-lamp): An incandescent filament or electric discharge lamp in which the sides of the outer blown-glass bulb are coated with a reflecting material so as to direct the light. The light-transmitting region may be clear, frosted, or patterned.

reflector lamps: A class of lamps that have reflecting material integrated into the lamp to direct the light. Types include common reflector (R), parabolic aluminized reflector (PAR), ellipsoidal reflector (ER), and multi-faceted reflector (MR) lamps.

sconce: A decorative and/or functional wall-mounted luminaire.

screwbase compact fluorescent lamp: A compact fluorescent lamp with a ballast that has a medium screwbase that fits into the standard incandescent lamp socket. A screwbase compact fluorescent lamp may either be modular, in which the lamp and ballast are separate pieces, or self-ballasted, in which the lamp and ballast are inseparable. Both types are designed to replace incandescent lamps. See also modular compact fluorescent lamp and modular compact fluorescent ballast.

self-ballasted compact fluorescent lamp: A one-piece screwbase compact fluorescent lamp.

service life (of a lamp): The total time that passes, including time that the lamp is on and time that it is off, before the lamp must be replaced.

shade: A device on a luminaire that is used to prevent glare (by hiding the light source from direct view), control light distribution, and sometimes diffuse (and perhaps color) the light emitted.

simple payback: A term used in the Economics chapter to define the time required to save enough in operating costs by using Design 2, compared to Design 1, to pay back the incremental cost of Design 2.

single-pole switch: Single-location on-off switch that controls one luminaire, or group of luminaires.

skylight: A clear or translucent panel set into a roof to admit daylight into a building.

socket: The fitting on a luminaire that electrically connects the luminaire to the lamp.

soffit luminaire: An architectural luminaire that directs light downward from the cornice or soffit between the wall and ceiling to light the wall surface below.

specification-grade luminaire: A luminaire that is produced with high-quality construction and materials. See also commodity-grade luminaire.

specular surface: A surface from which the reflection is predominantly directional. Specular surfaces are mirror-like or shiny, as opposed to diffuse.

spot lamp: A lamp that provides a relatively narrow beam of light.

surface-mounted luminaire: A luminaire mounted directly on the ceiling or other surface.

suspended luminaire: A luminaire hung from a ceiling by supports. Also called a pendant luminaire.

switch: A device that turns a lamp or lamps on or off by completing or interrupting the power supplied to the lamp(s). See also single-pole switch, three-way switch, and four-way switch.

task lighting: Lighting that is directed to a specific surface or area. Task lighting provides illumination for visual tasks.

three-level lamp: Incandescent lamp having two filaments. Each can be operated separately or in combination with the other, which provides three different light outputs. A special socket is required to use the three levels of this lamp.

three-way switch: One of two switches that control the same luminaire or group of luminaires. The luminaire(s) may be turned on or off from either of the two switches.

timer: See interval timer.

torchiere: An indirect floor lamp sending all or nearly all of its light upward.

track head: An adjustable luminaire that connects to the track in a track lighting system.

track lighting: A lighting system with an electrically fed linear track that accepts one or more track heads. The track heads can be easily relocated along the track.

trim: Baffles, cones, rims, and other treatments for apertures of downlights. Trim is usually the part of the luminaire that is visible from below the ceiling.

trim ring: A plastic or metal ring used to cover and seal the edges of holes that are cut into ceilings to install recessed luminaires.

triphosphor: See rare-earth phosphors.

troffer: A recessed luminaire that is installed in the plenum with the opening flush with the ceiling. Typically rectangular or square in shape, as in a 2-foot by 4-foot luminaire.

tungsten-halogen lamp: See halogen incandescent lamp.

twin-tube lamp: A single-ended fluorescent lamp with the tube bent into a very tight "U" or "H" shape.

U-shaped lamp: A fluorescent lamp with the tube bent in the middle so that the ends fit into the same side of a luminaire.

UL: Underwriters Laboratories; conducts safety and materials tests. UL-listed products have passed UL's tests.

ultrasonic (type of motion detector): Ultrasonic motion detectors emit high-frequency sound waves (too high for the human ear to hear), which are reflected by objects and room surfaces to a receiver located in the detector. The reflected waves set up a static wave pattern; any disturbance in this pattern alters the frequency of the reflected wave, which is detected by the receiver. The receiver then activates whatever device the detector controls (usually an alarm system or one or more luminaires). See also motion detector.

ultraviolet (UV) radiation: Any radiant energy within the wavelength range of 10 to 380 nanometers.

under-cabinet lighting: Luminaires mounted on the underside of cabinets to provide task lighting, typically in a kitchen.

uplight: A luminaire that directs the light upward onto the ceiling and upper walls of a room.

valance luminaire: An architectural luminaire with a longitudinal shielding member mounted across the top of a window or along a wall and usually parallel to the wall, to conceal light sources giving both upward and downward distributions. See also architectural luminaires.

vanity light: A wall-mounted luminaire located next to a mirror. See also "Hollywood" lights.

voltage (V): The electric potential difference that drives the current through a circuit.

wall washing: A technique that lights a wall fairly evenly from top to bottom without spilling or wasting light away from the wall into the room.

watt (W): Unit of active electric power; the rate at which electric energy is used.

watt-hour: Unit of electric energy. One watt-hour is the amount of energy consumed at the rate of 1 watt during a 1-hour period.

wattage: The active electrical power consumed by a device.

wavelength: The distance between two similar points of a given wave. Wavelengths of light are measured in nanometers (1 nm = 1 billionth of a meter, or 1×10^{-9} meters)

Associations

American Council for an Energy-Efficient Economy (ACEEE)
1001 Connecticut Avenue NW, Suite 801
Washington, DC 20036
Tel: 202-429-8873; Fax: 202-429-2248

American Lighting Association (ALA)
P.O. Box 420288
Dallas, TX 75342-0288
Tel: 800-605-4448; Fax: 214-698-9899

American Solar Energy Society (ASES)
2400 Central Avenue, G-1
Boulder, CO 80301
Tel: 303-443-3130; Fax: 303-443-3212

Association of Energy Service Professionals (AESP)
7040 West Palmetto Park Road
Suite 2315
Boca Raton, FL 33433
Tel: 407-361-0023; Fax: 561-361-0027

Association for Energy Engineers (AEE)
4025 Pleasantdale Road, Suite 420
Atlanta, GA 30340
Tel: 770-447-5083; Fax: 770-446-3969

Energy Efficient Building Association (EEBA)
2950 Metro Drive, Suite 108
Minneapolis, MN 55425
Tel: 612-851-9940; Fax: 612-851-9507

Green Seal
1730 Rhode Island Avenue NW, Suite 1050
Washington, DC 20035-3101
Tel: 202-331-7337; Fax: 202-331-7533

Illuminating Engineering Society of North America (IESNA)
120 Wall Street, 17th Floor
New York, NY 10004-3404
Tel: 212-248-5000; Fax: 212-248-5017, -5018

International Association of Lighting Designers (IALD)
1133 Broadway, Suite 520
New York, NY 10003
Tel: 212-206-1281; Fax: 212-206-1327

National Lighting Bureau (NLB)
1300 North 17th Street, Suite 1847
Rosslyn, VA 22209
Tel: 703-841-3274; Fax: 703-841-3374

Further Reading

Advances in residential lighting technologies, EPRI TR-100868, by W. A. Hendrix and K. Ushimaru. Palo Alto, CA: Electric Power Research Institute, July 1992.

Bringing interiors to light, by Fran Kellogg Smith and Fred J. Bertolone. New York, NY: Whitney Library of Design, 1986.

Choices for residential lighting: Light sources, EPRI BR-101436, by Robert G. Davis, Catherine Luo, and Sally Sledge. Palo Alto, CA: Electric Power Research Institute, January 1993.

Commercial lighting efficiency resource book, EPRI CU-7427, edited by Kathryn M. Conway. Palo Alto, CA: Electric Power Research Institute, September 1991.

Concepts and practice of architectural daylighting, by Fuller More. New York, NY: Van Nostrand Reinhold, 1985.

Concepts in architectural lighting, by M. David Egan. New York, NY: McGraw-Hill, 1983.

Daylight in architecture, by Benjamin H. Evans. New York, NY: McGraw-Hill, 1981.

Design criteria for lighting interior living spaces, IES RP-11, by the IES Residence Lighting Committee. New York, NY: Illuminating Engineering Society, 1969.

"Energy-saving tips for home energy lighting," by the IES Residence Lighting Committee. Lighting Design & Application, 1974, 4(4): 40-42.

Environmental standard for energy efficient lighting: Compact fluorescent products, Green Seal Standard GS-5-1992. Washington, DC: Green Seal Inc., July 22, 1992.

Guide to performance evaluation of efficient lighting products, by Robert G. Davis and Robert A. Wolsey. Troy, NY: Rensselaer Polytechnic Institute, Lighting Research Center, June 1991.

Interior residential lighting: A guide for builders and designers, by Sharon Johnson. Bellevue, WA: Puget Sound Power and Light, 1991.

Light: Effective use of daylight and electric lighting in residential and commercial spaces, by Jane Grosslight. Tallahassee, FL: Durwood Publishers, 1990.

Lighting answers: T8 fluorescent lamps, by Robert Wolsey. Troy, NY: Rensselaer Polytechnic Institute, Lighting Research Center, April 1993.

The lighting book, by Deyan Sudjic. New York, NY: Crown Publishers, 1985.

Lighting handbook: Reference & application, 8th. ed., edited by Mark S. Rea. New York: Illuminating Engineering Society of North America, 1993.

Lighting options for homes, by Bonneville Power Administration. Portland, OR: Bonneville Power Administration, April 1991.

The passive solar energy book, by Edward Mazira. Emmaus, PA: Rodale Press, 1979.

Perception and lighting as formgivers for architecture, by William M. C. Lam. New York, NY: McGraw-Hill, 1977.

Residential energy efficient lighting: Assessing preference for light sources [thesis], by Sally J. Sledge. Troy, NY: Rensselaer Polytechnic Institute, August 1992.

Residential energy efficient lighting survey, prepared by Linda Dethman and Sally King. Seattle, WA: Seattle City Light, August 1991.

Residential high-efficiency lighting: An assessment of utility programs, EPRI TR-101221, prepared by Aspen Systems Corporation. Palo Alto, CA: Electric Power Research Institute, December 1992.

Residential lighting acceptance pilot for Pacific Power and Light Company: Final report, prepared by Delta-T Inc. Eugene, OR: Pacific Power and Light, May 11, 1990.

Specifier reports: Electronic ballasts, by the National Lighting Product Information Program. Troy, NY: Rensselaer Polytechnic Institute, Lighting Research Center, December 1991.

Specifier reports: Occupancy sensors, by Dorene Maniccia. Troy, NY: Rensselaer Polytechnic Institute, Lighting Research Center, October 1992.

Specifier reports: Screwbase compact fluorescent lamp products, by James Barrett. Troy, NY: Rensselaer Polytechnic Institute, Lighting Research Center, April 1993.

Index

This book is set in
Palatino Roman, Bold and Italic
with Futura Heavy, Book and Condensed.

Book design by
Nager Reynolds Design, Westport, CT

Cover and illustrations of lighting designs by
Mark Patrizio, Kemp Building Graphics, Waterford, NY

Illustrations of technologies by
Bruce Kaiser, Kaiser Illustration, Watervliet, NY

Printed and bound by
Quebecor/Kingsport Press

To order this book contact:
The Lighting Research Center
Rensselaer Polytechnic Institute
Troy, NY 12180–3590
Facsimile (518) 276–2999
E-mail: lrc@rpi.edu